SCHOOL AND CHILD

SCHOOL and CHILD

A Case History

by

CECIL V. MILLARD

Research Professor of Elementary Education
Director, Child Development Laboratory
Michigan State College

1954
MICHIGAN STATE COLLEGE PRESS

COPYRIGHT, 1954, BY CECIL V. MILLARD
LIBRARY OF CONGRESS CATALOG CARD NUMBER 54-8842
MANUFACTURED IN THE UNITED STATES OF AMERICA

Contents

58- 04860

Preface..	xi

General purpose, xi; The illustrative case, xiii; Source of the material, xiv.

PART ONE: THE NORMATIVE APPROACH TO ANALYSIS

Introduction...	3

Chapter I - GRADE ONE—THE SIX-YEAR-OLD CHILD

A. The First-Grade Mode......................................	5
B. Behavior and Interpretation.................................	11

Motor performance, 11; Emotional reactions, 12; Anxieties and security threats, 13; Personal-social development, 13; Play and recreation, 14; Academic status, 15; Ethical and moral behavior, 15.

Selected References...	16

Chapter II - GRADE TWO—THE SEVEN-YEAR-OLD CHILD

A. The Second-Grade Mode....................................	19
B. Behavior and Interpretation.................................	24

Motor performance, 24; Emotional reactions, 25; Anxieties and security threats, 26; Personal-social development, 26; Play and recreation, 27; Academic status, 27; Ethical and moral behavior, 29.

Selected References...	29

Chapter III - GRADE THREE—THE EIGHT-YEAR-OLD CHILD

A. The Third-Grade Mode.....................................	31
B. Behavior and Interpretation.................................	34

Motor performance, 34; Emotional reactions, 35; Anxieties and security threats, 36; Personal-social development, 36; Play and recreation, 38; Academic status, 38; Ethical and moral behavior, 39.

Selected References...	39

v

Chapter IV - GRADE FOUR—THE NINE-YEAR-OLD CHILD

A. The Fourth-Grade Mode.. 43

B. Behavior and Interpretation...................................... 48
Motor performance, 48; Emotional reactions, 48; Anxieties and security threats, 49; Personal-social development, 50; Play and recreation, 50; Academic status, 50; Ethical and moral behavior, 52.

Selected References... 52

Chapter V - GRADE FIVE—THE TEN-YEAR-OLD CHILD

A. The Fifth-Grade Mode... 55

B. Behavior and Interpretation...................................... 59
Motor performance, 59; Emotional reactions, 59; Anxieties and security threats, 60; Personal-social development, 61; Play and recreation, 61; Academic status, 62; Ethical and moral behavior, 62.

Selected References... 63

Chapter VI - GRADE SIX—THE ELEVEN-YEAR-OLD CHILD

A. The Sixth-Grade Mode... 65

B. Behavior and Interpretation...................................... 70
Motor performance, 70; Emotional reactions, 70; Anxieties and security threats, 71; Personal-social development, 71; Play and recreation, 73; Academic status, 73; Ethical and moral behavior, 73.

Selected References... 74

PART TWO: DEVELOPMENTAL ANALYSIS AND INTERPRETATION

Introduction... 77

Chapter VII - PHYSICAL AND MENTAL DEVELOPMENT

A. Physical Development... 79
Comparative growth, 79; Progress in height and weight, 82; Factors affecting physical development, 83; Aspects of motor growth, 83.

B. Mental Development... 84
General applied intelligence, 84; Mental-growth curve, 88; Significant implications from the curve, 91.

Selected References... 93

Chapter VIII - ACADEMIC LEARNINGS

A. Available Data.. 95

B. Reading Achievement.. 96
Conventional evaluation, 96; Character of curve, 98; General conclusions, 99.

C. Arithmetic Achievement.. 101
   Conventional interpretations, 101; Comparison of achievement with teachers' reports, 103; Nature of achievement curve, 103; Longitudinal look at arithmetic performance, 104.

D. Spelling Achievement... 105
   Comparison with Stanford norms, 105; Character of curve, 106; Qualitative analysis, 107.

E. Miscellaneous Achievements... 108
   Social studies, 108; Science, 109; Language, 111; Literature, 111.

F. The Total Academic Picture... 113

Selected References... 115

Chapter IX - PERSONAL-SOCIAL DEVELOPMENT

A. General Personality... 117

B. Personal Habits and Traits.. 118

C. Character and Ideals.. 120
   Integration, 120; Ideals and standards, 120; Miscellaneous traits, 122.

D. Emotional Characteristics... 124
   The use of longitudinal growth patterns from objective data, 124; Miscellaneous characteristics, 126; Over-all picture, 127; Grade-to-grade picture, 127; Character of shift in the developmental matrix, 128; General analysis, 128.

E. Social Development.. 131
   General data available, 131; Status inventory, 131; Sociometric status (sixth grade), 133; General longitudinal interpretation, 135; General factors, 136; Specific factors, 137.

F. The Effect of the School.. 137
   The school as part of the total force, 137; Some limitations, 138.

G. An Evaluation... 139
   Concept of individuality, 139; Role of the teacher in modification, 140; Limitations in opportunity, 140; Importance of social development not recognized, 141; Use of sociometry, 142; The value of grouping, 142; More projects for human understandings, 143.

Selected References... 143

Chapter X - PERSONAL ADJUSTMENT

A. Adjustment Profile.. 145

B. A Definition of Mental Hygiene.. 147

C. Behavior Mechanisms... 147
   Compartmentalization, 148; Compensation, 148; Daydreaming, 148; Displacement, 149; Distortion or sour-grape attitudes, 149; Identification, 149; Negativism, 149; Projection, 149; Rationalization, 150; Regression, 150; Sublimation, 150.

D. Summation and Interpretation.. 150
   General behavior pattern, 151; Behavior and personality, 151; Behavior and goal, 151; Recommended treatment, 153.

Selected References... 154

PART THREE: GROWTH INTER-RELATIONSHIPS

Introduction 157

Chapter XI - DEVELOPMENTAL PATTERNS

A. The Problem 159
B. Growth Analysis 160
   Range of various measures, 163; Uniqueness of total pattern, 163; Interpretation in relation to growth needs, 163; Prediction of future performance, 165.
C. A New Method for Studying Inter-relationships 165
   The problem of obtaining the true picture of growth, 166; Differences in the equations, 166; Fit of the equations to the actual measures, 166.
D. Findings from the Data 168
   Time considerations, 168; Maturity points, 169; Inter-relationships, 170; Percents of development at various chronological ages, 171.
E. The Over-all Organismic Design 172
Selected References 175

Chapter XII - DEVELOPMENTAL DESIGN—SOURCE FOR THE DISCOVERY OF PRINCIPLES OF GROWTH AND DEVELOPMENT

A. Procedures in Child Study 177
   1. Introduction—General Purposes of Child Study 177
      Significance of child study, 177; Purpose of child study in the schools, 177.
   2. Current Child-Study Approaches 178
      Description of status, 178; The longitudinal approach, 178.
   3. Specific Study Devices 179
      Rating scales, 180; Check lists, 180; Achievement and intelligence tests, 181; Physiological measurements, 182; Miscellaneous measures, 182; Journal records, 183; Case study, 183.
B. Some Problems of Child Study 185
   1. The Statistical Barrier 185
   2. The Longitudinal versus the Status Approach 185
      General advantages of longitudinal study, 185; Difficulties and problems in its usage, 186.
   3. Types of Longitudinal Study 187
      The continued-measurement series, 187; Cumulative multi-observation series, 188.
C. Principles Demonstrated in Patricia's Record 191
   Growth is quantitative and qualitative, 191; continuous, 191; individual, 192; modifiable, 192; The cyclic nature of growth, 192; Growth and learning are complementary, 192.
D. Evaluation and Summary 193
   1. Limitations 193
      No record of diagnostic and remedial efforts, 193; No carry-over into the school program, 194; Infrequency of testing periods, 194; Lack of clustering of testings at significant maturity periods, 195.

2. Contributions of the Study.................................... 195
   Illustration of principle, 195; Several new hypotheses, 195; Illustration of a new technique, 196.

Selected References.. 196

APPENDIX—EXCERPTS FROM THE JOURNALS

FIRST-GRADE OBSERVATIONS... 201
SECOND-GRADE OBSERVATIONS.. 201
THIRD-GRADE OBSERVATIONS... 203
FOURTH-GRADE OBSERVATIONS.. 206
FIFTH-GRADE OBSERVATIONS... 208
SIXTH-GRADE OBSERVATIONS... 214

Index... 219

Preface

1. General Purpose

THE GENERAL CONCEPT of child development contains potentialities which promise an increasing influence on elementary-school organization and instruction. It is a concept which enters into almost all discussion related to teacher training, in-service education of teachers, and guidance of elementary-school children. No other questions are more frequently raised than those inquiring into the principles of child development, its generalizations, and its implications for instruction.

Specialists working in this area have done much in responding to the demand made on them to satisfy this need. Books, monographs, and research findings are now available which, when thoroughly understood and applied, can greatly aid in improving teaching and the direction of children. Child-development research today has moved far beyond its philosophical beginnings. It is now a young science and consequently something much more than a point of view. It thereby side-steps the possibility of becoming identified as progressive education or as an ally of liberal movements in education. It likewise resists the possibility of capture by the traditionalists in education. As a science, its findings can be applied only to the question of how the child will react under various conditions. Education has sadly lacked this necessary reservoir for fact finding. The ability of child-development research to meet this need is becoming more recognized day by day. Thus it is offering to teacher training the frame of reference which it has long sought to become a true profession. During the 1920's and the early thirties teacher training felt it had discovered its basic framework in the great test development which took place. A little later the curriculum movement occupied the center of the stage. The following years of disagreement and controversy between the progressives and the traditionalists, regarding effective methods of teaching and the appropriate selection of subject matter, gave warning that methodology and curriculum selection were entirely contingent on the purposes of education and consequently were but the periphery of basic professional knowledge. Where this controversy still reverberates it is but a sign of a sorrowful lack of discovery of child-development principles and consequently of a way to harmony and cooperative effort. In the application of the findings in child development much clarity is to be gained in the appropriate choice of criteria for method and curriculum. A common beginning point, a solid foundation of this kind, is necessary if teaching is going to raise materially its professional level.

Many books in this field have appeared in the last decade. General principles have been outlined. Steps to be taken in administrative procedure have been suggested as they relate to ways and means of the child's growth and development. Up to this point the most neglected area is the elementary-school period in the child's development. This book is one of few attempting to describe the behavior of childhood during this critical time.

There are three objectives which this book aims to accomplish. First, it attempts to bring added light to the knowledge of development sequences of the pre-adolescent. Only a few of the most recent hypotheses and theories of behavior have been directed toward the child of this age. Mental hygienists and others, through want of attention, have allowed the idea to formulate that here was a dull uninteresting period of development which scarcely justified attention. As a result the early childhood and the adolescent areas have received the major share of scrutiny and report. The pre-adolescent child has been allowed to reflect the very untrue picture of one who is easily directed, has no problems, and can easily be taught. The author believes that such a dust-covered concept is due for a much-needed replacement.

Secondly, this book attempts to refine many of the broad principles and generalizations as to how the elementary-school child grows and develops, revealing basic revisions and shadings as they apply from one age to the next. A child at one age, for example, is quite ready to respond to democratic procedures with considerable permissiveness of choice. It is generally held that all he has to do to respond more generously at a later age is to have more maturity and continuing experience under these conditions. Unfortunately such a simplified belief is untenable. Maturity differences bring conflicts into what previously existed as a happy and responsive situation. It is hoped that in these pages over-simplified concepts can be brought into a better perspective, and particularly, as they relate to increasing maturity, during this important period of the child's development.

A third objective, and one not previously attempted, is to illustrate with one single case principle and generalization of the child's growth and development. This is no place to hold a brief on the need for longitudinal study or to point out that what is most lacking in our teacher-training literature today is case-history material. Comprehensive studies on one child throughout his elementary-school career are almost completely lacking in our training materials for the prospective elementary-school teacher. This book, however, is not exclusively a case history. It is foremost an exposition of principle as seen in the life of one child. Its exhaustive treatment of data collected in school tends to give it a case-history status but its purpose is to establish and to point out to teachers and others how principles can be explained in the life of one child. The illustrative material is longitudinal in nature and as broad and comprehensive as could be conceived under the circumstances of the study of which this child was one case. There are two possible contributions to be found in this presentation.

One is believed to be represented in the uniqueness of the data used for illustration and the manner in which they have been handled. The data can be called unique because they differ considerably from those usually presented in case-study efforts. There is little which can be called a psychiatric or psychological probing of the recesses of a child's mind. No particular attempt has been made to include an explanation of the psychological vagaries back of the many observed behavior manifestations. No analysis has been made of dreams, personal feelings, or sensations. The over-all objective has been to illustrate a procedure for understanding and to interpret manifest child behavior at the pre-adolescent stage as seen in school. All data utilized can be classified as kinds which can be seen, heard, or otherwise objectively measured. The case selected is an average child found in an average school.

Second, among the possible contributions of this book is the manner in which the illustrative material has been handled. Part One contains certain general impressions of the child in relation to age-grade expectations. Briefly, general principles are pointed out in reference to age-grade maturities, accompanied by comparisons with the behavior of the child under scrutiny. Some of the analyses reported may be called highly tentative and subjective, based almost entirely on observation. In Part Two objective data are picked up and played against the first impressions. At this level of interpretation the Part One conclusions are weighed and screened and additional hypotheses and generalizations reported. The reader will find in this section considerable identification with conventional interpretations and handling of material. In Part Three a final study of the data is presented with some new and generally unknown approaches to analysis. No new data have been explored. The presentation is limited to the utilization of new tools and techniques in the analysis of behavior and the illustration of principle.

The entire approach covered by the several parts is believed to be unique. It might reliably be called a three-dimensional study of a child in school.

2. The Illustrative Case

The child under consideration is one of 70 on whom the following objective measures and test results were collected: Height, Weight, Mental Age (Kuhlman-Anderson), Academic Achievement (Stanford Achievement test), Durrell-Sullivan Reading Achievement, Durrell-Sullivan Reading Capacity, and Iowa Basic Arithmetic Skills tests. In some grades the Courtis Motor Measures and General Development Test were administered. Other materials included a personality inventory for the study of pupil adjustment, supplementary data such as report cards, samples of work, teachers' comments, and school records.

In general the presentation hews to purposes established for research in the Child Development Laboratory, Michigan State College. These have been reported with the following in mind:
1. To get an over-all view of each child's total development;
2. To understand better the effect of cyclic change;
3. To determine the degree of relationship of the aspects of development studied;
4. To identify as closely as data permit any influencing factors or changes in conditions;
5. To determine relative usefulness of objective and subjective data.

It will be seen that all of the above are recognized scientific aspects of child study. In a presentation of this kind, however, the writer must be pardoned for going somewhat beyond the data. This can be condoned only in the belief that the investigator, in dealing with a single child, must necessarily be interested and concerned with the future welfare of that child. Is the child happy? How is he progressing in school? What is the school and community contributing to his growth and general welfare? The answer to such questions—and case study should attempt to provide the answers—requires some departure in prognosis from the facts at hand.

The group of which Patricia was a member consisted of suburban public-school children going through school together. The school is located in a fringe area adjacent to a city of approximately 100,000 people. During the course of the study the community grew rapidly. Its population consisted primarily of people employed in the industrial plants of the metropolitan area. Consequently the neighborhood would rate as a low-normal or low-middle status on a socio-economic rating scale.

Patricia was first observed in the kindergarten and thereafter repeatedly observed through every grade of her elementary-school years. In general this child was representative of a normal trend in her growth and development. There were however two deviations from such a characterization. Her home background demonstrated first-generation foreign parentage. If this be a disadvantage it was minimized in this community since at this social level it had less significance. Second, she showed a possible departure from normal development in her increasing weight. This tended, in the upper grades, to set her somewhat apart from the other children. Aside from these factors there appeared to be nothing else to suggest handicaps to normal development throughout these years.

3. Source of the Material

The material on Patricia was collected through the activities of the Child Development Laboratory, Michigan State College. The child presented here was one of one hundred and forty at the beginning of the study and one of approximately seventy at the end who continued in school in this community and on whom complete records were available.

Description of the general over-all conditions of the study will prove of some interest as will its specific procedures and purposes.

MAJOR PURPOSES: The following are considered to be the major purposes:
(1) Research to determine the relationship of the child's growth and development to the school program;
(2) Observation of children as part of a program for training teachers to understand better the principles of child growth and development.

TYPES OF MEASURES: The tests and measurements, recorded by a trained graduate student or staff member according to schedule, covered five areas: (a) Physical Development, (b) Mental Development, (c) Subject-matter Achievement, (d) General Development, and (e) Social Status.

(a) *Physical Development:* Height and weight were recorded in the fall, winter, and spring for each child. A measure of grip was recorded along with height and weight to get a picture of the child's strength.
(b) *Mental Development:* The Kuhlman-Anderson tests were administered once each winter. They were processed in terms of mental age, grade age, and I.Q.
(c) *Subject-matter Achievement:* The Stanford Achievement was the only standardized subject-matter achievement test utilized continuously in the study. It was not, however, the only measure of achievement. Samples of work, scores on teacher-made tests, and progress reports by the teacher were included in each child's record file.
(d) *General Development:* The Courtis Motor and the Courtis General Development Tests were administered each spring. These tests, which are not generally known, are constructed on a differential basis. They are designed, when used in conjunction with each other, to give an accurate measure of the rate at which the child is developing.[1]
(e) *Social Status:* To get a picture of the change in each child's social status in the classroom, a sociogram was compiled each fall and each spring.

CASE INVENTORY: At least once each year a case inventory was compiled for each child by a college student in child development. The case inventory included information relating to the following six areas:
1. General School Background;
2. Physical Growth and Health;
3. Mental Development;
4. Academic Learnings;
5. Personal and Social Development;
6. Home and Family Environment.

[1] Not utilized in the earlier groups of which our case was a member.

An anecdotal record of the child's behavior for one-half day each week for twelve weeks throughout the years was included in the inventory, as well as:

1. Samples of the child's work;
2. A brief characterization of the child by the observer;
3. A photograph of the child;
4. A recording of an unstructured interview with the child;
5. Information from the child's school records. This included health and attendance records.

ORGANIZATION OF THE PROGRAM: Each child-development student was assigned to a specific child who was observed one-half day each week throughout the term. The observer made out a complete case history of the child in addition to keeping an anecdotal record of the child's behavior, as noted above. The observer was able to supplement his case history with the tests and measurements obtained by the research personnel, as well as through conferences with the child's teachers and the reading of earlier case histories prepared on his child. In some cases the observers gave to the classroom teacher an assistance which, in addition to enriching the observers' training, also served to enable the classroom teacher to be more effective by relieving her of certain tasks and thus permitting her to attend more adequately to others. All parties, of course, governed their actions on the basis of whether or not these activities contributed to the welfare of the child.

The observer, although recording anecdotes on only one child, was aware of the total classroom situation, and was able to appraise the effect of the whole room on his child as well as the impact of his child on the room. The child was also observed on the playground so as to evaluate behavior in more than one kind of situation.

East Lansing, Michigan
March, 1954

PART ONE

The Normative Approach to Analysis

Introduction

THE CHAPTERS in Part One are devoted to separate age-grade considerations of the behavior of children. Each chapter, one for each age-grade level, has been organized into two main sections: A. the particular age-grade expectations; and B. an interpretation of the behavior of our illustrative case at this time.

The age-grade "mode" includes materials in terms of an expectancy range for a child found in this classification. It is recognized that wide individual variations within any age-grade category are so vast that a concept of normalcy as a fixed limitation is entirely untenable. Consequently, when the words "mode" or "average" are used they may be expected to denote considerable range.

There may be found at any age-grade level a spread of behavior which overlaps somewhat with the age-grade limit of the group immediately above and below. Consequently, the important point to be made in these pictures of behavior may be found in the shifts of focus as the description moves from the mode of one age-grade level to the next.

The B section in each chapter introduces the illustrative case—Patricia—to the discussion. This section, however, is not entirely devoted to her. Occasionally an elaboration of a hypothesis or a statement of principle appears. These are usually followed by a comparison as found in this child's behavior. Briefly, then, this section is a mixture of principle elaboration and case illustration.

Each of the two sections is likely to be read in sequence as the student progresses through the book. Each section, however, may be seen in a longitudinal framework if the student on a later reading will progress from chapter to chapter covering first, in order, all of the A sections; and second, the B sections. It is believed that either perspective will present a cumulative picture of a growing child.

IN THE FIRST GRADE

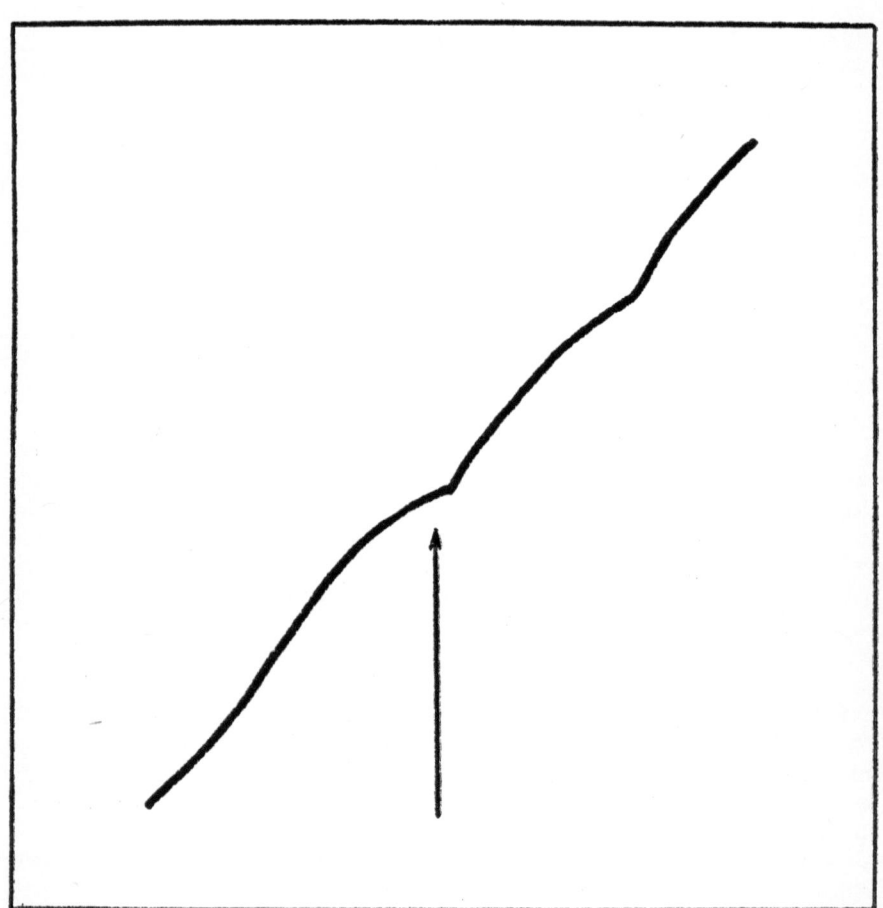

Period of Maturation

Chapter I

GRADE ONE—THE SIX-YEAR-OLD CHILD

A. The First-Grade Mode

"WHAT has happened to my child?" is an oft-repeated question of parents of the six-year-old. If the occasion for this question comes shortly after admission to school, "other" children or "wrong" schoolmates will be blamed for what appears as "degeneration" of a formerly "nice" boy or girl. Teachers who have little opportunity to see and understand the child in the process of change—an insight that is not necessarily forthcoming even when they move along with their group through a two- or three-year period—frequently are as unaware of gradations in behavior as the parent whom we have quoted. Other teachers, more familiar with the behavior shifts which accompany growth, are not surprised when parents make such complaints.

The explanation runs somewhat as follows. The child is ending one phase of development and beginning another. His development as seen at five appeared to be well-organized and integrated. He seemed happy with himself and with his surroundings. As a child in the kindergarten he played well, developed some self-control, and displayed a streak of sociability. Such an achievement has been his goal since his early days. He has proceeded toward this end without interruption. In a sense he is a grown up baby-youngster. He has reached the end of his first cycle of growth.

At six he is projecting himself into a new cycle that will not mature until eleven or twelve or thirteen years of age. Everything he is to become at the peak of his pre-adolescent development has its beginnings in the six-year bracket.

This does not deny the significance of the years from birth to six. Many previous developmental phases continue, but at new rates and with varied sensitivities to growth effects. He is the same child but in many ways he is a different child.

Many abrupt somatic and psychological changes enter the picture. The first teeth are abandoned and the first permanent molars make their appearance.

Glandular and other chemical processes take place that tend to produce a changed child.

Along with change comes a pattern of progress that at first is insecure and hesitant. The child is characterized by instability and organismic refusal to follow a consistent rate of growth. Speaking less technically, the child is up one day and down another. One week he may be able to spell a few words which are totally unfamiliar to him a week later. If he is given a series of intelligence tests he is more likely than not to show considerable variation—much more than he would show a year or two later. Growth sequences which are struggling to begin, such as reading, spelling, etc., fail to respond uniformly. Starting points although often occurring within the range of this grade level do not all begin at once. Some start before others. "Getting everything going" is the problem of the six-year-old. This is quite a task and often there is delay and hesitation in its accomplishment.

Thus the six-year-old is quite different from a five-year-old with an added year of development. What he was at five seems to have become dis-arranged at six. Actually he is progressing in his development. The difference can hardly be called "qualitative" and the word "quantitative" scarcely applies. Perhaps the best way to describe his condition is to use the words, "growing pains". The total picture of instability applies even to general health. He is more susceptable to disease. Nose and throat infections are more common. Changes in patterns of physical and motor growth detract from his stamina and robustness. His neuro-motor responses are less dependable and changes in the mechanics of seeing affect his school work. Children, for example, may be found to need glasses at this age which later may be discarded when various growth processes become coordinated and more reliably inter-related.

Accompanying the somatic and psychological changes are new attitudes and feelings, new moral and ethical developments, and a concept of self in relation to others. All of these—the somatic, the psychological, the cultural, and the spiritual—manifest themselves with some shock and insecurity. Six, then, can be seen as crucial in its lack of balance and its over-all behavior which rather adequately can be called experimental and exploratory.

The consequence of exploration is reaction in terms of extremes. The child is not predictable. He performs far below par at one time and considerably above it on another occasion. Which it will be, high or low, is almost entirely a matter of chance and temperament and thereby not strictly accountable at this time to conventional effect for its deviations.

It is questionable whether the typical first-grade school environment is compatible with the inevitable stormy beginning in a new developmental cycle. The first-grade child has difficulty in arriving at decisions as compared with the kindergarten child and the second-grade child. This would imply that considerable teacher influence and authority is essential. This certainly is not a propitious time for going all out for group decision and selection. Even under the best of circumstances the inability of first-graders to behave consistently will result in much confusion. Also in favor of considerable teacher decision and domination is the child's need for direction and control. His natural indecision should not be exploited to the point where teacher domination becomes a heavy burden to him. Teacher and parent aid of the right kind not only meets a need but will generally be welcomed. Teachers may, and often do, capitalize upon his characteristic indecision to the point where the child has no opportunity at all for choice and has little chance to see the results of his actions. A nice balance between teacher control and opportunity for developing independence is more satisfactory. Consequently some conventionality and restriction must be present in the classroom as well as some freedom, opportunity for group decision, and provision for individual explorations.

Instability and bipolarity on the part of the child have their effect in the home. He shifts from one emotional extreme to another. While he is crying he may come up with a smile, or when laughing may go into a crying spell. He may express love and hatred almost in the same breath. The only explanation for the drastic shift in expression is the child's inherent lack of ability at this time to distinguish whether the action causing the emotion is friendly or attacking.

The six-year-old, consequently, is confused in evaluating social relationships. With brothers and sisters he is loving and friendly at one moment and antagonistic and mean a moment later. This charactertistic leaves him somewhat short of adequacy in looking after a baby brother or sister for even a short time. He is neither mean nor jealous in spite of what his actions bespeak. Again, inconsistency of this kind is merely a growing effort without the background of coordination and integration to provide necessary constancy and control. His health inconsistency, temperamental vagaries, inadequate social relations are all characteristic of development at its early beginnings.

In school affairs he often appears to be regressing. As a kindergarten child he often made letters without any particular difficulty. As a first-grader he may write them backwards. He may read a few lines in a story one day but on the next day fail to recognize any of the words. His play is usually harmonious when only one other child is involved. When he becomes a member of a larger group he needs direction and guidance. Left alone with others the situation easily becomes chaotic. Attempting to induce him to be friendly or punishing him for faulty behavior is useless. He does not know why he acts as he does nor should teachers and parents expect explanations from him. His culture—in our attempt to justify his behavior—is beyond his natural propensities. His movement, thinking, attitudes, social development are all too immature for the complexity of the situation he is required to face. It is difficult to find words, expressive enough, to emphasize the kind of teacher and instructional program that will best meet his needs. The conventional first-grade teacher has but little insight into and understanding of his particular needs. He requires very gentle handling. He deserves attention to his comments, his queries, his drawings, and his stories. The teacher who wishes to become apt in meeting necessary conditions should be relaxed, friendly, and completely convinced that the solution to his problems is mainly that of providing the opportunity to grow.

Parents should present a similar environment, one that has an over-all climate of love and indulgence for his seeming indecision. They must remember that as his social developmental panorama opens for him he is faced with the problem of decision among many alternatives. When he makes the wrong choices, when not too bad, his action may be ignored; when his decision is extremely faulty he needs aid, not criticism. His problem is one of orientation to the world about him. Because of his lack of maturity in personal-social relations he naturally will and must make mistakes since he has insights into more problems than he is ready to solve. His errors usually are those of going to one extreme or another. He becomes insistent and aggressive or meek and hesitant, or he may attempt tasks beyond his potentialities. In school and on the playground he has the urge to win, to conquer, to subdue. If competition is an accompaniment of school work he wants to be first. He will boast about being first and will quite innocently copy from others in order to attain his goal. Conventional marking systems bring into prominence this trait in quite an undesirable fashion. He is combatative enough in his own right without school motivation and encouragement.

Social occasions for the six-year-old are much like those of seventh-graders but without the sex cleavage which is outstanding at the early adolescent age. Plans go awry and confusion reigns. Children may be coached to be polite and to greet other children courteously. However, they hardly ever take advantage of pre-planned ways of acting. At best, curt greetings are the order of the day followed by a growing crescendo of confusion. If presents are to be given, they are pounced on by scrambling, boisterous children. Social affairs in the first grade which include mothers may go-off with a little more decorum. Parties for children under more control with forced courteous behavior are quite unnatural and therefore without any real benefit. Children of this age who appear cute by imitating adults' standards during social occasions are merely playing an out-of-place role and consequently receive benefits of a limited nature. Some confusion must be present to give a party real social value. How much, however, is hard to determine. Children of this age need group social activity but in a climate that contains a satisfactory mixture of control and freedom. This of course is a climate that only the most skilled teacher can engender. At best the proper atmosphere allows opportunities for creative, adjustive behavior although the general tone may be one of confusion and highly motivated action.

The school room can provide a real opportunity for the first-grade child. He is so much more adrift, so much more confused, and has such a long way to go in his development as compared with the second-grade child—who also has his peculiar problems—or with the third-grade child who normally is well on his way. The first-grade room properly equipped offers just the right kind of supplementary environmental resources for providing the cultural surroundings necessary for his needs. Most important, without any doubt, is the teacher. And, most important of all the insights the resourceful teacher includes in her repertoire of understanding is that the six-year-old, in all his confusion, indecision, and "rambunctiousness", is a child going through a growth process which is natural and appropriate for the culture in which he finds himself. Tolerance and understanding should mark her general attitudes. Security, freedom to dramatize, create and explore, and recognition of friendly authority are the end points of reaction between such a person and a group of children of this age.

First-graders need room to move in. Motor and muscular movement are common accompaniments of creative and emotional expression. Their actions are more natural than dramatic although the latter seems to describe them well. The six-year-old's physical and muscular entity is alert and ready to act. Perhaps this is Nature's way for seeing that sufficient movement is brought into play to stimulate a paralleling of various growths at the beginning period of a new cycle of development. When the child is pleased his smile is not enough. He must show his pleasure with a jump, a cheer, or a clapping of hands. He does not cry quietly. He veritably bawls, kicks, and throws himself around. Even his dreams are violent, often marked by crying, falling or jumping out of bed. In less emotional situations he gestures, points, talks loudly, or rushes out of his seat while expressing himself orally.

Such a child is easily misunderstood. The right teacher for him is a person not easily startled by unexpected actions, questions, or comments. Of all possible phases of development which are taking place in him, the motor, social, and emotional are most closely joined and most readily seen as a triumvirate. Seemingly, one cannot be thrown into action without the active cooperation of the others. It should be readily seen that the instructional organization must be flexible, diversified, and supplemented with a richness of material and opportunity. The routine for these children must be carefully planned but, in order to capitalize on the opportunity shown by an unexpected happening, plans must be readily shifted. This kind of program requires greater resources than the kind built into the framework of a teacher's pre-plans followed to the letter. Drill and rote learning play a minor role in the proper setting. This child learns best through action and creative expression.

A popular and never-disappointing experience is the visit to a community enterprise. The post-office, dairy, fire-department, or neighborhood grocery store are popular choices. When opportunity is ably exploited much activity is the natural outcome of one of these trips. Children will use blocks or sand tables to reconstruct the scene of their visit. They may rig out a facsimile with orange crates, tables and other paraphernalia, make models from clay, or make crayon and wrapping-paper reproductions in mural form. When possible, children will act out the drama as seen by them. The goal is to develop meaning as to the various relationships witnessed on the trip. Many variations are possible on this theme. The work activity itself may be re-enacted for the personal values accruing to the child as he plays a role which brings something of himself into the necessary interpretations.

Obviously the kind of learning atmosphere suggested above is superior to the basic plan of formalized instruction in the skill subjects. Two reasons may be cited in support. First, the developmental upswing in various growths is still several months away. For some this is only a few months, for others it is six months, and for a few an entire year. There can be no particular advantage in bucking organismic lag although traditionally this is exactly what is being done in the majority of first grades throughout the country. The result is confusion, mixed results, indictment, castigation of children as failures, etc. The second reason for withholding formalized presentations in reading, arithmetic, and spelling is that the child's mind at this age has insufficient background to give meaning and interpretation to these kinds of efforts. Most six-year children still prefer picture-reading, dramatization, etc., which represent more primitive forms of communication. They are not yet socially or organismically developed for satisfying utilization of the kind of formal work that they often must endure at this age.

There must be sufficient readiness for reading so that the halting, hit-and-miss, limited vocabulary utilization that accompanies beginning formal reading must take up as short a time as possible. There is no particular fun in word-recognition reading at this stage. Beginning too early results in unduly stretching-out this somewhat boresome necessary phase. Consequently, this activity should be delayed until the time arrives when it will be least painful. The process of reading is best handled when the proper delay as to time is coordinated with an introduction which utilizes experience, creative reconstruction, with full motor accompaniment and utilization.

The first-grade child looks for much in the schoolroom situation. He is ready to accept his teacher as a supplementary mother. Consequently, he seeks attention and is generally pleased by it. When given the opportunity he shows a great deal of affection. He does not want his teacher to take his mother's place but rather to carry on the kind of atmosphere which he looks for at home. Teacher and parent need early contacts to facilitate understanding of each other for the purpose of establishing unanimity and coordinated effort. The child, in continuing his forays (he has been to kindergarten) beyond the home, needs security and encouragement of his efforts. When these are granted he is greatly aided in his broadened explorations in the social-cultural milieu. The child can only experiment successfully when he leads-off from a basis that remains rather fixed. If he has to scurry back he wants to know that the base has not been moved in his absence. He likes some convention and routine. But he does not like routine that denies exploration and experimentation.

The problem of the first-grader is to adjust to home and school demands, pressures, and challenges. His early years provided him with a single active environment. The school should broaden his base of activity while providing controls and guides but not frustrate or provide additional conflict. Thus the two environments should try to merge into one with the school regarded as an extension upon the home. This is not easy to achieve. The home offers dominant emotional security and expression which must not be too sharply challenged by school relations requiring behavior modifications. At best, in the way of unification of the two activating environments, the child must shift his behavior pattern as he moves from one to the other. The lesser the unanimity of purpose, challenge, and demand, the greater the shift required. Relations between parent and teacher generally should be above-board and fully explained to the child. A suggestion of this kind does not imply that the child should be present during a parent-teacher conference. The child should be informed of impending conferences and given security as to their purpose.

Coordinated effort is often lacking because both teacher and parent are more frequently unaware than not of the myriad of factors that stand ready to undermine the child's attitude toward school. First days in the first grade not infrequently produce high emotional tension as evidenced by lack of appetite or outright stomach upsets. Many children are sufficient to themselves in making a rough transition successfully. Others can receive injury that reflects itself in one or more deviational patterns. The child may not read, for example, when by all physiological maturity tokens he is ready. He may become aggressive, or withdraw to himself. He may foster a frustration far into his total elementary-school career. Such children are particularly vulnerable to a disciplinary attempt to solve their problems. Only the tough, rugged personality can adjust easily to an extreme authoritarian environment. The child with a background of freedom tempered by loving control will waver and become confused. The sensitive, immature, more emotional child will suffer the extreme effect of a disadvantageous school climate.

Some strain is inevitable and a normal accompaniment of adjusting to home and school atmosphere. It is innate in the physiological instability of this age level. It is also cultural in that all societies demand a normal amount of facing-up to life's expectations. Unfortunately, the cultural demand comes at a time when the child is not quite ready psychologically and maturationally. He is not quite ready to demonstrate new growth patterns, to proceed toward new levels in his development. And further, not all children of this age show the same maturational readiness. Some are later, some are advanced. In addition to the complex task of the first-grade teacher in dealing with the modal child with all his potential behavior variations, she must be ready to cope with exceptions to the rule. Thus flexibility, patience, and understanding must be the keynote in all instructional planning.

B. Behavior and Interpretation

1. *Motor Performance*

Patricia appeared to be somewhat less composed than the usual six-year-old and quite restless. She showed the usual picture, running in and out of the house in her play at home and moving from one play center to another when on the playground at school.

Six is usually described as a continuous-action age. Patricia fitted such a characterization when seen around home and on the school playground. She could be in all places almost at the same time—running, jumping, and constantly moving about. While working at her desk in school she gestured and often jumped up and down from her chair. Unlike other children who appeared to be all legs and arms at at this age she seemed to be better coordinated in her movements.

Patricia, like most six-year-old children, was pleased to assist in keeping the room clean and in picking up materials scattered or thrown about during work activity. Typically, she was not particularly efficient in her efforts or in her rather crude methods. Seats might be banged together and the broom whacked against wall or furniture.

Patricia always demonstrated a rough-and-ready attitude in her play. Bull-in-the-ring and other games demanding muscular action and physical contact were her favorites. Because the conventional first-grade teacher demands much "gentility" of her children, particularly of girls, the normal child who climbs high, jumps down from too great a height, wrestles or rolls around on the ground with other children, is regarded as the exception and something of a roughneck. Patricia was this kind of a child and consequently never quite gave in to teacher pressure to be a lady. Other children in her room substituted teacher approval and commendation for natural motor expression. Patricia, although struggling to sublimate her motor and physiological drives, never quite made the grade.

2. *Emotional Reactions*

Six years marks the age at which the modal child is about ready to start a new upward trend in his emotional development. Phrasing previously used will be effective in portraying this thought. The typical child at this age has a *maturational readiness* to proceed to new levels of emotional expression and reaction. Readiness implies not alone achievement of a stage of maturity but also a new inter-relationship between all organismic facilities. This represents a mobilization of forces for interaction with a broadened environment. Readiness also includes a more favorable sensitivity of inner faculties to outer environmental forces. Consequently the parent or teacher may expect a whole new panorama of behavioral and developmental manifestations. Living harmoniously with such a child requires manipulation and guidance based on complete understanding of him and of his behavioral manifestations, or in lacking understanding, a patient give-and-take with some lee-way for emergency withdrawal of authoritative bonds and restrictions.

As stated previously he is at the point where behavior ranges widely from expectations. The child may be cooperative and nice at one time and a short time later challenging and negative. A long list of adjectives recorded in Patricia's files notes typical six-year-old inconsistency. These are "good disposition", "shows her feelings", "poised", "calm", "happy", "well behaved", "cynical", "sensitive", "reserved", "contrary". Such a mixture of behavior characteristics is typical of the age as so ably demonstrated by this child.

Moodiness, with-drawal, reserve, and other similar categorizations recurred frequently in our anecdotes. Patricia provided a fine illustration, with perhaps more than average evidence, of six-year-old children who are quite inept at the finer more demanding small motor coordinations but somewhat more than typically skilled in large muscle coordination and movement. These children typically show recessive characteristics. They become moody, bored, restive, and self-engrossed. Patricia with her frequent getting-up from her seat, looking at a neighbor's book, sharpening her pencil, etc., was representative of this type of child.

3. *Anxieties and Security Threats*

There is no evidence in our file on Patricia to indicate that she showed the anxieties and fears of the typical six-year-old. Imaginary wild animals, fear of dogs, thunder or lightning could not be charged against her. Most children of this age live with imaginative beings that are awesome and fearful. The child visualizes ghosts or bears in a dark room. He also is likely to believe in witches. Some children fear other children to whom they attribute inhuman deeds. Patricia was a stranger to such phantasy. If she was ever afraid of the dark, of persons on the street, of bullies or gangs, it was during her pre-school life. Her first year in school included no circumstances in which she indicated fear of bodily injury, the flow of blood, or the many other six-year-old fears of physical harm.

4. *Personal-Social Development*

The implication of the idea of new emerging potentialities would lead one to expect of the six-year-old new developmental manifestations of strong interests in other children. Since this is not the case, two possible hypotheses are in order. First, Nature may have ordained a developmental lag in personal-social growth so that the influencing factors may be well in focus before the child is required to venture into this new and most complex area of action. It is possible that Nature may have given him this kind of organismic protection which she has so generously granted to other kinds of animals in the way of coloration, bodily conformation and equipment. It is possible that she has seen fit to adequately equip him physiologically, to give him personal information, or as the facts stand, to make him clearly aware of himself before making him clearly aware of the relations of others to him. A self-centered personality at this age does not attest to an undesirable time-lag in this phase of his development but rather bespeaks of a successful future personal-social development in which early recognition of self is a paramount prerequisite.

Certainly, the six-year-old sees the world in relation to his own universe. He is not appalled by it because it is so much more complex than his own world. What he values are his own interests and needs. What he wants is love, affection, and ego recognition of all kinds. He wants to be first. He wants to be praised. He wants to be the center of attention. When he is sure he has obtained these he is ready to widen his contact circle.

Patricia in a mild way was this kind of child during her stay in the first grade. She talked pleasantly about home and her part in it. At school she sought teachers' attention and approval. She was somewhat pleasant with other children but made no untoward efforts to gain approval. Because of her typical self-centered activity she was regarded by observers and teachers as somewhat shy, retiring, and insecure. It is likely that she demonstrated these characteristics but they were exaggerated because of typical teacher pressure to "socialize" than because of deep-rooted and significant insecurity.

In general, her first-grade year was marked by harmony between school and home environment. This is not unusual for many first-grade children. Among the others who attended school with Patricia, this could be said of the majority. It is interesting to speculate upon the reasons therefor. In Patricia's case there was almost a complete lack of contact between teacher and parents. Report cards were sent home without any response from parents. Since the reports were innocuous and could be interpreted by parents as indicating satisfactory behavior and school performance, the lack of parent reaction would be regarded as insignificant. The report was sent; it was satisfactory. Therefore no answer was necessary.

A high degree of cooperation has been suggested as helpful in aiding the child to make the proper transition from home to school. Since this was not the case in the rather successful transition made by a majority of children in this particular school, one wonders if the next best method to cooperative relationships might not be a complete lack of contact between teacher and parent. In such reasoning, partial "cooperative" effort may lead to conflict and misunderstanding. Here is a situation in which it is possible that an all-or-none attitude is representative of the best policy of operation.

5. *Play and Recreation*

Patricia was very typical in her play and games. Like most six-year-olds she was all over the place. On the school playground where the equipment or play space was more or less scattered, she moved from one to the other as fancy dictated—a child she wanted to see, a high swinging child she wanted to out-do, a ball game in session where she sought participation for herself.

In the classroom she was fond of paints and of cut-outs, engaging in these at every opportunity. She was not so skillful as most other children in small-scope and detailed drawing or tracing but enjoyed what she did even when it was crude and messy. At all times she wanted to please the teacher and was a little conscious of what other children thought of her work. She played equally easily with boys as with girls and at times showed a preference for playing ball with the boys. More than other girls in her room she liked rough games. Running, swinging, playing tag, and playing ball were her favorites.

Patricia also showed some interest in collections. This is typical for children of her age. She never developed collecting into a real hobby. Her swag was rather meager but she was fond of what she had.

6. *Academic Status*

Patricia demonstrated interest in her early reading activities. She enjoyed recognizing single words in various story books, mostly pictorial with some description of the content of the picture. She learned early to print her name and easily learned to make letters. Her early work in arithmetic was not satisfying. She reported a greater dislike for this subject than for any other.

Patricia greatly enjoyed the first grade and on the first day was not accompanied by her mother. Due to the fact that she had attended kindergarten in an adjacent room, the first-grade transition caused her no worry or anxiety. Like most first-grade children she reflected interest in nearly everything that was presented and was always excited and intrigued when new plans were introduced. Patricia's attendance was regular. She did not fall victim to the usual chronic colds of most first-graders but invariably evidenced a slow-down toward the end of the week.

Unlike many children her imagination did not run away with her. Many children become frightened by seemingly harmless stories around which they build fantastic interpretations. Such children frequently develop a fear that lasts several days. These are built up into feigned illnesses or actual upsets that keep them away from school. Teachers of this grade might well give attention to the factors that cause absence rather than show concern for the reasons parents give for it. Such a strong connection exists between insecurity and illness that it is often difficult to separate one from the other. Certainly a child who is often absent because of ill health should be carefully studied for signs of anxiety, fear, or insecurity.

7. *Ethical and Moral Behavior*

It is only the exceptional child that gives in school a true picture of what we traditionally call ethical-moral behavior. Unless the child steals a pencil, shears or paper from another child or from the teacher, the typical ethics of this age are not resoundingly demonstrated. Well planned controls, organization, and supervision prevent much from happening that happens easily at home and in other circumstances out of the scope of the teacher's range of control. Consequently when the child is "caught" stealing quite a fuss is made. He will deny the allegation, even when he is caught "red-handed", and will put up quite a defense for himself. A child may even filch materials from the teacher's desk, if he likes the teacher, much as he would do at home in taking something desired from his father's desk or den, or from his mother's source of supply.

Patricia was never accused of taking things from other children or from her teacher. As a result she was regarded as "honest" and a "good citizen", responsible and a good group member.

In reality, at home and in situations without strict supervision, the child's ethical-moral development is in a state of flux. A child may confiscate things which do not belong to him. Parents are greatly disturbed because he previously had not shown such a trait since he was very young.

The occasion demands much less in the way of correction than is usually applied. Merely restoring the displaced article without comment or issue is usually sufficient. The occurrence is not representative of regression but rather of having arrived at a new stage of development. All performance at this age is inconsistent, generally unreliable, and experimental. The child must first fix his own ego realizations before he can adjust to others and to regulations which define individual and group rights.

Teachers of first-grade children are quite unaware of their real developmental problems. Home contacts and conferences certainly should be slanted heavily in the flow of information from parent to teacher instead of from teacher to parent. Teachers who are successful in collecting information may at first judge a child to be one kind of person at home and another kind at school. The purpose of learning everything possible about a child is to enable the teacher to see him in a variety of situations. She will then realize that it is often the circumstances under which school is conducted that cause normal behavior to appear abnormal.

Patricia gave some evidence of fluidity of rightness-wrongness in playground situations. In the classroom she would not hesitate in turning around in her seat to pick up a pencil or crayon belonging to her neighbor and use it momentarily. She usually returned it promptly and was never surreptitious or sly in the act.

Patricia liked toys as well as other children and was proud of her possessions. Like most children she was proud of their quantity and diversity but in her play gave them only slight interest and attention. She was typically careless of them and when brought to school frequently left them scattered about the room.

Selected References

Louise B. Ames, Janet Learned, Ruth Metraux, and Richard N. Walker: *Child Rorschach Responses*, pp. 207-19. Hoeber, New York, 1952.

Arnold Gesell and Frances L. Ilg: *Child Development*, Part II, "The Child From Five to Ten", pp. 88-120. Harper, New York, 1949.

Faculty of the University School: *How Children Develop*, University School Series No. 3, pp. 18-28. Ohio State University, Columbus, 1946.

Ilse Forest: *Early Years at School*, pp. 60-62. McGraw-Hill, New York, 1949.

Gladys G. Jenkins, Helen Schacter, and W.W. Bauer: *These Are Your Children*, pp. 38-61. Scott-Foresman, New York, 1949.

Celia Burns Stendler: *Children of Brasstown*, pp. 37-38, 42-44, 57-59, 66, 73-77, 82. U. of Ill. Press, Urbana, 1949.

Ruth Strang: *An Introduction to Child Study*, pp. 315-364. Macmillan, New York, 1951.

E. H. Watson and G. H. Lowrey: *Growth and Development of Children*, pp. 103-8. Year Book Publishers, Chicago, 1951.

IN THE SECOND GRADE

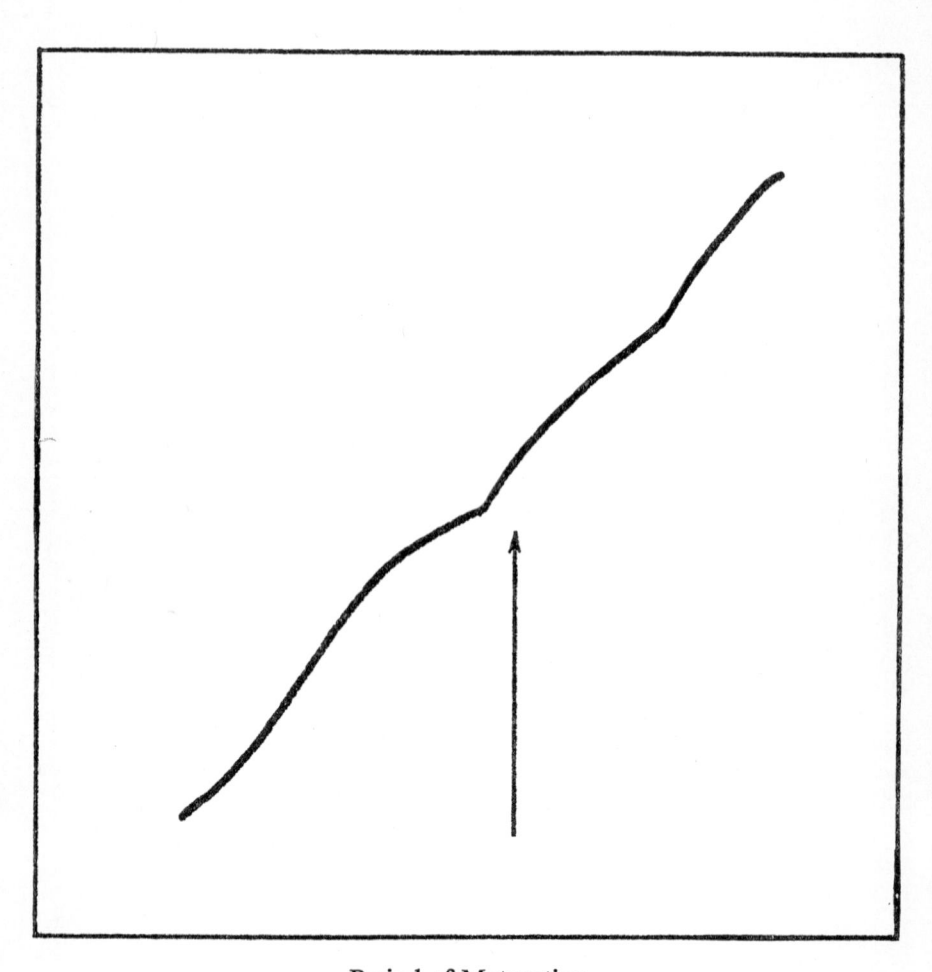

Period of Maturation

Chapter II

GRADE TWO — THE SEVEN-YEAR-OLD CHILD

A. The Second-Grade Mode

THE SEVEN-YEAR-OLD CHILD has stabilized himself typically in his pattern of development.[1] His various growths are smooth and progressively upward. He presents a picture of a child "quieting down" in respect to his earlier up-and-down irregular progress. Also in contrast to his earlier uncontrolled reactions and spontaneous outbursts, he now can endure extended calm and personal self-absorption. In the midst of self-study he can ignore the outer world and its potential interruption or challenge. In many respects development at this stage is accompanied by a reflective evaluation of experience in preparation for those many interesting things which the child thinks are coming to him.

The average seven-year-old is a good listener. He enjoys stories read to him and will request repetitions. The radio and television both intrigue him greatly. He is entranced typically by these instruments and greatly resents intrusion or interruption. If given the opportunity he will haunt the movies for his favorite pictures and spend unlimited time in watching repetitions. Unless the seven-year-old shows such characteristics in a culture in which they can be found, he is somewhat immature and lagging in his development. The normal pattern is one of abandonment of callow insensible behavior. The teacher who is assigned to a roomful of such children—it sometimes happens in spite of wide variations of maturity at any age—will inevitably feel that she is indeed fortunate in having such a large number of *nice* boys and girls.

Seven can be a happy age if parents and teachers allow reasonable freedom. The boy or girl can withdraw to his or her room and play for lengthy periods. Parents, overly conscious of the dangers of introversion and fearful of withdrawal tendencies, are inclined to protest and prevent full enjoyment of a natural characteristic.

[1] See preceding chart for start of seventh year.

School and home both need to provide the opportunities this age demands for reflection on the happenings in the child's world. He is ready to react to many events which heretofore passed him by. He needs the opportunity to dwell upon the meanings of his variegated contacts with children and adults. Meanings are primarily in the category of feelings which will form the basis for later emotional and creative reactions.

This whole process consists not only of development but also of many accompaniments of development. It results in a maturity beyond that of the experimental and uncontrolled behavior of the six-year-old. It is something more than an indication of growth processes at work. Fundamentally it indicates the beginning of reactive struggles with the cultural surroundings. Such surroundings are broad, diversified and often cruel in their demands. Both parents and other children fully test inner and outer resources. Significantly, the seven-year-old must be allowed, within reasonable range, periods of needed preoccupation and reflection. And of equal significance, this age is marked as the time at which there is the beginning of the joint utilization of inner and outer resources in achieving necessary life adjustments.

Teachers and parents interested in cherishing full potential developmental maturity must bow in their demands to this particular personality need. Adults can best serve the inner psychological urges of the seven-year-old by curtailing requirements that prohibit satisfactory mental reflection. What may occasionally appear as mild perturbation, neglect of social demands, melancholia, shyness, depression, or even rejection, should be carefully scrutinized before being assayed as a trend toward psychic digression. Behavior often so characterized should be expected at times on the part of most seven-year-old children.

Obviously, this kind of child receives more than he gives. In view of what can be expected of him a year hence, his preoccupation must be regarded as preparatory. Apparently what he is seeking is a safe foundation on which to branch out—a necessary foundation based on satisfactory adjustments between self and environmental impact. *Of all the years regarded as basic for later personal development, this is one of the most significant and important.*

Such behavior categorization does not mean that the seven-year-old is not greatly interested in things around him. He is thinking when his physical counterpart gives the opposite impression. He may explode out of a seeming relaxed or indolent mood into a dynamic, moving child of action. Or, seemingly paying little attention to what is going on, he may literally throw back the answer to a problem or question when least expected.

In between extremes, from isolation to dynamic action, there may be found the beginnings of wholesome, social behavior. The child at this age while seeking insights into himself is becoming increasingly aware of others. He sees other children not only in relation to satisfaction of his own personal drives but in reference to their attitudes toward him and their attitudes and value judgments toward life in general. His parents take on a new perspective. They are seen somewhat apart from the child himself as he explores contacts with other children. He often expresses a desire for a new brother or sister or he may attempt a pal relationship with an older child. Movement away from parent identification includes exaggerated fondness of his teacher. Thus he begins a new guarded relationship with those who are close at hand. This indicates the beginnings of growth in independence and of the trend which in the later elementary-school years will take him almost entirely away from his parents.

The school has great potentialities in its opportunity sequences for this age level, particularly in reference to the teacher. Acceptance by this new friend in his life is sought, and conversely, teacher disapproval brings unalloyed unhappiness and despair. A smile, a friendly pat on the head, a readiness to hear his story or experience causes a bubbling over of friendliness and good-will. The typical child will go to all lengths to attract attention. He will ask for directions, cues, and starting signals even when directions are known and thoroughly understood. These are indicative of social development.

The second-grade teacher should realize that she must maintain person-to-person relationships with the majority of her children. She must be quite free and easily approachable, moving around the room and thereby providing equal opportunity for access to her. Of all the elementary grades, the need is greater here for a friendly democratic type of personality than in any other grade. These children need expanded contacts and it is the teacher's responsibility to see that they are provided. In this way she encourages emotional and personal development so necessary to the present and future happiness of the child. A by-product of free, informal, individual contacts is the opportunity given for development of speech and narrative skills so essential to the child's personal development. Stories and anecdotes presented to her by children strengthen security, give challenges, and encourage experimentation with new contacts.

As at school so at home! In spite of the withdrawal tendencies mentioned the child shows an increased interest in affairs that are not exclusively concerned with his own welfare. He has periods of genuine companionability. He will volunteer and respond to requests for help if not isolated in performing assigned tasks. He wants to help his father in mowing the lawn, but of course will not like to do it alone. These bursts of helpfulness are occasionally trying in that he will want to do things that are beyond his ability. The wise parent will be patient and graciously accept his assistance and compliment him for his help.

To already mentioned characteristics of broodiness and helpfulness let us add independence. Although the child occasionally becomes argumentative and disagreeable, let us not infer that such behavior is a counter attack to infringements upon personal plans but rather a display of a naturally developing trend toward a desire to express his own thoughts and decisions. It is not manifested through verbal aggression or direct physical attack on playmates but instead through a half-courteous, half-sulky expression.

Diversified behavior, as described, adds up to a personality that at times is agreeable and receptive and at other times mildly aggressive and considerably assertive. This does not mean that developmental trends are at cross purposes with each other or that the child is unstable or unpredictable. What appears as a variety of personality traits is nothing more than wide ranged behavior all-expressive of natural development, viz., growth of independence, improved adjustive processes, and a feeling-out of environmental surroundings which he needs not only to endure but to use for his own personal improvement. From day to day, nevertheless, he shows a moody, changing, shifting type of development.

In terms of social contacts brought about on the playground or in the family back-yard, his beginning independence is somewhat undisciplined and non-group centered. Games that appeal to him are quite informal with a minimum of rule and regulation. He is likely to take a dim view of such controls as may apply to himself but becomes demanding, quarrelsome and critical of minute infringements by others. If his side loses he makes alibis or claims that the other side was unfair. He is not above tattling on other children or dubbing them as cheats or teacher's pets. Or he may become indignant enough to quit before the game is over and proceed home by himself.

For he can really become indignant! His ethical values are forming and although he may omit evaluation of his own performance in reference to them, he readily applies standards to others. Again we have here the beginning of a new growth phase in pre-adolescent development. Such behavior is natural and an accompaniment of a growing consciousness of what is good and bad. Oftimes his gripes and criticisms are merely a mechanism for surveying opinions and attitudes of others as to what is right and wrong. Punishing this child in the presence of other children is not helpful. Such a child can appear to be wrong to others but right to himself. He will avoid crying before others and consequently should not be pressed through punishment to reach this stage of confusion.

The seven-year-old does not often resort to tantrums, particularly in the presence of non-family members. Disapproval as he may typically register will be manifested in displays of sullenness, a hasty exit accompanied by slamming a door, or outright placement of blame on others. All are normal, are definitely on a maturity trend, and not to be greatly deplored. Particularly common are his alibis and scape-goating efforts. Parents and teachers so frequently attempt to use "reason" to prove to the child that someone else could not possibly be to blame. Treatment of this kind is utterly worthless and confusing to the child. He is at the age where he needs an easy out in order not to weaken, as he feels it, his security and group belongingness.

It suits the mood of the seven-year-old child to find indulgence of his minor deceptions. If his excuses are accepted, he is not thereby necessarily encouraged to go to greater lengths to explain the next unapproved episode. Rather, with understanding and a minimum of adult disparagement, he himself can provide the necessary self-discipline for gradually discarding this manner of justifying his actions.

Sensitivity to property rights is likewise at an immature stage. This child may help himself to community property, as would be the situation in school, or occasionally appropriate the property of individual children. In essence this is not theft but more essentially the dominant drive of a new interest, or an old one, which appropriation of property satisfies.

Children demonstrating such behavior should not be accused of or charged with theft. The development of acceptable ethical codes takes time and accompanies total maturation as it relates to experiences. As contacts and horizons broaden, the child is given his best opportunity for stable growth. Without them, and living rather restrictedly from broadening contacts, he must learn by precept and dogma. In the natural situation his problem is one of relating personal desires to social and cultural sanctions. This is of course the problem of all individuals at all ages. Parents, although recognizing the complexity of the individual-cultural demands at the adult level of maturity, are inclined to regard a child's problem as simple. This is not the case. The problem of the seven-year-old is, if possible, even more complex. He is just beginning to learn something of society's demands at a time when he knows little about himself in relation to others. The teacher should be most patient in dealing with such problems since the child, if circumstances permit, is naturally a social being and will progress toward a satisfactory maximum in this respect. "Teaching" is hardly necessary. What the child needs is patience and the opportunity to explore.

Age seven, it must be remembered, is found within the pre-adolescent developmental cycle at the beginning of a growth stage. The child is here ready for reflective thinking leading to generalizations and conclusions. In spite of argument and alibi on his part, he may be talked to regarding ethical action. Perhaps his critical attitudes and his experimentation in reaching for standards make him suspect of his own efforts. He does not mind "doing things over" at his teacher's suggestion. Also typical are his repetitive improvement attempts in his own individual projects —his drawings, his carpentry, etc.

In some ways the seven-year-old gives evidence of trying to make up for lost time. He is hard to satisfy, and constantly attempts to improve his achievements. He will draw sheet after sheet on the same subject with but little variation or difference. In sedentary games he will continue way beyond the point of boredom of children at other ages. His persistency for repetition—in asking for the same story over and over, in wanting to improve upon a task fairly well done—is somewhat annoying and easily misunderstood. Age seven, however, shows a "well-roundedness" in growth efforts which is entirely lacking in the experimental behavior of the six-year-old. Against his withdrawal tendency is his trend away from it as reflected in his beginning interest in others. Even his thinking has a personal-social cast. His moments of withdrawal and reflection are in the main taken up with a consideration of his reactions as they relate to playmates and family. And, as befits a beginning up-rise in a growth pattern his thinking is in terms of an over-all problem rather than with episodes or disparate incidents.

His general vision of the world and his environment contains more detail than was found at six. His landscapes now include not only sky, but also sun, moon, planets. He draws houses and people in action. He has a comprehension of some of the people in his environment. These of course include what to him are the more glamourous—the policeman, the fireman. He knows the grocery-man and the milkman. The teacher has meaning and significance. Time and season also have meaning for him. Time of day is unimportant. He is given to too much self-absorption to be depended upon to remember to do much in preparation for a later event. Activities should be directed to the present or he should be given reminders which will be welcomed by him. Such precautionary measures do not necessarily indicate restraint of freedom or restriction of potentially growing independence. They are merely aids and directions which his maturity stage needs for adequate blossoming-out.

Seven-year children show a mixture of realism and phantasy. The old fairy tales may still be of interest but so are stories and incidents relating to science. Sunday-school experiences raise questions. He wants to know about God and heaven, and has come to know something about death. All in all the seven-year-old child is growing up. His horizons have widened to accommodate all broad elements of the universe both physical and spiritual. His developmental stage is one of great receptive possibilities with the problem of adjusting inner drives to cultural demands. He is all boy or she is all girl. He romps, he plays, he climbs trees; he designs pranks on others; he is happy, mostly cheerful, and he is somewhat careless of adult standards.

Because of his ever widened areas for behavior he is easily misunderstood. A mood or a phase of his activity may be taken as an interpretation for his total being and outlook. Consequently home and school guidance must be understanding, elastic, and varied in its applications to fit his changing moods and reflections.

B. Behavior and Interpretation

1. *Motor Performance*

Patricia as typical of a child of this age was considerably more active during this year than was the case in her previous year. She showed many spontaneous conflagrations of physical action. She did not, however, at any time during the year show the usual caution of the second-grader. She was always ready to take a dare—climb a tree, jump the creek, etc.

Patricia gave little evidence of the desire for perfection shown by most children who take every opportunity to repeat over and over a special performance. Nevertheless motor activity and interest as evidenced by running, playing ball, and swinging seemed to endure continuously with but classroom interludes.

In the schoolroom this child presented the opposite picture. She lolled in her seat, was inattentive to most of the class discussions, and when the occasion presented itself to move from her seat sauntered casually about the room. At her desk she often rested her head in her arm while writing or reading. Also typical was her dropping of pencil or book without apparent cause or reason.

2. *Emotional Reactions*

At seven Patricia was conscious of the behavior of other children and their reaction to her. She did not display fear of success in the work of her grade although she was quick enough to curry her teacher's favor or to reclaim status through a smile or a planned contact when she felt that she had been somewhat indifferent or neglectful. Patricia never gave the emotional type of attention to stories read aloud that was expected and shown by other children.

Most children of this age withdraw from games, discussion groups and other places when differences arise, rather than remain and contest the aggression of others. Patricia did not withdraw in the face of conflict but more often withdrew from a peaceful well-balanced proceeding. She managed usually to remain on the fringe rather than risk her status by complete withdrawal.

The typical child of seven puts on displays of aggression which are more sham than real. Patricia was often like this, carrying a rather friendly bold front somewhat alarming to smaller children but never backed by vicious aggressive action.

Seven-year-olds differ from their year-younger contemporaries by frenzied vocalization and yelling as compared with the over-all motor (voice and actions) energy release of the six-year-old. The second-grader shouts to everyone—playmate, teacher, and parent. Patricia was quite like this, especially on the playground.

This child gave little indication during the periods under observation of the high-level standards attributed to the seven-year-old. Such a child is academic at heart; he strives for high grades, and will only call attention of parents to his best efforts. The perfection drive in him doesn't signify that he will not defend first tries. He may argue that his production—drawing, spelling paper, or whatever it may be—represents what was called for in the first place. If left alone, however, he will discard and try again. Patricia would have difficulty in qualifying for this kind of stereotype. In the first place her general manipulative pencil, crayon, or painted productions were messy. Detail rather than creative standards motivated her teachers in their assignments. Patricia, perhaps because of this, did not once present a well-finished product.

Nor did Patricia exhibit the usual seven-year-old tendency of persistency. Typically, this child goes on and on in completing a project of his own choice or one assigned by the teacher. Patricia was often reported as having difficulty in completing a task. The observer implied that a demonstration of this kind indicated poor work habits. A more critical evaluation of this child would be to the effect that she displayed normalcy in having difficulty in completing a task, but in the time consumed for the act showed little improvement, revision, or creative efforts in attempting to discharge the responsibility involved. Patricia's efforts might have been described as mere dabbling rather than as studious and concentrated effort to do something really well.

Other descriptive phrases characteristic of the child of this grade are more applicable to Patricia. She was really quite conscientious. Although often doing poorly she made plans and carried them out. She was ready to do errands for her teacher and to take assigned group responsibility. She was considerate if not thoughtful and was anxious to secure approbation of others. Although individualistic she liked to share with others, particularly if sharing was the result of selection of her by others.

3. *Anxieties and Security Threats*

During her whole elementary-school period Patricia gave the impression of being a mixture of a big girl and little girl. She was of course a few months chronologically advanced beyond the typical second-grader. She was larger than the other children and even during her first year in school there was something motherly and kind in her attitude and general personality. The "little girl" connotation did not spring from demureness, overt fears, or extreme shyness. Rather, it came from her bravado, dare-me type of personality exterior. To some extent such a a description qualified her for the sterotype of the seven-year-old vacillating on a scale from extreme deliberation and caution to unreasoned, abandoned behavior.

Patricia showed some anxiety about her relationship with other children. She tended to look down upon the "Brownie's" since she had but little to do in this organization. She also tended to compensate for some rejection at her own grade level by courting the attention of girls in the third and fourth grades. Generally speaking the second-grader is misunderstood in reference to social contacts. This is not a grade where social groups have much continuity. Enforced groupings, whatever their democratic goals, are somewhat artificial at this level. Patricia consequently was somewhat misjudged as non-social on the basis of inextensiveness of her friendship list.

4. *Personal-Social Development*

Seven is the time for a beginning of the process of acceptance of sex status and adjustment. Patricia seemed to show neither of two typical characteristics of a child of this age. She was not in any marked way a child that spent her time reading, listening to the radio or quietly contemplating her status and reactions with other children. Nor was she particularly devoted to awareness of her body with an ensuing sensitivity to sex and her identification as a girl. There was something in Patricia which became more marked later which indicated some hesitance to accept herself as a girl and to act accordingly.

Seven is a time when most children give signs of membership in the family group and happily assume home responsibilities. Patricia was such a child. She not only liked to have her share of work to do but was always ready to do more than her share. Circumstances surrounding Patricia made it difficult to determine whether the desire to help and the desire to prove her use to her family represented her dominant desire for family approval or whether it could be attributed to the fact that she had so much fun working around her parents' store. Anecdotes and records indicated that Patricia preferred helping with the gas pumps to aiding her mother in the kitchen. And further, to indicate more personalized reasons for responding to family demands for help was sustenance of interest in working at the store. Patricia in regard to these duties was quite unlike the typical seven-year-old child who tires easily of routine home work and prefers to move to new tasks rather than repeat daily the same old job.

Patricia generally played well with other children. Within a small group of favorites she was quite ribald—laughing, jesting—and in general played the part well of what one expects of a clown. She liked informal group play in which there were few rules but had inclinations toward the formalized soft-ball games. She was more like a boy than a girl in that she enjoyed friendly wrestling and pushing around.

She was not so shy as she was formerly and talked rather easily with our observers. She not only was responsive to their questions and interest but assumed some social aggression of her own as indicated by her "Hi, kid!" greeting one day to one of these.

5. *Play and Recreation*

Patricia gave little evidence of expanded play activities. Most girls at this age begin designing doll wardrobes and revert to endless coloring of designs and cut-outs of one kind or another. The modern progressive trend in art work toward free, sweeping movements should not overlook the desire girls have at this age for coloring and cutting out rather small designs and patterns. In other words, there must be an opportunity at this age for both kinds of work and each should be included some place in the school program but for totally different objectives. Cut-outs serve a personal-social motive and secondarily should be considered as a performance to develop manipulative coordination and movement. Patricia at times demonstrated this concept of the seven-year-old. In general however she avoided this activity when her efforts were to be compared with those of other children. She excelled more with big muscle games than with the less active manipulative activities. If these are a cultural and a sex-role accompaniment and thereby give evidence of adjustment to such, Patricia can be seen as an avoider. She did not really reject but seemed to give indication of extending for as long as possible the earlier non-sensitivity to sex cleavages. We must be warned, however, before going too far in characterizing Patricia in her play activities, that marked individual differences may be expected.

6. *Academic Status*

On the whole Patricia spent her year in the second grade in quite normal fashion. Her work was satisfactory enough as indicated by report cards, and her general over-all behavior was neither annoying nor at a level to justify commendation. She showed no fears of the second grade in the early weeks as might be expected, nor did she give indication of fatigue during her various school activities. In other ways Patricia was more typical. Her desk was filled with miscellaneous papers and other materials showing some transition of a feeling of belongingness from home to school. Patricia's attitude toward her teacher was somewhat indifferent. She spoke to her when she felt like it or quite ignored her on other occasions. She never ignored her teachers to the extent of jeopardizing her status nor was she consistently enthusiastic and demonstrative in her affections. She was somewhat quieter when she worked than she was in the first grade, but talked more to herself or mumbled. She readily wheeled around in her seat to talk to a neighbor and typically often demanded her teacher's assistance either by calling aloud or by walking directly to her before stating her request.

What was interpreted as personal disinterest and failure in cooperation by most of our observers may have been more of a natural kind of behavior which was *not* shown by a majority of her classmates. Behavior so characterized was Patricia's readiness to rest her head on her seat while a class was in session, getting up "impolitely" and walking about the room and then back to her seat, opening and closing her desk, taking something out, etc. Such behavior indicated natural restlessness, exhaustion of normal attention span, and readiness to move to another kind of activity. Anticipating and looking forward to a shift in school routine is characteristic of seven-year-old second-grade children. They frequently will interrupt on-going procedure to inquire as to the next-period's activity.

Dropping and manipulating pens, paper, pencils, etc., is also a natural reaction for children of this age. Correct schoolroom procedure should recognize these symptoms and make allowances for them. This would void the opportunity for children to be accused of being clumsy in doing those things that are natural and that they would do anyway but which are regarded as interfering and annoying in an instructional situation. Teachers who have no particular orientation to the peculiarities of the second-grader often choose this grade for teaching since it is amenable to conventional procedure. The child is ready to learn and invariably provides a performance which shows improvement. There is inherent in the situation a temptation to push these youngsters. Children at this age need help with personal-social needs. Their creative tendencies, their emotional expression, and their ethical-moral sililoquizing need nurturing. If not given attention at this age and grade, some of these more intangible traits may never emerge.

Teachers should realize that second-graders also need help on the playground. Their activity is expansive and quite uncontrolled. Patricia as an illustration of this kind of action exploded from classroom to playground. Big and active, she was one of the first to get out. Occasionally Patricia interfered with others, or was interfered with by others. She would confiscate a swing for the entire period or graciously give it up. All this is meant to point out that she showed many normal tendencies of the second-grader.

7. *Ethical and Moral Behavior*

Patricia's schoolroom behavior in the second grade gave no important insights into her ethical-moral consciousness. Because nothing distressing or symbolic was witnessed in her behavior, nothing was recorded.

In terms of general behavior, which usually is considered related to ethical-moral attitudes, Patricia showed many typical qualities. She responded amicably to directions. At no time was she disciplined in anything more than an all-inclusive manner. She was always reasonable, though sometimes not too alert, but never was found far from average behavior. Patricia definitely was the kind of child that wanted to be thought of as helpful and good, and healthfully for her own welfare found some ways to reach this goal.

SELECTED REFERENCES

Louise B. Ames, Janet Learned, Ruth Metraux, and Richard N. Walker: *Child Rorschach Responses*, pp. 220-39. Hoeber, New York, 1952.

R. G. Barker and H. F. Wright: *One Boy's Day*, pp. ix, 428. Harper, New York, 1951.

Barbara Biber, Lois B. Murphy, Louise P. Woodcock, and Irma S. Black: *Life and Ways of the Seven-to-Eight Year Old*. Basic Books, New York (59 4th Ave.), 1953.

Merl E. Bonney: "A Study of Social Status on the Second-grade Level". *Journal of Genetic Psychology*, 60, 1942, pp. 271-305.

Faculty of the University School: *How Children Develop*, University School Series No. 3, pp. 18-28. Ohio State University, Columbus, 1946.

Ilse Forest: *Early Years at School*, pp. 62-64. McGraw-Hill, New York, 1949.

Arnold Gesell and Frances L. Ilg: *Child Development*, Part II, "The Child From Five to Ten", pp. 131-158. Harper, New York, 1949.

Gladys G. Jenkins, Helen Schacter, and W. W. Bauer: *These Are Your Children*, pp. 62-79. Scott-Foresman, New York, 1949.

IN THE THIRD GRADE

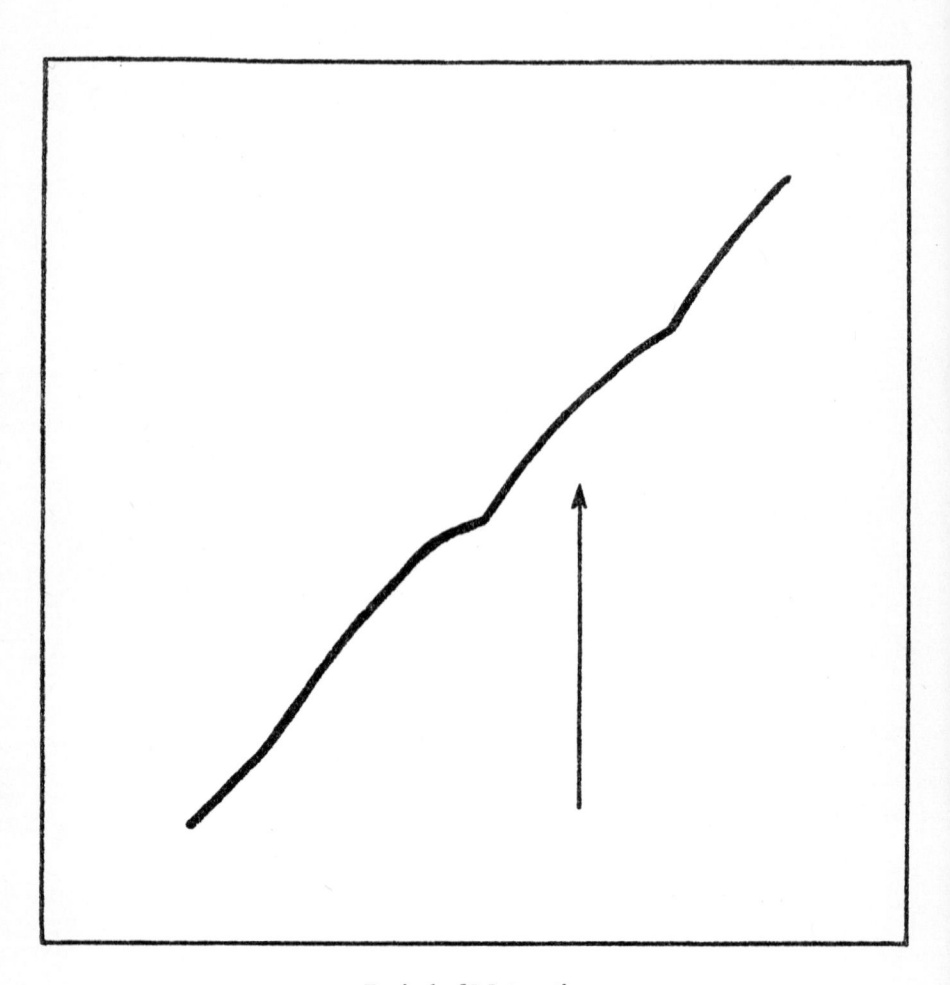

Period of Maturation

Chapter III

GRADE THREE—THE EIGHT-YEAR-OLD CHILD

A. THE THIRD-GRADE MODE

EIGHT HAS OFTEN been compared to age four with reference to growth potentiality. The comparison is not inappropriate since the two ages respectively represent similar stages of maturity but each in a different developmental cycle.

The eight-year-old is embarking upon a consistent growth trend in all phases of development. The sixth year was a year of uncertainty and exploration; seven gave evidence of development but with considerable variation and unreliability. Eight is the time for steady progressive development. It represents a period in which the child is responsive and a time in which teacher and parent can expect much gain in connection with good guidance efforts. It is almost a fool-proof year for teachers. The growth potential is powerful and resists ordinary threats and unfriendly impositions. Positively, it is a receptive period. Children show results. Character and ethical development, as well as the creative and emotional trends, are easily stimulated. What is true for these developmental motivations is also true for personal-social development. The child of this age easily covers a wide environmental range and demonstrates an improved adjustment to it.

Physically he is much more mature. Coordination is good and eyes are sufficiently developed for both near and far distances as they are for the more intensive reading activities which are his lot in this grade. He is less susceptable to disease, is ready for rough games and has the skill for more complex physical activities. He can dance, play baseball, and is interested in dramatics in which he may become most proficient.

Sex differences both in terms of interests and of maturities become noticeable. Girls begin to equal or to show height and weight superiority over boys. They tend to be more proficient in school subjects, definitely show better adjustment to instructional organization and to teacher demands and other typical school manifestations that are more likely than not "female-centered".

Up to this age boys and girls have played together rather harmoniously. At eight they begin to discover that the opposite sex has conflicting interests. This is likewise the age where they begin to discover themselves as manifested by activities to become identified with their own sex. They will occasionally gang-up and deride members of the opposite sex. Or boys will pick on girls sometimes crudely and in an unfriendly manner.

Occasionally a boy or girl will cross sex lines in an experimental mood but generally the two groups remain apart. The question of life and where babies come from is often raised and likewise often answered. This is the age of speculation and crude explanation. Sex interest however is not dominant nor does it have an erotic background. It represents more curiosity and a timeliness for broader information about self and the world. This would seem to be a good age for parent-child consultation on the matter of birth, a time at which he is seeking information and is ready to adjust to it easily. Mild homosexuality may be demonstrated but need not generally cause worry.

Although this is a period in which beginnings are laid for gradual withdrawal from parent and teacher behavior codes, it is still a time in which the child seeks both parent and teacher approval. Indicative of a kind of "in-between stage", the child will still be amenable but responds better to hint or suggestion than to outright dogmatic command. He is beginning to recognize conflict between peer and parent requirements. He wants status with both.

In school he demonstrates some withdrawal from teacher authority. The closeness of his fellows makes him strongly conscious of their expectations for him. He is beginning the stage where he wants their approval more than that of his teacher. The teacher's role should become that of arbiter or umpire. She becomes less involved with him emotionally unless she attacks or threatens group continuity and alignment. A teacher who has followed along with a group of children through the first and second grades may be quite amazed with the change in these children. They no longer need her as they did in the earlier grades nor do they seek her approval and attention as was earlier the rule. Any school program which indorses such a policy of teacher continuance should prepare teachers for this shift in children's loyalties. A teacher dealing with this age level can be more withdrawn in inter-personal relations but will be active in providing environmental challenges and opportunities. He or she will also be less dogmatic and demanding.

One should not infer that these children are all at once socially minded and group-conscious. Eight is only the beginning point of a development leading to group stability and organization. The child is attracted by small-group activity but his attachments are temporary and shifting. Planned group manipulation by the teacher should follow the natural inclination of children. Since the child himself has exploratory social drives, teacher manipulation should parallel this pattern. Children of this age are not ready for independent group decision nor are they impressed or aided by formal conduct of meetings. In their games they are more likely to make their own rules than to follow official rules or those used by others. They will stick to what they have accepted as official and if necessary will argue out a controversy over interpretation. They will not become angry and go home as would be the case at an earlier age.

In school this age child is ready to profit from simulated enterprises such as a store, or a post-office, and if allowed to work in a school supply center, will do quite well in assuming responsibility. The lemonade stands, circuses, and other enterprises put on by children for other children and parents on the front lawns during the summer, are typically promoted by eight-year-old children. A school carnival will be actively and effectively supported by children of this age.

The desire of the child to experiment and to enlarge upon his immediate environment leads him easily into dramatic activities. He has by now sufficiently established his basic personal drives so that he is ready for creative exploration and experimentation. Teachers, in organizing such activities, should make arrangements for casts to shift their roles. The child is more ready for diversity than for improvement in a role that might be thought fitting for his kind of personality. Allowing a child too soon to become pigeonholed or typed is contrary to natural developmental drive at this age and is limiting to full emotional and personal developmental opportunity. The eight-year-old is very much alive and is rapidly projecting himself into the future. It is a growing age.

He takes enthusiastically to new learning areas. If not introduced to them by his teacher he will ask questions about earth and sky, trees, leaves, flowers and animals. He is interested in his body, outside and inside, and wants to know how it works. All he needs is an open door to rush enthusiastically into a study of Indians or pioneers. Cowboy and Indian stories, radio and television programs entrance him. Studies involving race, family, and national relationships are given interested attention when the opportunity is offered. Science and social science work should be broad and comprehensive. Containment within specified units or limited subject matter offerings is contrary to his expansive, reaching, grasping mind. No one can tell the specific direction a given group of third-graders may go when provided with facilities and opportunities for action. Books, working materials of all kinds, laboratories, science equipment, storage space for collections should all be standard equipment for this age and grade. Fundamentals can be learned easily and naturally in a challenging and inviting environment. The teacher for such a group should have broad, diversified interests and be a handyman in all meanings of the word. Studies of children of different races and cultures greatly intrigue the third-grader when given informal treatment. This child has few prejudices and biases and is expanding in every sense of the word. He can learn to understand other children and can go a long way from the adult prejudices of his community in respect to racial and national problems. He is a true internationalist and stands ready to receive unbiased and fair impressions toward other people.

Intellectually, including measurable aspects of learning, he likewise is on an upward trend. Mental development as expressed by scores on intelligence tests will show an increase. If he has been tested annually it is more likely than not that his I.Q. ratios will now be somewhat higher than the earlier ones. If comparisons for grading purposes were made on the basis of the child's own previous growth curve, third-grade children in general would receive all A's. Unfortunately, grades are based on comparative scores with other children. Hence some third-grade children must be graded as below average and some even as failures. What an artificial and frustrating device to throw in the path of this growing, enthusiastic child!

The third-grader is increasingly stable in his ethical-moral behavior. His regard for rules, ideas of right and wrong, are falling into a definite focus. He now makes judgments of his own behavior and that of others. He knows when he deserves punishment and is ready to accept it. He knows what belongs to him, what belongs to others, and acts accordingly. When he helps himself to a neighbor's pencil he knows that he has done something wrong. He feels that rules are necessary and puts up little protest when they limit his own action. He differs from the six- and the seven-year-old who struggle for parent and teacher approval for security's sake alone. The eight-year-old usually will do the right thing without reward but is greatly appreciative of commendation, not because he was good but because he exercised good judgment.

All in all the eight-year-old is characterized by beginning independence, diversity of interest, and the start of individual and sex interests. Individual differences among children in any particular phase of learning greatly exceed those at an earlier age. Identification with other members of his sex is a dominant need and its beginning should be assured by the kind of group operation brought about by the teacher.

B. Behavior and Interpretation

1. *Motor Performance*

Typical of a child of eight, Patricia possessed better motor and physical coordination than was her lot at seven. Unfortunately she also at this age found this advantage somewhat curtailed by her obviously beginning oversizeness. She was tall for her age but beginning to be heavy for her height. Nevertheless she possessed her share of grace of movement along with a marked dramatic tendency. She showed no decrease in her habit of sitting in her seat in any way except the right way. She still sprawled and stretched out at most times. Some of this was still typical of her age but some of it seemed to represent a protective front and compensation for her imagined and real handicaps.

Like most children Patricia was active as soon as she was released for playground activity. She was cheerful, she was merry, she wanted to be in all things at once. Here she outdid the other girls. From some she excited admiration, from others she received only indifferent attention. None opposed her or outwardly condemned her. She was always received but not particularly was she ever sought out.

Most children at this age show considerable improvement in fine motor expression. Drawings are improved. Handwriting shows signs of individualization. There was very little opportunity for Patricia to demonstrate such maturational effects since her school program offered so little in the way of encouragement and challenge. Art work was infrequent, unimaginative, and absolutely uninspiring. Such development as we found in Patricia was felt to be considerably below optimum levels and merely satisfactory and somewhat low-average. Handwriting and drawing were desultory and unimaginative.

2. *Emotional Reactions*

Patricia seemed to be a child that learned what she learned practically flat on her back. She was scarcely ever up and alert in her physical accompaniments to learning. The effect on observers was that of indifference and reluctant indulgence with what the teacher prescribed and assigned. However, Patricia was not indifferent. She was anxious to please and under circumstances which permitted her only a pittance of teacher and classmate acknowledgment she did quite well. Physical restriction along with a dearth of variety kept her at a slow learning pace. There was little in her environment to bring out the typical characteristic of unbounded interest in accepting new assignments and challenges that are typical of this age and, we believe, might have been found in Patricia. Most children of this age are ready to face anything. They, when given the opportunity, outline projects far beyond their scope of action, and, when this happens, do everything possible to meet their commitments. They do have the countercharactertistic of running off on tangents and proceeding to something else. There is however a general continuity of action which was lacking in this child.

Teachers who are afraid of children getting out of hand in project or developmental activity need be less fearful with third-graders than with second- or fourth-, or fifth-grade children. The third-grade child not only thrives by this kind of activity but strangely enough is easy to handle. His interest span is elastic enough so that he may be diverted back to conventional procedure or to a new activity. He looks for certain elements of control from his teacher or parent and subsides without protest. Teachers do not need to be "yellers" to control the third-grade child. Patricia as such was easily controllable. Even on the playground where she felt less untrammeled she could be brought to "heel" like a good, well-trained hunting dog. Like most third-grade children she was impatient, but got to work immediately, and if the task was not too great got it done without too much diversionary action. If the task was too denamding, too difficult for her, she ran out of steam—dawdled, looked around the room, and waited for something else to happen.

Paralleling the demands made by children of this age on their parents are occasional negativeness and resistance. Patricia fell into this descriptive category. At home she was always willing to help but frequently delayed or gave excuses when attention was requested to a specific task. This personality trait was likewise displayed in the classroom. She often pleaded "busy" as an excuse for carrying out a definite responsibility but in general was willing to help—cleaning up the room, putting books away, etc.

Children of this age are helpful and Patricia was such a child. Teachers may feel with some justification that they may call on certain children to help others with their work. The busy but competent and understanding third-grade teacher is not hesitant in using such aid, not only because of the value to the children in the experience but also as an appropriate instructional resource. Parents may protest when this plan is overdone. Third-grade children are not ready to take over teaching duties nor should one of them be delegated to grade arithmetic or spelling papers.

Responsibilities assigned should be those of giving aid to other children, assumption of responsibility to see that a committee does its job, or of doing a piece of planning, or handing out books and looking after the reading corner. This age is sufficiently mature to produce a goodly number who can be depended upon for carrying out such responsibilities.

3. *Anxieties and Security Threats*

Patricia showed very little in the way of anxiety and fear during her eighth year. In repose or in watching other children she gave some evidence of not obtaining enough of their attention. For the most part, however, she played the role of a bold, happy, and courageous child.

The typical child of this age has some back-log of fears from the sixth and seventh years. In the case of Patricia these seemed to have been dissolved. She was thoroughly oriented to the dark. Shadows, street noises and persons held little fear for her. In this regard Patricia was much of the same pattern as are children of that segment of society, not necessarily the lower class, that prescribes no rigid evening restrictions. Working around the store in the evening was not unusual for her. Consequently she abandoned childish fears of the dark much before the age of eight.

4. *Personal-Social Development*

The pre-adolescent developmental impetus, gaining momentum in the eight-year-old, is reflected in his personal-social relations. The completion of the earlier years results in a beginning consolidation and integration of the inner self. The child develops a personality adjusted to a small, controlled environment. In a sense the kindergarten and first- and second-grade arrangements represent a culturally controlled and limited environment but one in which the range of action is broader than the earlier home-centered experience. The kindergarten and first- and second-grade activities provide experimental and exploratory forage into the land of new personal-social contacts. The effect is to provide a readiness for growth that is both inner and outer motivated without conflict or confusion from each other. The product of the experiences of these years is a child who is ready to respond to new and more varied stimuli. Patricia was a true representative of this kind of behavior sketch.

Patricia gave clear indication of being cognizant of herself as a person, and

GRADE THREE—THE EIGHT-YEAR-OLD CHILD

as a person in contact with others. She perceived differences between herself and other children. She recognized her own particular ethnic background. She realized her own particular abilities as a showman and more and more utilized these to solicit attention and to make herself acceptable. She saw that humor and fun is a desired group social asset, and she sensed her ability to meet this kind of group need. The result was wholesome and aided Patricia in finding a place in several informal groupings. Patricia in her dramatics varied somewhat from the typical child. Instead of imitating or identifying herself with characters in stories or incidents, she tended to portray or project her own personal characteristics.

Patricia was quite unusual in her relationship with boys. She liked to play with them and on occasion would wrestle around with them, piling on when they all fell down in pulling on a rope, chasing, being chased, etc.

Most children of this age have some knowledge of the act of procreation. Our records do not indicate just how much information was possessed by Patricia at this time or, if any, how she came by it. Her look of superiority when talking about baby kittens and her lack of questions about such things would seem to show that she was sufficiently informed. Most children of this age request rather detailed information. Girls as a rule are not hesitant in asking questions of their mothers. Characteristic of the maturity achieved at this time, they are discreet. They will not blurt out a question in the presence of others but will wait until an intimate moment arrives involving only themselves and their mother. Children of eight are generally ready to absorb such knowledge appropriately. Pets will interest them in this regard as will studies of other animals.

Patricia, like most eight-year-olds, presented more mature social behavior away than at home. The child at home must still fit in with an earlier pattern of parental dominance. Away from home he is more on his own, and almost invariably can be depended upon to be at his best.

In school he looks for recognition of achievement. Third-grade children are much more sensitive to grades (marks) than are first- or second-graders. If they do well they want recognition. If they do not receive good grades they are hurt and confused. Patricia gave much evidence of this characteristic. She beamed brightly when her work was noticed. She rather retired into herself when achievement was not recognized.

Patricia made the appropriate kind of pal relationship required by this level of personal-social maturity. She looked forward to getting to school to meet her friends. When necessary she waited for a chum after school. Observers who feel that children of this age have "few" friends misinterpret the social needs of this age. A teacher might more justifiably be concerned with the child that has many friends but no chums or pals. Grade organization at this level should provide a few minutes before formal school work begins to allow these contacts to be made, for boy to see boy, girl to see girl, to get their secrets and their plans made for the day. When no opportunity is available children find difficulty in thinking about anything else and will wait impatiently doing scarcely anything until the contact is made.

These children also begin to develop a liking for older children. Patricia was often seen with girls in the fourth or fifth grades and seemed to enjoy the identification greatly.

5. *Play and Recreation*

Patricia's play habits were a prototype of the eight-year-old. She greatly deplored isolated play and abandoned it for group play almost invariably when the opportunity presented itself. School and home equipment at this age should facilitate group activity. Choice games involve action and increased motor accompaniments. Even their work, pictures, etc., depart from still life. Their drawings now tend to tell a story or to depict action.

The typical eight-year-old will always welcome games that involve running, throwing, or jumping. The little-lady concept is quite foreign to natural inclination except when visiting or in contact with adults. Less active games that intrigue children of this age are card games, checkers, chess, and dominoes. Patricia showed greater favoritism for action games but would indulge in these others on invitation.

6. *Academic Status*

Patricia's case records presented a very interesting sidelight on some of the problems of school organization and instruction. Records were available to us after she had completed a given grade that were not available to her teachers as they saw her that year. Thus what we learned about Patricia in a larger perspective gave an evaluation opportunity that her teachers did not have.

We know that for her the third grade was a time of increased academic growth as compared with earlier and later years. Her teacher admitted that her work was "satisfactory" and at times "above average". The grave injustice done Patricia was not the bare fact of inaccurate interpretation. It was, as we see it, the fact that her teacher failed to recognize her contact with Patricia as a time for her greatest potential developmental year. Recognition could not have failed to encourage more enthusiastic and enriched opportunity. As it was, Patricia more or less participated in a series of take-it-or-leave-it assignments which placed full responsibility on the child. Her teacher seriously discharged her responsibilities, as she saw them, by treating the third-grade year as just another year in which materials were presented conscientiously and evaluation conducted objectively. It would seem that this grade-level should be the place where teachers should try especially hard to bring out more of an emotionally accompanied, dramatic, creative program of activities.

Patricia was rated as doing satisfactorily in reading. She enjoyed it in a sort of desultory fashion, not expanding her school-reading activities to home-reading interests. Although she was not interested in perusing various kinds of story books, she showed some interest in comic books given her by other children. Although children of this age generally prefer the animal or funny stories, they do begin to show an interest in westerns and the more imaginative or blood-and-thunder epics. Patricia followed this pattern in a mild way.

It has been mentioned that for the eight-year-old the teacher assumes lessened importance for providing behavior guides. Accordingly, Patricia was less inclined to solicit her teacher's favor and less inclined to lean on her for approval and direction. At this age, however, the child shows no abrupt departure from acceptance of teacher control. He is pleased to have the teacher join his play groups and will respond wholesomely to sincere teacher participation.

7. *Ethical and Moral Behavior*

The eight-year-old is much more dependable in situations that involve ethical decisions than he was at seven. Consequently he expects a more adult level of treatment from his teachers and parents. Parents do not need to forewarn the child as was previously necessary. Nor does the eight-year-old like to be treated as irresponsible by his teachers. If a child loses a plaything and another child is suspected of taking it, the remainder of the group will not willingly submit to cajoling urgings to "confess" or to searching of their persons.

Patricia was somewhat typical of this concept of ethical-moral maturity. She was increasingly capable of managing her affairs and of making her own decisions. Nevertheless she wanted her "goodness" to be approved. Children of this age quite frequently relate incidents to teachers and parents in which their role is deliberately portrayed as the kind that demands approval. In line with growing dependability, their exaggerations will not be extreme. When wrong, and particularly when caught in a wrong act or decision, some alibi will be offered. Patricia found little occasion for exercise of this perogative of her age expectations. She was more inclined to present a playful, rebellious role that was inoffensive and harmless and elicited such comment as, "You little clown", or, "Now, Patricia, that is enough!"

Selected References

Louise B. Ames, Janet Learned, Ruth Metraux, and Richard N. Walker: *Child Rorschach Responses*, pp. 240-50. Hoeber, New York, 1952.

Edna W. Bailey, Anita D. Laton, and Elizabeth L. Bishop: *Studying Children in School*, pp. 57-61, 108-117. McGraw-Hill, New York, 1939.

Alvina T. Burrows: *Teaching Children in the Middle Grades*, pp. 23-35. Heath, Boston, 1952.

Ruth Cunningham and Associates: *Understanding Group Behavior of Boys and Girls*, pp. 13-204. Bureau of Publications, Teachers College, Columbia University, New York, 1951.

Faculty of the University School: *How Children Develop*, University School Series No. 3, pp. 18-28. Ohio State University, Columbus, 1946.

Arnold Gesell and Frances L. Ilg: *Child Development*, Part II, "The Child From Five to Ten", pp. 159-87. Harper, New York, 1949.

Gladys G. Jenkins, Helen Schacter, and W. W. Bauer: *These Are Your Children*, pp. 80-95. Scott-Foresman, New York, 1949.

Earle L. Reynolds and Grace Schoen: "Growth Patterns of Identical Triplets from 8 to 18 Years". *Child Development*, Vol. 19, 1948, pp. 130-45.

Ruth Strang: *An Introduction to Child Study*, pp. 315-64. Macmillan, New York, 1951.

E. H. Watson and G. H. Lowrey: *Growth and Development of Children*, p. 106. Year Book Publishers, Chicago, 1951.

IN THE FOURTH GRADE

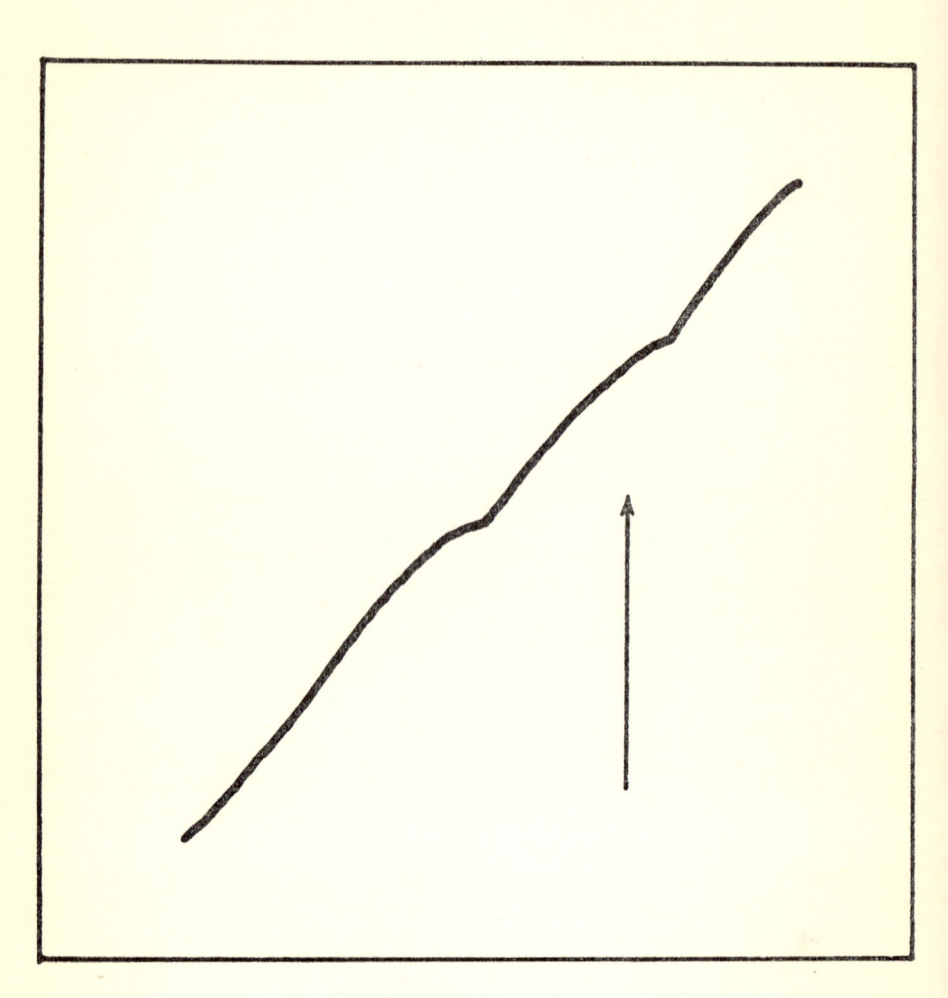

Period of Maturation

Chapter IV

GRADE FOUR—THE NINE-YEAR-OLD CHILD

A. The Fourth-Grade Mode

THE NINE-YEAR-OLD period has two important characteristics. First, it presents a continuation of that part of the pre-adolescent growth cycle in which the rate of growth and learning is the most accelerated. Second, it presents noticeable shift toward compelling peer-group relations. Since this child has not reached the point where there is strong or persistent rebellion to adult suggestion and domination, and because, in the first instance, he is in a period of rapid learning—the nine-year-old is a teacher's delight.

Grade four covers approximately the middle span in the pre-adolescent growth cycle.[1] Placement here is not a mere arithmetical calculation in determining the mid-point between six and twelve. The various years do not divide themselves equally in terms of growth years. Nine, organismically, only happens to represent the mid-point segment of the total pre-adolescent developmental sequence.

Orientation to life in general proceeds advantageously. What the child promised to be at eight, in his "better" behavior, is favorably encouraged by a growing self-dependence which provides him with assets for pleasant parent and teacher relations. The emergence takes place gradually, not abruptly. It is only parents and teachers who all at once come to the realization of what has happened. Return to school after a couple of weeks of absence, for other reasons than of illness, almost invariably surprises the teacher. She is startled to find Johnny so grown up and "bigger". Teachers and parents, in attempting to adjust to the child where he is, frequently discover that, during the search for understanding, Johnny has left them behind. This is a time when planning must be done almost overnight to keep up with the child's constantly progressing development.

The upward swing in the developmental sequence brings about the desire for

[1]Notice in the figure preceding that Patricia is a little beyond this point as the result of being a few months older than the other children.

self-direction. The child feels his increasing powers and is self-motivated into a need for personal direction and guidance. At the five-six-seven stage, when developmental progress is not so indicative of an upswing but is orienting itself to both old and new stimulations, there is a greater need for adult domination and direction. Again at about eleven or twelve (but depending on the child) when development takes on similar new orientations, adult guidance and direction is again desired and needed. At the eight-, nine-, and ten-year levels the situation is quite different. The child at this stage has expanding capacities for work. There is no uncertainty as to his progress. It is definitely upward! In school and at home he should have some opportunity to make decisions, to be his own boss and to exercise considerably direction of his own affairs. He may be disturbed by authoritative interruption which takes him away from his particular project of the moment. He may then appear surly and impolite. If he has been assigned tasks he should be allowed to help in making plans for them. In spite of some power of regulating and ordering his own affairs this child frequently loses himself. Self-drive will not deter him from occasionally running off on a tangent or from changing his own plans. He is susceptible to slight motivation; he is sensitive and alert to stimuli and responds accordingly.

Consequently his plans often get beyond his ability to execute. He can jump from one thing to another and right back to his original project. His learning needs, imposed by his organismic drive and ability to perform, are mainly those of organization, choice, and self-control. School activities should be over-all planned to suit this particular panorama. His attention span is greater than before and can be imposed upon for lengths of time up to two or three hours when there is some essence of personal choice and direction in the ensuing activity.

The nine-year-old's ease of learning makes him ready to accept monotonous drill assignments. If he is on his own, he will practice patiently in order to perfect a detail. If he is in school he will quite readily accept teacher direction in practicing essentials in the skill subjects—reading, writing, spelling, and arithmetic. This is part of the period in which he can be induced to do things over and over. Although at a later age he will rebel, he will now accept a reasonable amount of such assignments as fair and logical. Coupled with his ability and desire for broad problem activity and his desire for self-direction and self-planning, he becomes quite overloaded in his curricular and extra-curricular activities.

A further characteristic, or perhaps an accompaniment of his rich growing period, is considerable toughness. He can be over-loaded with, in many instances, no particular damage. Nevertheless, teachers and parents should not capitalize upon this trait in their planning but recognize it rather as an anchor or safeguard. Constructively, what this child needs is intelligent and understanding manipulation of potential environmental stimuli. He responds to everything so well that he can be led into blind alleys or inconsequential learnings. The job of guidance for parent and teacher alike is to see that the child is provided with stimuli that will bring out his most important individual characteristics related to his temperament, emotion, personal-social needs, and cultural surroundings.

It is believed that the child has fixed potential ceilings. It is also believed that many children have potentialities that lie unawakened because of minimum challenges. This applies particularly to emotional development where the challenges always lay some place between minimum and maximum richness, and often are conflicting, while some are even damaging. The emotions are concerned primarily with the adjustment of the child toward achieving a happy existence and in the coloration which they give to his behavior. Here is a field of which we know very little insofar as guidance and direction of children are concerned. Consequently, children reach this age conditioned in their emotional development primarily on a trial-and-error basis. Such a child may at times be moody; he may be timid or he may be aggressive and bold.

On the positive side—related to emotion, personal-social development, attitude and feeling—the nine-year-old shows much more mature understandings of his relationships to his teacher and parents than the eight-year-old does. Attitudes are generally compatible with adult concepts of what they should be and in the main contribute to amicable and friendly relations with them. The urge toward peer-group recognition and acceptance is just beginning to be strained and as yet poses no threat to family or to teacher-pupil harmony.

Nine also displays other characteristics which invariably produce adult blessing and approval. He quarrels less with younger brothers and sisters. With these, and with children of his own age, he demonstrates fairness and a let-live consideration. He makes fewer excuses for himself and pours less abuse on others for his own failures. He will take blame individually or as a member of a group when it is provided in fair measure and not as aggression and attack. He is punishable and under proper circumstances will believe that punishment is due him.

His senses of fairness gives him a judicial aspect. He evaluates the responsibility of each member of a mis-behaving alliance. He particularly wants to know who was the ring-leader and places greater responsibility on the boy or girl who initiated the mis-deed. He is interested in drawing up rules, constitutions, and by-laws. He likes to act as a monitor and accepts the full implications of such responsibility. But children of this age, while responsive to schemes of student government, councils, or rule-making committees, will over-govern and over-penalize. They need self-governing responsibilities with some challenge but likewise need suggestions and assistance. Their sense of fairness renders them receptive to studies of prejudice and bias. At this time they can act and live in the most tolerant manner with children of minority groups.

Ethically, the nine-year-old has made considerable progress toward adult standards of honesty and truthfulness. In many ways he is more honest than most adults as he will walk back to a store to return a nickel given him in excess of the right amount of change. He can do errands and handle tasks that are generally considered beyond his maturity status. He likes to be considered important and to be entrusted with errands of importance.

In view of his quite exalted opinion of himself he does not like to be given the "baby treatment" when guests are around. To be introduced as "my little man" is quite disgusting. Too much attempt on the part of guests to bring him out is also nauseating. He likes plain, down-to-earth, man-to-man recognition. He would rather participate in adult conversation than have the adult obsequiously "condescend" to his level. Although he likes his home, his associations to it, he feels some tendency to draw away from it. In another year this tendency will be more marked. He may, however, at nine, show more interest in something he has planned with other children than with a family group.

He must have this contact and when granted (by parents and teachers) he somehow marvelously maintains a judicious balance between both home and peer loyalty. Much of the gang-spirit shown invests itself mainly with chatter about this and that, what he is going to do when he grows up, his ideas on school and home, some organizational activity—but all lightly done and innocuous. He is feeling out the group and his possible relation to it. He can show loyalty to it but can react in a very enthusiastic fashion to chance grouping as occurs through choosing sides for a spelling contest, ball game, or any other kind of contest.

Money or special favors are not as effective as formerly in challenging his interests. He is so busy on his own initiative that he needs little in the way of encouragement to keep him going. He likes to make out schedules, to plan rules and procedures, and to make lists of one kind and another. If a teacher likes to make specific assignments and suggests that they be written down, she will quite generally receive a cordial response. The child has become statistic-minded. Many boys follow the batting schedules of big-league ball players and can quote them correctly. During the war it was boys of this age that could identify planes of various kinds and many varied service insignia. Comic books that carry information have appeal. The futuristic comics, particularly, take their eye.

The fourth grade demonstrates the first real separation of the sexes in their interests. The boys like to rough-house when they are standing around without much at hand for constructive efforts. Girls will giggle and whisper to each other. Boys get a mild sensual sensation if the opportunity offers for wrestling around with a girl but in general are inclined to keep away from them. Boys will tease each other about girls and girls will talk of boy-friends.

Withdrawal of sexes from each other at this time is natural. It seems to be a cultural designation so that the developing child may make an orientation to his own sex without confusion and conflict from competing urges. School activities must take this into consideration. Parties are difficult because of this cleavage and contribute little to personal social needs unless cleverly planned. Contests which involve one group against another are usually successful but invariably rough and noisy. Considerable separation of sexes for special occasions is often desirable and contributive to fun and genuine enjoyment. Boys and girls would not like to be entirely separated. They like to spy on each other, yell derisively, and do other things that indicate distinction and difference.

Children of this age usually have added to their knowledge of the reproductive process. Most nine-year-old girls know the meaning of menstruation. Some of them understand the relation of the father to the sex act. Much of this knowledge has been passed on to them in a garbled fashion. The nine-year-old is not obscene or flagrant in discussing or in talking about these things. His inquisitiveness is shown with some poise and considerable modesty. The child of this age treats such information rather objectively. There is too little of the romantic about him to give it a subtle or personal meaning. Sex education treated objectively may be profitably explored with children of this age.

Individual differences among the nine-year-olds are more marked than ever. Girls have caught up with boys in size and are ready to go on to greater growth and maturity differences. Consequently, the modal picture of the nine-year-old must bow to wide individual variation not only in terms of maturity differences but also with reference to individual personalities. The child has acquired by this time a personality core. This stamps him with increased unanimity of behavior from day to day. Explorations become less, behavior ranges lessen, but not necessarily accompanied by a narrowed personality. Personality can and should be broad, but as it develops it will be more consistent and repetitive in its manifestations. His gestures, mannerisms, facial expressions, moods, depressions, are patterned to fit in with his emerging personality design. As is true with his more obvious learning opportunities in their rapid growth progress toward individual limits, personality traits are likewise progressing with lessened variation toward specific levels.

Nine is assertive! The child of this age is not only organizing his behavior but is beginning to show the results of organization. Whatever he is, is more readily observable and measurable.

The work habits of the nine-year-old are pleasing. The eight-year-old showed speed of reaction and prompt application to the task at hand. The nine-year-old combines control and self-discipline along with speed. This combination tends to obscure speed as a characteristic and to give the impression at first of a slowing down. Further insight will indicate that this is not true. He now wastes less time in his organizational efforts and will plan before pitching into the task at hand. Better organization and self-discipline result in an enduring quality which will enable him to stay interested for longer periods. Because he is cognizant of his growing powers and is able to see the results of his energies he becomes interested in improving himself. He can be kept at practice on mechanical skills—drill in arithmetic and spelling, or practicing the violin. He responds readily to self-evaluation devices, test scores, etc. He will be particularly responsive to drill exercises and studies that enable him to keep records on himself. He learns rapidly, seems to know it, and is intrigued by it. He will repeat drills and exercises which can be timed or scored just for the reward of self-recognized improvement.

His enthusiasm in his work habits makes him susceptible to unimaginative as well as creative teaching. His program undoubtedly should be broad. He will respond to pure routine and mechanical teaching and will often approve such direction of his energies. He is more frequently than not found in situations which are quite exclusively based on this kind of a program. Because he can learn he is often led to learn. He can be pushed in spelling, phonics, and other mechanical processes. Teachers frequently are unaware that his total personal-social being is equally responsive and equally hungry for stimulation. It is to be hoped that in more and more schools a balanced program can be provided which serves both objectives, (1) stimulation and environmental surroundings that minister to his rote learning needs, integrated and coordinated with, (2) activities that test his potential personal-social development possibilities.

B. Behavior and Interpretation

1. *Motor Performance*

The characteristic fourth-grade syndrome of hard work and hard play was demonstrated at least by Patricia's play. Her behavior in school was so desultory as to make a decision regarding her interest and effort mere speculation. Neither drill nor broader learning opportunities were organized in such a way as to make a particular appeal to a girl of Patricia's kind. To please her teacher was insufficient motivation to get much out of her.

On the playground matters were different. Patricia clearly indicated coordination and skill in motor activities. She could throw and bat with even the best of the boys and was often sought out by them. And, compatible with her age, she preferred the game that offered the greatest competition and opportunity to display the urge to win.

Patricia gave evidence of well differentiated eye and hand skills. Handedness was marked and dominant superiority of one over the other well established. Patricia's work in art had improved and demonstrated some attention to improvement of skill and ability. The work assigned was conventionally stereotyped and often gave the impression that it provided limited motivation.

In reference to posture Patricia was most casual. She was never observed sitting up in her seat. She sprawled and seemed to enjoy experimenting with unique positions while working or reading by herself. She demonstrated ability to do almost any kind of work with her head lying on her arm, or sprawled at full length. Patricia seemed to be quite unaware of the extravagant picture which she made because of her size.

2. *Emotional Reactions*

Most children of nine show less outward symptoms of tension than the eight-year-old do. They are less quarrelsome, less rowdy, and less willing to fight without definite purpose. Patricia undoubtedly reflected this pattern. Tension release for her was combined with activities that gave her recognition and pleasure. This is undoubtedly a common occurrence for many individuals but is then demonstrated during later years when it represents more of an adjustive process than a device for lowering emotional pressures and fears. It would appear that Patricia discovered qualities in herself at an earlier age which brought her pleasure and recognition, and at the same time gave her emotional release. Clowning and playground activity were the reactions so demonstrated. When she was neglected in the classroom, or had gone long enough on a vacant-eyed self-engrossment, she could always be depended upon to come through with a remark that brought a laugh, some dramatics that gave her the center of attention, or some Gargantuan feat on the playground. She displayed few of the usual signs of tension release as are so often expressed through finer motor response. Like many children, however, she twisted constantly in her seat, fussed with her hair, and picked at her hands.

Patricia, similar to most nine-year-olds, showed increasing independence. She was always ready and willing to assist in a room clean-up, to go on errands for her teacher or to aid other children in planning a reception for mothers.

Emotionally, the nine-year-old is less susceptible to persisting flare-ups, continued or intense anger, or recurrent bitter feelings and attitudes. At this age he may be said to be approaching the pre-adolescent peak of emotional stability. There are several reasons for such a relationship between stability and the particular age. First, greater maturity should result in better emotional control and expression. Second, the period of development represented chronologically by the nine-year-age span is a time remarkably unaffected by factors which produce variation in the growth pattern. In other words, *nine generally is a time when the maturational drive is the dominant factor in the kind of growth design produced.* Teaching, illness, emotional upset, etc., are less effective at this time than the potentiality of growth itself. Patricia as a nine-year-old approximately fitted this concept of appropriate maturational-chronological relationship. In many ways, this year, as seen at school, was her best. And there was nothing in her records to indicate that this was not true for her life at home.

A reflection of the stability characteristic of this age was Patricia's loyalty to her friends. Her attachments were stronger than they were previously. Her contact with friends showed greater continuity and endurance. Also characteristic of this age were her beginning interests and contacts with girls somewhat older. She liked to go to the movies with them and when seen in their company made it a point to speak to her other friends so that she would be noticed as a member of the older group.

3. *Anxieties and Security Threats*

Patricia gave but little indication of anxiety and insecurity during this age range. She seemed to show no fears nor tag-ends of doubts and worries carried over from an earlier age. She demonstrated some concern about her work in academic fields but not enough to indicate real worry. Social niceties gave her concern in that she indicated a desire to do the right thing and to conduct herself appropriately when conversing or speaking with adults. A particular singling-out or special notice, such as was the case on the occasion of her birthday party, brought forth unusual appreciation and satisfaction. All in all Patricia appeared to be the kind of child at this age that was quite inured to anxiety and insecurity but especially appreciative and responsive to kindness and special attention.

4. *Personal-Social Development*

The nine-year-old's dominant maturational drive gives the child an unusual sense of self-sufficiency and personality well-being. Patricia, as representative of normalcy for this age, manifested these characteristics. She showed improved self-direction and control. For the first time she began to indicate some interest in her remote future as demonstrated by her statements to our observers concerning her career interests.

In terms of personal-social development the nine-year-old begins to show the need of and the desire for social groupings. These are confined usually to the sex of the child concerned and are accompanied by but minor rebellion to parental and teacher guidance and control. Patricia demonstrated this need in her efforts to attract attention from peers. She talked much of her girl-friends and their activities and seemed anxious to be identified with them. In this respect she barely made what might be regarded as minimum contacts. Her friendship circle was small and limited, and gave no appearance of being potentially expansive.

The main deficiency in her motivations came as a result of a school and home program that lacked broad stimulation, lacked encouragement to explore areas of competency that would have added to her personality and made her more interesting and attractive to others. Home and school were at equally low levels as sources for such challenge.

At this age Patricia was also affected by organic factors which were somewhat hindering to optimum personal development. In her case this factor was excessive weight which tended to break down personal security and needed confidence for increasing her competence area. All these—home limitations, school limitations, and personal limitations—kept down her developmental ascendancy to minimum levels.

5. *Play and Recreation*

Patricia, as a prototype of most nine-year-olds, liked to continue doing what was pleasant for her. Rather than in playing with dolls for unlimited hours, she was interested mainly in more vigorous activities. Bicycling, playing ball, and other activities more commonly associated with the play of boys, seemed to intrigue Patricia most. And curiously, in vigorous activity she seemed to show the antithesis of what she appeared to be in the classroom where she was indolent, ponderous, and somewhat reluctant in her physical movements. It is possible that she found her excessive size turned into an asset on the playground and took full advantage of it to promote herself.

6. *Academic Status*

The graphic picture of Patricia's academic progress, to be shown later in detail, leads one to conclude that the fourth grade was a year in which "quite satisfactory progress" was made. This would hardly lead us to conclude that satisfactory progress in her case was anything in particular to cheer about. Most nine-year-olds are voracious readers. Either they read a number of books or read the same book over and over. Animal stories, children's classics, and the old favorites need but little encouragement for avid perusal. Patricia, in commenting about the book given her on her birthday, confessed that she had read no other book.

Comic books, radio programs, and the juke boxes were another matter. Patricia was well aware of the most popular radio programs, music, and comic serials. In this respect she was quite normal but unfortunately was given almost no challenge to broaden these interests into something more worthwhile and lasting.

Patricia, however, enjoyed school. Like most children she was more verbose in describing her life at home before children and teachers than in conversing at home on school happenings.

Fourth-grade teaching is often very mediocre. There is frequently over-attention to the rudimentary skills resulting in neglect of the creative areas and a conscientious effort to give all children, with their wide variation of performance, individual attention. Consequently some tension is aroused and the faithful fourth-grader tries so hard not to "let his teacher down" that the whole situation becomes involved with details plus an over-all emotional coloration. It is unfortunate that the fourth-grade child cannot be made to feel that he is success-bound and be given some encouragement to abandon his fear of failure or of not doing well or of displeasing his teacher. Patricia was quite typical of such a child in such a situation. She demonstrated some fear of failure, gave some indication of tension, and generally was a little unsure of herself.

It is believed by many that children who previously have been progressing slowly show a natural spurt at the fourth-grade level. In Patricia's case the most rapid learning took place in the third grade with the fourth-grade span represented as a continuation of rapid growth. Other data show that this is quite typical and that the fourth-grade spurt is an exception rather than a common phenomenon. Also typical was Patricia's growing ability to work independently of her teacher and of other children. This in spite of many occasions in which she sat staring out of the window transfixed with some idea, plans, or mere daydreaming. Patricia also represented the typical fourth-grader in her desire to succeed. Children of this age *want* to be graded, to be given some sign of success. When they do not attain what they consider a satisfactory recognition they are hurt and become slightly peevish. They like competition but respond admirably and more suitably to the group rather than the individual brand. However, they are inclined to become harsh and unjustly critical of a team member who lets them down in a game crisis.

In handwriting and arithmetic, Patricia showed typical traits. In arithmetic she did quite well. She "liked" it at one time and "disliked" it at another. Most of such judgments are more emotional than real and are usually expressed in reference to the work of a specific day which was either unsuccessful or satisfactory. Such judgments are quite unrelated with, nor are they indicative of, real progress or the lack of it.

7. *Ethical and Moral Behavior*

The substance of the nine-year-old's ethical and moral-behavior pattern is a sense of fairness. Patricia had this quality to a substantial degree and at almost no time demonstrated departure from such a background. She indicated this trait in her relationships with others and in positions of trust given her by her teacher. She would alibi and make excuses when she had done wrong, but never showed any tendency to shift blame to another child. She knew when she was right and when she was wrong, and at times showed considerable disgust with her efforts. Sometimes she was slow in responding to a suggestion but never made any outright display of disobedience.

SELECTED REFERENCES

Louise B. Ames, Janet Learned, Ruth Metraux, and Richard N. Walker: *Child Rorschach Responses*, pp. 251-63. Hoeber, New York, 1952.

Edna W. Bailey, Anita D. Laton, and Elizabeth L. Bishop: *Studying Children in School*, pp. 57-61. McGraw-Hill, New York, 1939.

Merle E. Bonney: "Sex Differences in Social Success and Personality Traits". *Child Development*, Vol. 15, No. 1, 1944, pp. 63-79.

Alvina T. Burrows: *Teaching Children in the Middle Grades*, pp. 36-44. Heath, Boston, 1952.

Ruth Cunningham and Associates: *Understanding Group Behavior of Boys and Girls*, pp. 13-204. Bureau of Publications, Teachers College, Columbia University, New York, 1951.

H. B. English: *Child Psychology*, pp. 499-534. Holt, New York, 1951.

Faculty of the University School: *How Children Develop*, University School Series No. 3, pp. 29-39. Ohio State University, Columbus, 1946.

Arnold Gesell and Frances L. Ilg: *Child Development*, Part II, "The Child From Five to Ten", pp. 188-211. Harper, New York, 1949.

Gladys G. Jenkins, Helen Schacter, and W. W. Bauer: *These Are Your Children*, pp. 96-111. Scott-Foresman, New York, 1949.

Earle L. Reynolds and Grace Schoen: "Growth Patterns of Identical Triplets from 8 to 18 Years". *Child Development*, Vol. 19, 1948, pp. 130-45.

Helen Schacter and W. W. Bauer: *Guide Book for the Health and Personal Development, Book 4, The Girl Next Door*. Scott-Foresman, New York, 1949.

E. H. Watson and G. H. Lowrey: *Growth and Development of Children*, pp. 106-7. Year Book Publishers, Chicago, 1951.

IN THE FIFTH GRADE

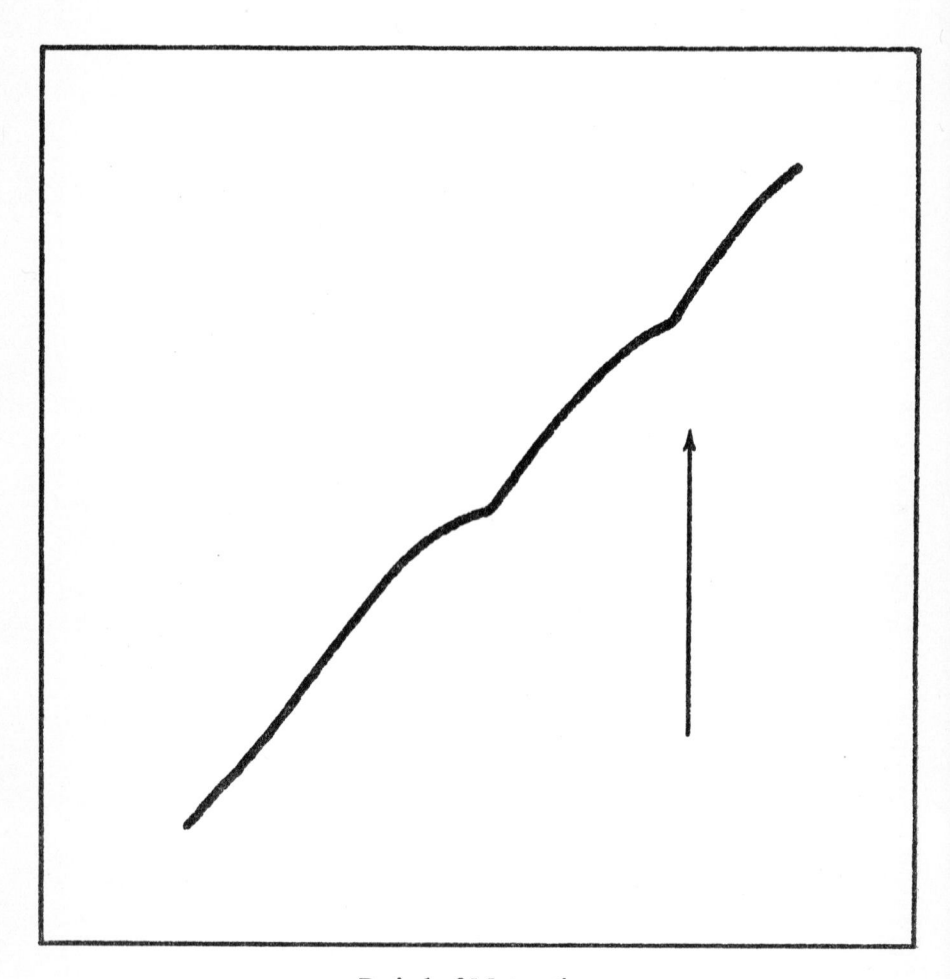

Period of Maturation

Chapter V

GRADE FIVE—THE TEN-YEAR-OLD CHILD

A. The Fifth-Grade Mode

TEN IS generally the age at which pre-adolescent development nears completion.[1] This means that the child achieves finally what he promised to become at eight and nine. Previous ages have been those of reaching out and striving for the future. Ten is the age of arrival. Pleasant as such a thought may be to parents and teachers, they must be warned that there is a corollary to the maturational concept of "final arrival." The corollary is that when a maximum (or destination point) is approached there is a consequent slowing down in growth increments. This does not necessarily mean that the unit of growth, although showing a gradual reduction of gains made, diminishes in its qualitative values. Teaching, handling, and direction of the child maintain a consistency of importance no matter what the grade level may be. Therefore the child at ten approaching his destination needs to be evaluated along other lines than on mere quantitative gain.

What is his station? What is the kind of person that usually is representative of this period of maturation? In comparison with the nine-year-old who is busy learning and growing, the ten-year-old is relaxed, poised, and somewhat reflective. If given the proper opportunity he demonstrates sufficient skills for the tasks at hand. His interests and drives respond to challenges to put skills to work. In contrast, rote learning and other mechanistic assignments seem to intrigue him but little. In the larger project or core-assignment area he can easily learn to budget his time, plan with others, and arrive at decisions. For the teacher who is effective when utilizing group procedures—decisions, pupil planning, etc.—the fifth-grade group is a much better prospect than either the fourth or the sixth.

The fifth-grader has maximum self-possession in comparison with children of all other elementary grades. This characteristic renders him susceptable to learnings which have social significance. He can easily learn to act politely and cour-

[1]See figure on preceding page.

teously. Social information and adult ways of behaving are frequently demonstrated.

He also takes an interest in the broader social area. Social-science work involving the study of social problems will be readily accepted. He is sympathetic and open to new understandings. He is idealistic and quite free from bias but can be easily influenced into either direction. Teachers who ignore this opportunity are of course leaving him unawakened. Parents who recognize their own faults and biases should realize that this is a very formative age. Teachers who have chosen the fifth grade because of its special opportunities should be aware of the potential influence that they have for providing direction and purpose not only to the child's social thinking but likewise to his over-all moral and ethical behavior.

The ten-year-old gives a limited preview of what he will become in the future. It can not accurately be said that such talents as he possesses have fully demonstrated themselves. Those that have emerged are well developed and speak favorably for the future. Those that have been aborted will still be given a later opportunity, but in most schools and homes explorations which have been ignored to this point have little chance of later encouragement. Personality traits are sufficiently mature to be appraised for future vocational interests. The evaluator should not exclude, however, the possibility of hidden resources which, under proper circumstances and events, can easily be brought to the surface in the early adolescent years.

Ten represents a period in which basic socializing foundations are laid. The child of this age is developing group loyalties and has the need to find his proper sphere within a group of his own age and sex. Group acceptance gives him security and a feeling of belongingness. Sex identification and realization is essential before he can make the necessary later adjustments to the opposite sex. Initiation ceremonies and group secrets are common, serving to weld him with others. The strong group affiliation with its attending processes leads his interests to mysteries, jungle stories, adventure, and superheroism.

Boys and girls of ten keep quite apart from each other. Conflict and quarrels are common. They can be brought together at times with some social gain but the occasion must be rare and for a specific purpose. "Old-fashioned" or square dances are often enjoyed by both groups. When a party is allowed to drift or to extend into informality, chaos and confusion almost inevitably result. Boys really enjoy wrestling and pushing each other about. Girls are more endeared to each other, gossiping, whispering, writing notes, etc. Girls are more cognizant of themselves as persons. They become aware of their ongoing physiological change and give great attention to dress, mannerisms, and general appearance.

There would be question on the part of some authorities of the accuracy of the preceding sketch. Much has been written concerning the rebellion that takes place among nine-, ten-, and eleven-year-old children with reference to adult standards and controls. Such children are pictured as going "off the beam" from good to bad, hating parents, quarreling with them, ignoring their directions and control. There are several reasons for the discrepancy which may be found in the literature. The discussion of two of them will be sufficient at this point.

In the fifth grade there are children with nine-year maturities as well as children with eleven-year-old maturities. It is altogether possible that these two groups—the one below and the one above—outnumber the typical ten-year-old. Consequently the picture is not clear as to what really may be expected as fifth-grade behavior. The child we have described is a child in terms of maturity who is almost at the end of his childhood cycle. The eleven-year-old, as we shall describe him later, is a child who is beginning a new cycle of growth with its ensuing confusion, instability, expanding group relationships, and increasing disregard of parent and teacher mandate. Since some children at this stage of maturity may be found at the ten-year-old level, it is no wonder that many children of this age are regarded as disobedient and trying. In our opinion this characteristic is more marked at a later age and should not be described as ten-year-old modal behavior.

Second, the background and social climate under which the child lives is important in determining the kind of person which he becomes. The typical ten-year-old is beginning to arrive at his preadolescent social destination. He may be directed toward a productive, creative life or he may be innocently pushed toward a rebellious, destructive, frustrated future. Children under influences which tend to bring out the latter condition utilize their gang spirit and interest to harmful ends. They aggressively rebel against parent and teacher domination and lean more and more on gang rule. Some of these may become delinquents. So many children in metropolitan areas are of this latter brand that they may be regarded as typical—typical only to the extent that they reflect an environment which has done little to understand them or to raise them to satisfactory levels of social adjustment.

The ten-year-old in his learning pattern is also typical in that he is arriving at his pre-adolescent maximum. He should show gains but they will be less than those made by him during his stay in the fourth grade. The child often recognizes his slowing-down. If he is a low-average performer in previous grades he may at at this level be regarded as non-responsive, uncooperative, or retarded. Teacher suspicion that this is true is easily noticed by the child and he may then, in reality, become uncooperative and unresponsive, perhaps even antagonistic.

The fifth grade is not a place for extensive remedial work, drill, or pressure to do better. In some ways his development may be described as coasting. The developmental drive of the third and fourth grades should carry him through this year, and, oftimes, the next. The fifth-grade level for the typical child is a time in which the resistance to instructional pressures is unequalled by any other elementary grade.

A most productive situation is one characterized by rich creative opportunities in which there is considerable opportunity for self-direction. In this particular objective surprising results can be expected if the activity represents a culmination of three years of practice (2nd, 3rd, 4th) in self-direction during which there has been a direct increasing ratio between increased maturity and increased experience. These are undoubtedly the three most productive years for laying the groundwork for the development of this kind of ability in personal and group relations. The sixth, seventh, and eighth grades are not nearly so appropriate for this particular kind of developmental encouragement. Thus, the developmental gradient of this characteristic does not follow, through the next three years, a proportionate compatibility between increasing chronological maturity and personal and group freedom. In the earlier three grades mentioned (2nd, 3rd, 4th) it comes close to this kind of picturization.

The fifth-grader is typically the executive type. He wants to start at the beginning and proceed to the end. He is an organizer. If his teacher utilizes various sections of the textbook irregularly he may protest. In his mind progress should be orderly from one page to the next. Consequently he will not necessarily rebel against extensive utilization of conventional methods even at the expense of creative and more challenging curriculum plans. On the other hand, his ability to plan, to be creative, to apply skills, etc., suggests that for well-rounded development he be taken into consideration, be given explanations and asked for advice.

Unlike the nine-year-old, the ten-year-old will not respond very heartily to monotonous drill assignments, particularly if he has already undergone these experiences in the third and fourth grades. The more competent children, academically, will not show so much improvement as formerly. The less competent children, likewise, levelling off, will often be over-motivated and consequently will begin to develop feelings of inferiority.

In reference to skills, these children are more appropriately located maturationally for applications rather than for reviews or for further mechanical learnings. The fifth-grade child who reads well needs little routine class work in reading. His ability will be more richly fostered by encouragement toward wide, diversified, free reading. Consequently the classroom should be richly endowed with accessible materials. This should be the case in the fifth-grade room to a greater extent than in any of the other elementary grades.

In this grade considerable difference is found between the behavior of boys and that of girls. This difference needs to be understood by teachers in order to work with children effectively. In the earlier grades, differences are quite negligible as they affect classroom organization and instruction. In the fifth grade a discerning teacher can detect changes.

One of these is the antagonism between boys and girls that is beginning to become evident. This is due to the fact that the personal-social-sex developmental gradient demands a sex-withdrawal and orientation as a condition of readiness for later extra-sex orientation and adjustment. Secondly, the now obvious superiority of girls generally sets up a competive learning climate which boys can meet only through withdrawal and mild attack. Consequently misbehavior is more frequent. Clinics for child study report a greater incidence of behavior deviation. As cited by one investigator, the frequency among ten-year-old boys is three times that of girls of this age.

Maturity difference is the usual explanation for sex segregation in the upper elementary grades. There can be no doubt of the more rapid development of girls. Physical-growth records document this conclusion. Similar findings are reported in studies of mental development, and likewise portrayed by comparisons of the achievement curves of boys and girls.

B. Behavior and Interpretation

1. *Motor Performance*

Patricia utilized this year to progress to the end of her pre-adolescent cycle and to begin progress on the adolescent cycle of development. The fifth grade witnessed a consolidation and improvement on big-muscle control but demonstrated a rather low maximum in hand and eye coordination, small-muscle manipulation, and those finer motor movements usually demonstrated by a child of this age in hand-writing and in art work. The promise of her early school days was never fully realized. Without further reasonable explanation this must be attributed to lack of motivating experiences.

2. *Emotional Reactions*

Patricia showed almost no tension-release activity. Life looked good to her. She had but little occasion to complain, to be worried, to be jealous of the other girls, to alibi her shortcomings or to do many of those things usually coloring the behavior of the unhappy or poorly-adjusted child of this age. Picking at her fingers, twisting around, jumping up and down were much less a part of her "sitting"-behavior pattern than was true a year previously.

Emotional development during Patricia's tenth year was seen as a smooth coming-into-focus of what was projected for her in her earlier years. Patricia was constantly seen by the writer as a child with narrow deviational ranges as she progressed from six to eleven years of age. Her development proceeded evenly without threat of breaking away on tangents. Small behavior annoyances were dropped at the proper time. Ten found her dependable, friendly, and an easy child to have around.

Perhaps this analysis seems haloed and out of order in comparison with the statement made in the preceding section. We have recorded our perturbation regarding the absence of activities that might have awakened artistic and creative drives. Creativity can only result when the artistic and the emotional are brought together; when an attitude, an appreciation, or a deep understanding can be expressed in a reading, a production, or a work of art. Obviously the omission of curriculum activity geared to this end left Patricia unstirred and with a low-level emotional-growth impact. Such maturity as she achieved, however, was easily obtained. The reader should not necessarily infer that smooth and untroubled progress is necessarily an easy accomplishment even when a low maximum is in prospect. This in itself reflects a kind of emotional control and adjustment which is salutary to the child and satisfying to those who live with him. Smooth, easy progression therefore is not necessarily a correlate of a low prospective maximum.

It is a definite emotional counterpart which can be just as affected by problems and frustrations regardless of the level to which it is progressing. Our diagnosis of Patricia in this respect was always promising and optimistic. She showed at an early age a kind of developmental progress which would have responded readily to modification activities. In the face of the available evidence it would seem that these were denied her.

3. *Anxieties and Security Threats*

There are three main drives on the part of the ten-year-old child. These are (1) the desire to please, (2) the desire for more adequate expression of personality, and (3) the desire for sex and peer identification. Eleven and twelve is a time in which these drives are perhaps more dominant and demanding, but at ten any frustration to their realization can cause anxiety and insecurity. Patricia, although reaching the age of eleven before completing the fifth grade in school, was quite typical in that she presented plenty of evidence to conclude that these drives were part of her being and that in her daily life she showed some concern about them.

Here was a child that did not go out of her way to please others. She did not "wait on" the girl "stars" nor did she exert herself to please her teacher. Her daily standard pattern was one which might be characterized as an indrawn neutrality. She slouched and appeared, many times, as far away. Occasionally she did something so well that special commendation was offered. This pleased her greatly. She became almost sentimental and effusive in expressing her appreciation. Little question that she sought love and approbation.

Children that have had opportunity and encouragement present well-rounded personalities at the age of ten. Owning one, their drive is to show it off. The ten-year-old has the greater need, in comparison with the nine-year-old, of this kind of expression. Patricia unfortunately had few qualities to parade. Latent potentialities that never came into being produced in her a shortage of those characteristics that are generally considered as part of a well-rounded personality. Consequently she gave signs of anxiety. They were but the beginnings of feelings that never developed into significant problems later on. But they were present. Patricia of course was helpless in the matter. Her total development of personality traits was of a kind that brought mere maturation to those that came into being at an early age. Her development gave no promise of expansion horizontally as it moved longitudinally to its maturity. Faked listlessness, extreme emotionalized appreciation of attention, and oft repeated demonstrations of her physical-recreational abilities are but a few of the demonstrations documenting this observation.

Tied in with both of these was Patricia's desire for sex and peer identification. An observer seeing Patricia only on the playground involved in large-muscle sports—ball, running, batting, etc.—might conclude that she was undergoing difficulty in accepting her sex role. Seen year after year and in a variety of situations, other conclusions can be made. Playing with boys, or with girls in the more boyish sports, undoubtedly was a compensation rather than an escape. Patricia enjoyed girls' play and participated enough to indicate satisfactory identification with her own sex.

4. *Personal-Social Development*

Patricia was described at this age as a "child with a very good disposition. She was conscientious, reliable, courteous, cooperative, and neither too aggressive or submissive." This description can hardly be called colorful or individualistic. Nevertheless it has some significance in that it indicates she had achieved some balance in her personal-social development which might reasonably be expected of a child of her age and grade.

Patricia reflected the maturity expected of her by her tendency to dress like the other children, to use the same slang expressions, to enjoy the same type of movies, juke-box tunes, and comic serials. She was not entirely average, however. Occasionally she departed from the others in peer-accepted customs, likes and dislikes. She reverted to a costume or dress habit reflecting her ethnic background or expressed interest in or liking for a tune or movie more popular with older girls than with her own group. Some of this represented recognition of a lack of total acceptance and an inability to achieve status in her immediate group. Perhaps such a strong ethnic background intensifies the conflict beginning to emerge at this age between home and peer group.

A typical characteristic is membership in and promotion of clubs and secret societies. There was almost no evidence of this kind of interest, nor was there among the other children. Undoubtedly such activity would be observable had it existed. Perhaps formalized clubs for children of this age need a cultural background or some educational stimulation. In this particular school, club activity received almost no encouragement. The scattered stores and the lack of recreational hang-outs, were, likewise, not exactly conducive to bringing gangs and groups of children within contact of each other.

5. *Play and Recreation*

Patricia presented some change in her play habits in the interval from nine to ten. This consisted mainly of a little more dignity in the way she conducted herself. Playground activities still interested her but they were given less spontaneous attention. She planned for them and did not rush quite so enthusiastically into a game without some preliminaries. Proper clothes for sports were given concern more often than formerly. She needed her own glove. In some respects she seemed to aspire to the proficiency shown by those older girls who make up the playground teams that play in city recreational leagues. Later observations showed that Patricia did not become so identified. Extreme weight probably frustrated this ambition if it ever really existed.

Unfortunately for her, pre-adolescent maturity brought little in the way of diversion and versatility. Her home provided some balance in its customary short-period summer vacation at a lake cottage. The family record seemed to indicate harmony, considerable sharing of planning and other responsibilities and genuine pleasure to all members.

In her particular recreational interests Patricia was a rather smooth, polished performer. Although less than at nine, she still seemed to need to embellish her performance at bat, in running, or in the field by mannerisms attracting attention. She not only wanted to perform well but had an equal drive to dramatize her efforts.

6. *Academic Status*

Patricia enjoyed school more than ever during this particular year. Skills in all subject-matter areas were rather equally developed. Patricia shifted somewhat when asked which subject she liked best. At one time it would be reading and at another time arithmetic or some other area of study. At no time did her teacher single her out for special deficiencies. Patricia seemed to have no worries about outcomes. She did her work as required although at times she lagged and then had to hurry to complete an assignment.

Wide academic ranges can usually be found at this age level. These existed in Patricia's grade but to a lesser degree than is often the case. Among the group, Patricia was to be found around the middle or slightly above. Her effortless, somewhat inattentive manner of working undoubtedly affected her grades which usually were those of plus-average quality. A little more disposition to act busily or industriously might have brought her slightly higher rewards.

It is unfortunate that her academic work contributed so little to her general personal interests and desires. Patricia could read "satisfactorily", spell, and do her arithmetic. However, outside of school she read little and she had no real dramatic or creative interests. The contributions to her development came from the radio, the comic books, the juke-box, limited travel, and a fairly good family integration.

7. *Ethical and Moral Behavior*

Ten usually has quite a sound background of beliefs and ethics. The ten-year-old is a responsible person and can be depended upon. He may resent being asked to help out at home but when this occurs it is usually because he has his own projects underway and is conscious of his responsibility to them. Tens, thus, are often too busy to have time to assist in family affairs. Patricia was not quite this kind of child. Unlike many modern homes her family needed her. She responded to this need and through this response gained much that would have been denied her if left to her own resources. She had too few motivations in other aspects of her environment to have gone far in self-developed projects.

Patricia was honest in her relationships with other children. She seemed to have some religious concepts but church attendance was irregular and without real significance. It is likely that her moral and ethical precepts came from her home where she was wanted, loved, and necessary for its wellbeing. Adequate success in school kept her away from petty dishonesty in doing her work or on occasions when she had to take tests or examinations.

Selected References

Louise B. Ames, Janet Learned, Ruth Metraux, and Richard N. Walker: *Child Rorschach Responses*, pp. 264-78. Hoeber, New York, 1952.

A. W. Blair and W. H. Burton: *Growth and Development of the Pre-adolescent*, pp. 264-78. Appleton-Century-Crofts, New York, 1951.

Ruth Cunningham and Associates: *Understanding Group Behavior of Boys and Girls*, pp. 380-91. Bureau of Publications, Teachers College, Columbia University, New York, 1951.

Faculty of the University School: *How Children Develop*, University School Series No. 3, pp. 29-39. Ohio State University, Columbus, 1946.

Arnold Gesell and Frances L. Ilg: *Child Development*, Part II, "The Child From Five to Ten", pp. 212-17. Harper, New York, 1949.

Gladys G. Jenkins, Helen Schacter, and W. W. Bauer: *These Are Your Children*, pp. 112-28. Scott-Foresman, New York, 1949.

D. A. Prescott and Others: *Helping Teachers Understand Children*, pp. 167-84. American Council on Education, Washington, 1945.

Earle L. Reynolds and Grace Schoen: "Growth Patterns of Identical Triplets From 8 to 18 Years". *Child Development*, Vol. 19, 1948, pp. 130-45.

Helen Schacter and W. W. Bauer: *Guide Book for the Health and Personal Development*, Book 5, *You*. Scott-Foresman, New York, 1949.

E. H. Watson and G. H. Lowrey: *Growth and Development of Children*, p. 107. Year Book Publishers, Chicago, 1951.

IN THE SIXTH GRADE

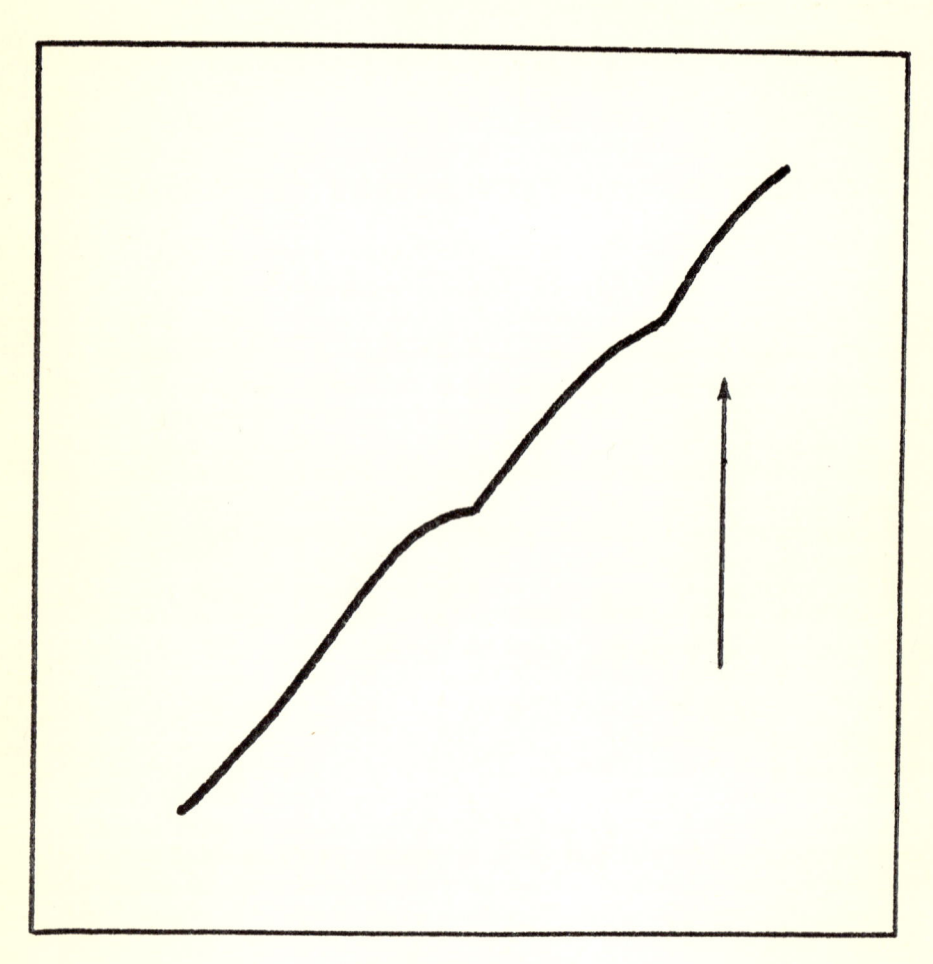

Period of Maturation

Chapter VI

GRADE SIX—THE ELEVEN-YEAR OLD CHILD

A. The Sixth-Grade Mode

THE SIXTH GRADE in school is the year in which a teacher can expect almost anything to happen. For the parent it is a time in which he may see great changes in his child, quite often for what he thinks of as the "worst." Redl describes this period as one which is most disappointing to parent and teacher, a time in which children are hard to live with and to understand. It is even said that investigators have turned away from these children for study because they are "boisterous, dirty, discourteous, secretive, and antagonistic, no longer babies nor yet grown up in our society . . . " (Zachary).

Recent investigators agree generally that eleven, particularly, is an age at which the child finds real conflict between peer and adult demands. Some beginnings of peer pressures were felt during the ages of nine and ten. At eleven it is difficult to maintain equilibrium between the two. The group makes real demands. Although outright rebellion to adult authority may not occur, continuous conflict and aggression are always at hand.

In school, discipline is always a problem. According to Jones, more behavior problems are cited for fourth-, fifth-, and sixth-grade children than for any other age group. Blatz and Bott report a peak frequency of misbehavior at the age of nine. Their cases, however, represent a special sample which cannot be said to be typical of the nine-year-old as he has been previously described. But the data do point out the significance of the personal-social drive which begins at nine and becomes particularly demanding at eleven. That the latter years should be the more climactic is a conclusion substantiated by Piaget who says that conflict with parental desires reaches its peak during the tenth and eleventh years. Redl concurs that these children are rebellious and likewise show accompanying physical manifestations such as facial tics, speech disorders, nailbiting, etc. He characterizes them as irritable, distrustful, suspicious and easily upset. They often show immature tantrum tendencies occasioned by demands for punctuality, obedience, and submission to family demand and dictate.

What kind of children are these? How are they seen in the sixth grade in school? The descriptions given cannot be called representative of all sixth-graders. They fit only a minority or roughly a third. This is the group that stands between two others of this age, namely, those that are making the transition from pre-adolescence to adolescence (Figure 1, B, following). The two groups less characterized by the various growth connotations are, firstly, the eleven-year-olds who are less mature. In reality their development at this age is more like that of the ten-year-old than that of the rebellious, more mature eleven-year-old (Figure 1, A). The other group for which the description is less accurate is made up of those eleven-year-olds who are precocious (Figure 1, C). These are the children who are most mature and inevitably will be found on their adolescent maturational level. They have grown out of the earlier period of instability and conflict. They have made certain adjustments, have found a new zone of satisfying activity and are moving closer to their new destination.

The disturbed group, the children who reject parental guidance with subsequent guilt, inner conflict, or outer aggression, may nevertheless be regarded as the modal group in this age-grade location. Consequently the discussion of the sixth-grade child will be related to these youngsters.

There are several reasons given for the kind of behavior reported. According to Finley, parents and teachers impose standards of conduct on these children for which they are not ready. The typical child of ten has been easy to handle. In his rather mature behavior, he has suggested optimistic promises for the future. When he turns away, adopts behavior a little more rowdy, more independent, more challenging than the former childhood rules and regulations, parents become disturbed. As the child withdraws more and more to his own peer standards the conflict intensifies. A kind of gradual mutual misunderstanding develops which becomes more and more confusing. In school the child is regarded as a misfit, or showing delinquency trends, and is often reported to the principal or to a child-study clinic.

There is another explanation for such behavior. It is based on the idea that at this time the child is ending one cycle of development and beginning another. Pre-adolescence (the childhood cycle) is approaching maturity and the adolescent-adult cycle is beginning to materialize. A hypothesis which can be offered in all sincerity is that the child's behavior, conditioned by a pattern of development underway for several years, is now threatened by new inner needs which cannot find satisfaction in the old ways of behaving and acting. The child is faced with alternatives or choices. Old drives and objectives are still retained while new ones are beginning to come into focus. As a result, conflict ensues. The old pattern attempts to force the new out of the picture. And the new, which by leaps and bounds gains internal reinforcement every day, gradually gains dominance.

There is also some substantiation for the thesis that the degree and kind of cyclic overlapping has some relationship with the amount of confusion, instability, and conflict which follows or accompanies this Dr.-Jekyl-Mr.-Hyde phase of the child's life. No child reaches complete (99 to 100 per cent) maturity of the

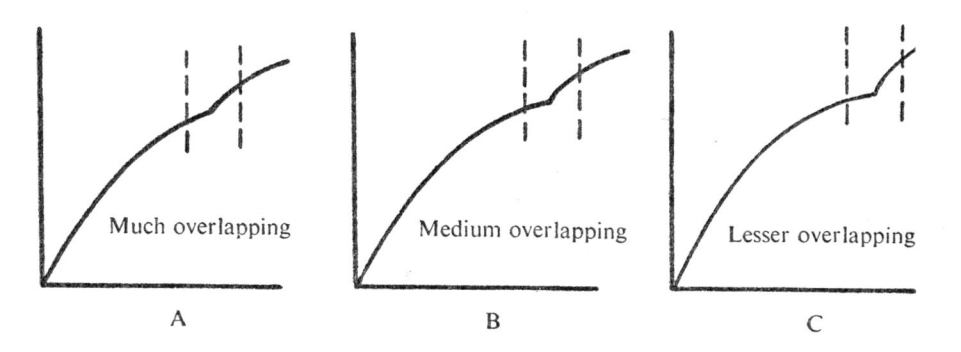

Figure 1. General Categories of Maturity of Eleven-Year-Old (6th-Grade) Children.

A—The More Immature Group: These are sixth-graders still on the pre-adolescent cycle of growth. Behavior is generally good, more like fifth-graders; become problems in the next grade.

B—The Median Group: Here may be found the sixth-grade problem children described in the literature as rejectees of adult control at this grade level. Conflict the result of contrasting needs as typically seen at the sixth-grade level.

C—The More Mature Group: These are the children that are the most likely to have been problems at the fifth-grade level. As sixth-graders they are already on the adolescent cycle and adjusting exclusively to the demands of this one level of development.

pre-adolescent cycle before beginning the adolescent-adult cycle of development. Some children start the latter cycle when they are only sixty per cent mature in the former. Others may reach as much as ninety per cent of maturity before beginning their adolescent period, Figure 2.[1]

Whether differences in the amount of cyclic overlapping are related with differences in behavior is a natural question and one deserving research attention. It is altogether possible that here may be found a clue as to behavior differences among children.

Behavior, as implied by these hypotheses, has a strong physiological base. Cyclic changes represent the framework, so to speak, upon which the whole behavior pattern is built. This thesis does not deny the effect of the environment. Children with differing maturity patterns, equal in every other way, will respond differently to the same environmental motivation. Likewise, the same child at different maturity stages will be more responsive at one time than at another to the same environmental stimulus.

[1]This problem is now under investigation in the Child Development Laboratory, Michigan State College.

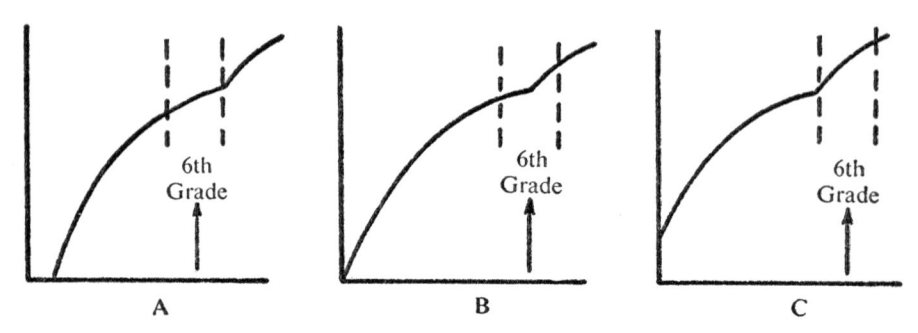

Figure 2. Difference in Relationships Between Pre-adolescent and Adolescent Maturities of Sixth-Grade Children Passing from One Cycle of Development to Another.

> A—The child who shifts early from one cycle to another: Change in behavior in relation to needs of new cycle is postulated as smooth and without serious problem; adolescent demands are mild.
>
> B—The child who lives under dual demands: One cycle is growing to completion at the same time that another is beginning to make serious demands. Problem behavior as the result of conflicting inner demands.
>
> C—The child who matures in one cycle before beginning the next: Shifts rapidly into adolescent behavior pattern.

A third explanation, but one at a secondary level of importance since it would not be a factor without the accompanying physiological phenomenon, is the lack of clear goals and objectives.

New growth demands are often confusing. The child who previously has been willing to accept adult explanation for some routine requirement, regulation, or behavior such as the time for coming home in the evening, now has a new reason for staying out. His wishes for companionship are developing, etc. Previously he accepted parents' mandate and without question returned home at a designated time. Now he wonders why he should return. It does not seem logical. He is doing no harm and is having fun. He therefore questions the old authority. Lacking any other, he may comply but with resentment, stay out anyway, or rebel with some feeling of guilt. In justifications of parents' mandate, it can be said that he has not yet established confidence in his ability, and in some instances he knows this. Questioning the old, questioning his own ability, he acts impulsively with confused objectives and goals.

A fourth way of looking at the problem is to point out that behavior at the end of a cycle or at the beginning of a cycle is always more deviational than during the upswing or rapid developmental times. This phenomenon needs little more explanation than to note that growth at the baseline or near the ceiling of the maximum can only deviate one way. If it is just emerging it can only show chance errors upward—it can not drop below a zero point. If it is proceeding near the maximum, chance errors can only show negative shift.

Deviations at this point should under the best of conditions be the result of chance or deliberate experimental effort. But unfortunately, the child's environment often will add increased pressures to accentuate or exaggerate these natural strayings. A teacher will insist that a child should read. Or if he can read just a little she will think that he should read better. Or, to illustrate what happens at the upper near-maximum levels, if the child is not so high as she thinks he should be, added pressures will be put on him. These generally do nothing but add to the confusion, demoralize the child, and lower the rapport level. Deviations not only become more frequent but depart with greater magnitude from the point of the child's real performance level.

There are certain other considerations that must be noted in order to understand behavior of this age group. First, there is the growing antagonism between boys and girls. Conflict seems to parallel increasing rejection of adult standards shown by both groups. Several theories to explain this are in vogue. One school of thought describes it as conflict originating among boys and directed toward the feminine sex in general. Breaking away from mother control generates an attitude of rejection toward all members of the female sex. Another viewpoint is quite different. It explains the antagonism between sexes as a process of mutual scapegoating; each takes out on the other the aggression that they dare not show adults. Perhaps a third theory is more reasonable than the two others. This theory would regard conflict as merely a representation of maturity differences. The maturity advantage in favor of girls stirs up antagonisms because girls are more successful in school work and in general adjustment to rules and regulations.

Whether such conflict as exists is good or bad is a matter of speculation. In general it has been deplored. Some authorities indicate that it is a secondary characteristic of development that is essential. This theory points out that withdrawal into sex groups is a natural accompaniment of development preparatory to assuming a later adolescent-adult extra-sex homogeneity. Thus the child preparing for later integrated well-being in adult life needs first to identify himself with his own sex. Segregation without interference provides opportunity, for example, for boys to adjust themselves to the idea that they are boys. The same applies for girls. By strictly following behavior codes of their own sex, boys and girls more easily accomplish proper identification.

Regardless of cause, it is a fact that rejection of adult and family codes is in many ways a part of the growing-up process. Both parents and teachers are inclined to look upon gang-age fads, frills and dress as undesirable. In consequence they do everything possible to counter-attack.

Nevertheless, it would seem that one of the requisites to adequate well-being, increased personal and social development, and satisfactory emotional maturity is movement toward acceptance of peer demands even in the face of some parental or adult opposition. Because the culture offers no alternative it is essential that the child devise his own course of action. He has a basic need of social contact and finds security and belongingness in some rejection of parental authority, and often, in regressing to earlier forms of behavior. In effect there is always the appearance of a certain amount of personality disorganization. To say that such a backward step is necessary to future development and well-being may seem to be an exaggeration of the facts. Nevertheless, much unanimity in research can lead to no other conclusion than the necessity of careful consideration of this idea. At this age the developing personality is given added impetus by the child's beginning desires for independence. Success in this undertaking, painful as it can be, seems to be a requisite to further independence and to adequate personal and social maturation.

Adequate peer status makes no mean contribution to the child's total development. It is in this accomplishment that he achieves considerable social consciousness. He becomes important to his group and the group to him. Thus he achieves belongingness and social security. His independence is expressed through activities of the group. In peer-group association there is no adult to tell him what to do. He expresses ideas of his own and learns to compromise with the ideas of others.

B. Behavior and Interpretation

1. *Motor Performance*

Patricia as an eleven-year-old was well started on her adolescent cycle. Since her eleventh birthday took place in late April of her fifth-grade year she chronologically was old enough, as a girl, to be found on this cycle of growth.

Motor performance as such reflected her stage of maturity. Gross motor action was smooth and more rhythmic than ever; so were her finer motor movements, as demonstrated by skill in writing, drawing and cutting. Hand and eye coordination also reflected this stage.

2. *Emotional Reactions*

In terms of her developmental maturity Patricia was a child representative of type C shown in Figure 1. As such, her emotional reactions could be anticipated to be mild with reference to antagonism toward boys and adults. As a matter of fact there was no antagonism observable anywhere in Patricia's behavior. She accepted the companionship of boys and was more pleased than disgruntled to be linked with a boy in the conversation and teasing of other children.

It was difficult to determine whether Patricia found conflict in shifting to an acceptance of standards of her peers. It was obvious, in her contacts with other children, that peer status was important and sought after. She obtained sufficient attention and acceptance but somewhat less than other children. Our analysis placed her on the fringe of the normal area reasonably expected of children of this age. This was a position that she seemed to have occupied since the fourth grade, a time at which these contacts began to assume importance and significance. Of some relation to a speculation as to what "might have been" is our conclusion that this school community offered little in the way of efforts to stimulate peer-group organization. A scattered community with neither good nor bad cleavage opportunities, and a school environment that did little to encourage club activity, left but little stimulus to this child except through home-to-home and after-school chance contacts.

Patricia, as typical of the mature eleven-year-old, and as a twelve-year-old in the spring of her sixth-grade year in school, showed the usual mimicry of the older adolescents. Langauge, dress, use of cosmetics, etc., were part of her behavior design but some reluctance was shown toward leaving her more secure childhood status. She still clung somewhat to family ideals and goals and to the preadolescent games in which she found security.

3. *Anxieties and Security Threats*

The particular potential conflict ensuing when a child has to make a choice between parent and peer domination seemed to be of little consequence in Patricia's life. Peer demands were minor but of course important. Patricia easily accepted them but in so doing risked no loss of status in her particular home. She worked in the home and in the store from an early age. Store work tended to give her mature status and to free her from the kind of rules usually imposed. Consequently anxiety and insecurity through usual channels were by-passed. The kind of home of which Patricia was a member—a "foreign" ethnic tradition with more male domination than in the typical American middle-class home—was the kind which would seem to produce a conflict at a later age. The time of course would be middle or late adolescence. At this time it is likely Patricia will want to do other things than work in the store. She may then seek the kind of independence which she does not now particularly desire.

4. *Personal-Social Development*

Personal-social development by Patricia may be summarized at this stage as having followed four main lines.

Firstly, Patricia had progressed in her maturity at this grade level to the early adolescent stage. She had completed the beginning try-out aspects of behavior which occurs between maximum pre-adolescence and the beginning of adolescence. Her developmental trend was well enough established to suggest that what she was at this time will in the future continue, but more clearly pictured. Personality and social characteristics of late adolescence were in the making and beginning to be obvious. Generally, when development reaches this stage, it is like a snow-ball going down-hill. It gains momentum and grows according to its emerging design. It is also hard to stop.

The challenge to teachers has been generally unrecognized. Very few see in sixth-graders the need for broadened contacts and diversified explorations. Criticism can be directed both to the conventionalists and the progressives. The conventionalist looks upon a child in Patricia's stage of maturity as one that needs review, consolidation of learnings and a sharpening up of skills. Patricia as a sixth-grader was past this stage. Conventional mechanical learnings were boresome, and in the light of our exposition took up time that might be better used. The progressives with a maximum of permissiveness and choice could lead such a child to the same barren end but with fun as an only advantage. It can hardly be debated that provision of creative opportunity, in areas of which Patricia and her classmates were almost totally unaware, would have been the best prescription for a broadened and diversified development. Children of this age know what they need in terms of a familiar environment. What they don't know are the opportunities for expression in an enriched environment.

Secondly, an appraisal of Patricia in reference to moral and character values, at this stage, was complimentary. She showed stability. She had almost no conflict between home and peer demands. She had no temptations of significance that would cause serious insecurity or would tend to divert her from attaining at maturity her own and her parents' objectives.

Thirdly, her social values were adequate for her in the environment in which she lived. Preparation for any other would have been unwise and is not implied by this statement. Such implications as have been pointed out refer to enrichment at her own level rather than training for a higher level.

Patricia was cooperative, helpful, and dependable. These characteristics were indicated at an earlier age and came more and more into focus with each passing year. With the home, school, and community environment as described here, one might question such a conclusion. She had but little opportunity to develop these traits in school. Nevertheless, she was honest and willing to help others. She showed many traits that *seemingly* were given no encouragement. One can only conclude that the most casual type of home, school, and community tends to bring out and encourage only necessary minimum inherent potentialities. Our plea throughout is an argument for providing greater opportunities for expression, appreciations, and creative living.

Lastly, an appraisal must be made of Patricia's limitations and handicaps. Chief among these was her physical development. It probably will not only curtail future peer-group acceptance which demands conformity even in body-build, but will also curtail essential energy expenditure.

5. *Play and Recreation*

Patricia's physical development at this time was more characteristic of the early adolescent than that of the late pre-adolescent. She had grown in both height and weight to the point where she became very large for her grade. In the main she seemed to lack feministic characteristics although clearly progressing on the adolescent cycle. She was both sluggish and active. Dynamic at one time and slumped at another was still descriptive of her physical picture.

6. *Academic Status*

There was nothing in Patricia's records reported by teachers or by the laboratory observers to suggest that she was much more than an indifferent, somewhat uninterested, reluctant pupil in academic learning situations. Both teachers and observers saw some hope in her at times but in general were disappointed to discover that a bright, interested reaction one day devolved almost instantaneously into lethargic, half-hearted attention. She performed well enough but no further. She seemed uninterested in driving herself to a high level of achievement in terms of effort, supplementary study, neatness of prepared papers, or well rounded-out presentations.

Nothing more need be said regarding her academic situation based upon the subjective observations of teacher or observer. The picture would have been the same if Patricia had been in almost any other school operating with about the same standards. The conventional criteria for judging a child are usually effort shown, interest, promptness and neatness of response, ability to pass such tests as are given by the teacher, and general attitude.

Part Two brings out certain data which indicate that at this time she was travelling through a responsive learning period as shown by permanent learning and objective responses of much better quality than either the teacher or observer would have believed. Her case is one in which quite good achievement was taking place without the usual signs and in spite of academic arrangements that had little challenge for her.

7. *Ethical and Moral Behavior*

The behavior of children is undoubtedly influenced by family, religion, community mores, and peer-group relations. Patricia in her sixth grade in school, as in other grades, presented a consistent pattern of ethical and moral behavior which seemed in accord at all times with the influences operating upon her. Her behavior was regular and in accordance with expectations and standards. Insofar as it was possible to make a determination, there were little or no conflicts between parental and peer codes nor did her own drives push her toward any kind of manifested rebellion. She appeared to be a child who was developing a rigidity of ideal and objective which may or may not cause her confusion and concern at a later time. Teacher and school attitudes introduced no new concepts of behavior or ethical concepts that would do anything but consolidate the pattern originally brought by this child into the school environment.

Patricia behaved as expected in this framework and judged other children accordingly. In general, judgments were limited to minor behavior defections. Where behavior was judged bad it was held against the child only temporarily. Patricia was always ready to forgive and was incapable of carrying over in her mind the thought that the victim of a minor infraction should be permanently ostracized.

Selected References

A.W. Blair and W.H. Burton: *Growth and Development of the Pre-adolescent*, pp. 178-96. Appleton-Century-Crofts, New York, 1951.

W.E. Blatz and Helen M. Bott: "Studies in Mental Hygiene of Children." *Pedagogical Seminar*, 1927, pp. 552-82.

Alvina T. Burrows: *Teaching Children in the Middle Grades*, pp. 18-23. Heath, Boston, 1952.

Faculty of the University School: *How Children Develop*, University School Series No. 3, pp. 29-39. Ohio State University, Columbus, 1946.

Malcolm Finley: "Developmental Aspects of the Latency Period Significant to Education." *American Journal of Orthopsychiatry*, XIII, 1943, pp. 271-5.

Gladys G. Jenkins, Helen Schacter, and W.W. Bauer: *These Are Your Children*, pp. 112-28. Scott-Foresman, New York, 1949.

H.E. Jones, H.S. Conrad, and L.B. Murphy: "Child Development and the Curriculum." 38th Yearbook, National Society for the Study of Education. Public School Publishing Co., Bloomington, Ill., 1939.

Jean Piaget: *The Moral Judgment of the Child*. Harcourt-Brace, New York, 1932.

D.A. Prescott and Others: *Helping Teachers Understand Children*, pp. 231-70. American Council on Education, Washington, 1945.

Fritz Redl: "Preadoloscents, What Makes Them Tick?" *Child Study*, Winter, 1944, pp. 44-8.

Earle L. Reynolds and Grace Schoen: "Growth Patterns of Identical Triplets From 8 to 18 Years." *Child Development*, Vol. 19, 1948, pp. 130-45.

Helen Schacter and W.W. Bauer: *Guide Book for the Health and Personal Development*, Book 6, *You and Others*, pp. 5-128. Scott-Foresman, New York, 1949.

Ruth Strang: *An Introduction to Child Study*, pp. 315-64. Macmillan, New York, 1951.

E.H. Watson and G.H. Lowrey: *Growth and Development of Children*, pp. 107-8. Year Book Publishers, Chicago, 1951.

Caroline B. Zachary: "Understanding the Child During the Latency Period." *Educational Methods*, Vol. 17, 1938, pp. 162-5.

PART TWO

Developmental Analysis and Interpretation

Introduction

THE CHAPTERS in Part Two will deal on a longitudinal basis with growth and development of the elementary-school child. Concern in this part will be directed toward over-all development in the total perspective of the elementary school. Utilizing the same case as furnished the illustration for Part One an attempt will be made to make three approaches to the analysis of data. First, we shall show the developmental picture of the child herself. Has her development been normal? What was outstanding about it? Wherein was it deficient? Second, we shall appraise environmental factors as they affected this girl. The home, the school, her associates, etc., will be given attention. And last, we shall be particularly concerned with "what might have been." Wherein could her emotional environment have been improved? What kind of educational organization would have been necessary to result in achievement of optimum potentialities?

The third approach is in reality a special application of the second dealing with environmental factors. In this instance attention will be directed to the school alone as an environmental stimulus.

The various approaches will not affect the organization of the presentation, but rather will underlie the presentations in all chapters thereby furnishing purpose and direction to the analysis.

Writing limitations make it necessary to project a series of pictures of the individual. It is hoped that these will lead to an over-all perspective rather than to segmental or discrete scenes of a growing child. Our analyses will be presented under the following various aspects of development:

Chapter VII—Physical and Mental Development
Chapter VIII—Academic Learnings
Chapter IX—Personal-Social Development
Chapter X—Personal Adjustment

The three objectives mentioned will be kept in mind throughout each chapter but none will necessarily receive equal emphasis. In one chapter, for example, it may be appropriate to place greater stress on environmental factors. This would be the case in discussing personal and social development. To the contrary, in appraising physical development, environmental background will attain only minimum attention. In the other chapters, the balance will shift likewise but each will be given some treatment.

The material presented will complement the interpretations recorded in Part One. In a sense the interpretations in this part represent an analysis of behavior at a level somewhat above the one of the previous part. The goal is to add to such understandings as have already been established and to show further the validity of principles either demonstrated or postulated in the previous discussions. Of secondary importance is the opportunity offered to demonstrate how data on one child can be appraised and evaluated in studying the interaction between him and his school environment.

Chapter VII

PHYSICAL AND MENTAL DEVELOPMENT

A. Physical Development

1. *Comparative Growth*

PATRICIA, like most young children, grew very rapidly. Increase in height was accompanied by increase in weight. In Pat's case, they were similar in pattern but her weight increased more rapidly than her height, Figure 3. Height and weight curves showed a paralleling in changes of rates and rhythms as would be expected of a child of normal development. The data available during her kindergarten and first-grade days indicated a rounding off of the *early* childhood cycle at from eighty to eighty-five months of age. At approximately eighty-five months a rapid rise occurred with a new spurt showing between 110 and 120 months of age. This would imply that Patricia began her pre-adolescent development around eighty-five months and her adolescent cycle between 110 and 120 months.

From all appearances there was an over-all normal relationship between the height and weight growth sequences. Shifts appeared at approximately the same time in each, and thereby may be regarded as an indication of normalcy.

Pat showed her most rapid pre-adolescent growth during the middle elementary grades. The lesser fifth-grade gains might conventionally be interpreted as a slowing-down of growth. Breckenridge and Vincent have defined this as " . . . a period of consolidation of earlier gains and a breathing spell before the changes incident to pubescence begin . . . " It is more likely, however, that such changes in rates and rhythms merely picture the phenomenon of cyclic growth.

The slowing-down in the fifth grade represents the approach of the pre-adolescent maximum, and the sixth-grade spurt dramatically points out the beginning of adolescence.

Signs of Adolescence: Research reveals that pubescence is signalled by increased rates of growth with new rhythms and relationships. Part Three discloses the information that Pat began her adolescent height and weight cycles at 116.8 and 114.7 months of age, respectively.

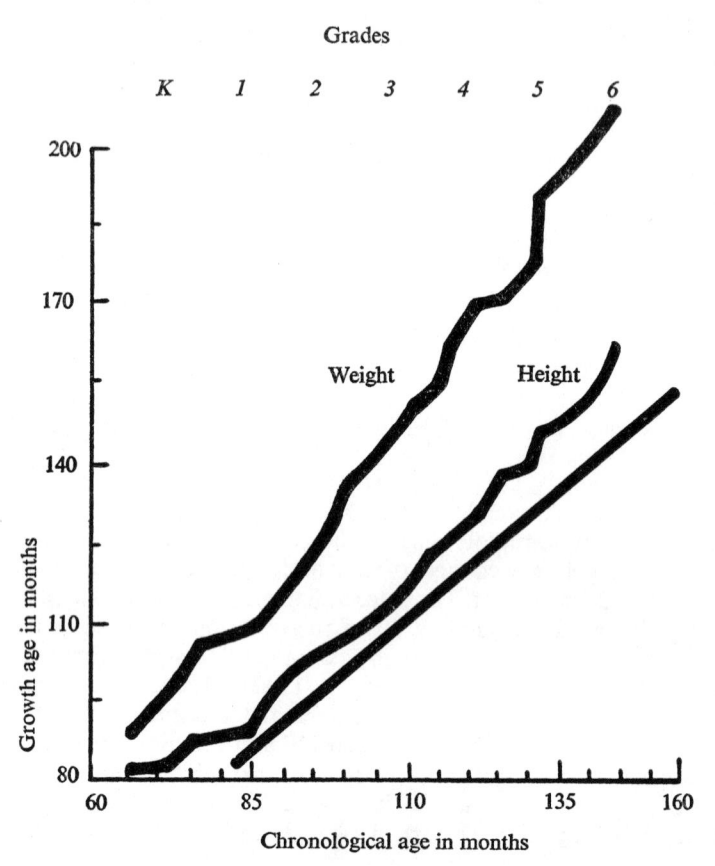

Figure 3. Curves of Height- and Weight-Age Equivalents

Some children enter pubescence at eight years of age. Others do not begin until they become sixteen years old. Girls range in general from eight to fourteen in the first signs. Pat's adolescent beginning points in her height and weight growths, and her first menstruation at 153 months (12 yrs. 9 mo.) place her well within the range of normalcy in this respect.

Effect of Adolescence on Size: Studies also disclose that rates of growth in both height and weight correlate with the degree of sexual maturity achieved. In reference to Pat this means that the earlier she showed the advent of pubescence, the greater should be her superiority over other children. Research reports that the average girl of twelve who menstruates before her thirteenth birthday is almost 4.5 inches taller and over 24 pounds heavier than the average girl menstruating at fourteen years or older. In Pat's case this was true in reference to both height and weight, Table I, in comparison with normal girls. As indicated in the table Pat was both taller and heavier than the child pictured by established norms. Her weight increasingly departed from the standard picture.

TABLE I

COMPARISON OF PATRICIA'S HEIGHT AND WEIGHT WITH REPORTED NORMS

Age	Height			Weight		
	Pat	Norm	Difference	Pat	Norm	Difference
132 mo.	58"	55.5	+2.5	123	75.8	+47.2
144 mo.	61"	57.5	+3.5	149	83.7	+65.3

In looking further for the effect of developmental status on height and weight we refer again for help to data provided by Shuttleworth. According to his findings the beginning of the period of rapid growth in height is usually found between two and one-half and three and one-half years before the first menstruation.

Measurements in height are reported below for Patricia from the kindergarten to the end of the sixth grade.

A study of gains made from one end-of-year measurement period to another, May to May, reveals that the span between 109 months and 121 months produced greater height increments than any previous period. Since Patricia menstruated for the first time at 153 months the period of greatest gain should occur between 30 (2.5 yrs.) to 42 (3.5 yrs.) months before the first menstruation. Since this event occurred at 153 months the appropriate age span for Patricia may be obtained by subtracting 30 and 42 respectively from 153. The "proper" age range for greatest gain, for her, then should fall between 111 and 123 months. Patricia showed little deviation from this standard in that her actual period of greatest growth was from 109 to 121 months. In this respect she was very close to reproducing exactly the norm suggested by Shuttleworth.

TABLE II

PATRICIA'S HEIGHT MEASUREMENTS

Grade	Month	Age	Inches	Gains (May to May)
K	September	65	46.2	
K	January	69	46.7	
K	May	73	47.3	—
1	September	77	47.8	
1	January	81	47.9	
1	May	85	48.0	0.7
2	September	89	49.1	
2	January	93	49.7	
2	May	97	50.4	1.3
3	September	101	51.0	
3	January	105	51.6	
3	May	109	52.5	2.1
4	September	113	53.9	
4	January	117	54.7	
4	May	121	55.3	2.8
5	September	125	56.4	
5	January	129	57.2	
5	May	133	58.0	2.7
6	September	137	58.8	
6	January	141	59.7	
6	May	145	61.0	3.0

2. *Progress in Height and Weight*

Evidence of Cycle Growth: Growth for any given child proceeds at different rates in different cycles. From birth to twenty years of age most normal children display two periods of rapid growth separated by a period of less rapid growth. The periods of rapid growth are (1) early childhood, and (2) adolescence. The period of less rapid growth is found in the intervening elementary-school years—late childhood—or, as referred to here, the pre-adolescent years.

Patricia gave evidence of this kind of physical development. There appeared in her graphed early-growth patterns the last vestige of the early-childhood cycle, and during the fifth- and sixth-grade years the beginning of the period of adolescence, Figure 3.

It will be seen in the figure that both Patricia's height- and weight-age equivalents were considerably above the straight-line ratio-norm. This is of course of no particular significance in and by itself. Her size in comparison to other children naturally had significance for her social development. This point, however, will be discussed in the section dealing with this phase.

3. *Factors Affecting Physical Development*

Home Conditions: Considerable data were collected on Patricia relative to physical characteristics and general health background. Most of these suggested consistency of factors which influenced the pattern of growth. Aside from the usual harmless childhood contagions—measles and chicken pox—she had no serious or persisting illnesses of any kind. Her school-attendance record substantiated this commentary. Economic shifts in the family are often likely to produce growth variations. In Pat's case there was no evidence of such an occurrence. Her parents remained on a constant social-economic level throughout her school days. Tensions, ability to maintain home and family living essentials, and other changes in family status did not materialize in the elementary-school life-span of this child.

General Energy Expenditure: No metabolism records were ever made on Patricia. Consequently we must depend on observation of other reactions for this area of analysis.

And it is to this point that other information is available. The story of Patricia portrayed in Part One indicated a constant shifting from a personality bursting with energy and drive at one moment to one almost immediately characterized by periods of apathy and indifference. This seemed to be the story reported over and over. Patricia was very heavy for her age and height. She hadn't yet reached obesity but it stands in the offing unless something is done.

Family standards tend to minimize a corrective opportunity of this kind. Her ethnic origin was such as to regard diet suggestions in the light of interference. The main hope for Patricia in this matter is to be found in her own desires. Perhaps she wasn't bothered by her weight as much as our records seemed to indicate. Her extremely good features will be of assistance to her regardless of her decision. If she is not unhappy enough to do something about her weight, she still has her good looks. On the other hand, her fine eyes, skin, and features might motivate her to become even better appearing. Continued school and consequent peer surroundings as well as ethnic ideals and goals, social life and contacts—in case she should drop out of school—will aid her in making a decision.

4. *Aspects of Motor Growth*

Limitations of Our Data: In the experimental study in which we first located Patricia no formal motor measurements were recorded. Subjective information bearing on this phase of her development, however, was available. First, Patricia illustrated well a basic principle of the development of motor response. Secondly,

Patricia demonstrated a tenable hypothesis with reference to the elementary school in its attitude toward motor activity in the classroom. These points will be brought out in the following discussion.

General Principle of Motor Development: Motor development, both simple and complex, may be defined as the process of learning, controlling, and integrating motor responses. The fine responses, such as those of the fingers, hands, or eyes and hands combined, depend on small-muscle development. The more involved movements of the body, especially those of the arms, legs, trunk and shoulders are dependent on large-muscle exercise and involvement.

Observations on Patricia during the six years of her elementary-school attendance pointed out that she was much more adept and interested in large-muscle activity and experiences than in small-muscle utilization as required in art, handwriting, work-book activity and the like. This conclusion is based upon consistent observer agreement of large-muscle superiority as demonstrated in running-games, ball-handling, and other playground activities. On the other hand, she showed only mediocre ability in tracing, drawing, and handwriting. Whether her size handicapped her in learning these or whether it was lack of curriculum motivation and adaptation to her interests is a debatable question. Nevertheless, repetitive comment noting discrepancy between the two characterizes judgments made.

Basic Skills Satisfactory: Nearly every child derives a great deal of pleasure from running and jumping, bicycle riding, roller skating, playing ball and other sports. Patricia certainly was a fine example of this generalization. If anything, she manifested almost too much interest in these large-muscle activities, particularly for a girl. Her skill in playing ball afforded her a great deal of satisfaction and perhaps greatly aided her in developing an improved gang status as she progressed through the elementary school. Unfortunately for Patricia, and for others for that matter, her opportunity for development along these lines was almost exclusively a limited recess period of incidental gang action. She would have greatly enjoyed a more extensive repertoire of games and sports.

B. Mental Development

1. *General Applied Intelligence*

General Mental Characteristics: The inventories used by our observers included two particular check lists which were employed in arriving at an understanding of Patricia's mental development. One was called "general mental characteristics" which contained the following sub-categories (numerals in parentheses represent the number of observers, of a total of seven, who ascribed to Patricia the characteristic noted):

Attention	*Understanding of Instructions or Explanations*	*Concentration on Task at Hand*
Alert—on the job	Grasps ideas readily (1)	Holds to task and achieves
Attentive (1)	Understands after questions (4)	Holds to task with occasional lapses (4)
Average	Average (4)	Average (2)
Dreamy (4)	Confused but knows she doesn't understand (2)	Means to concentrate but doesn't (2)
Non-attentive (3)	Thinks she understands but really doesn't	Has to be driven
Distracted		Attends more to others (1)
Confused	Confused and helpless	Can't concentrate even under supervision
Not there		
Scatterbrained		

Memory	*Imitation*	*Openmindedness*
Remembers well and retains (2)	Imitates easily and well (2)	Curious and interested in all novel experiences
Remembers fairly well	Imitates fairly well	Receptive to new ideas (1)
Average (2)	Average (4)	Progressive
Means to remember but doesn't (1)	Imitates little and with difficulty	Average (3)
Forgets easily	Can do things only his own way	Prefers the old and familiar
Never remembers		Conforms (5)
		Presents new ideas
		Conservative

Initiative	*Originality*	*Foresight*
Active in initiating	Has many good ideas	Always foresees possible consequences
A self-starter	Creative	Anticipates, looks ahead (4)
Has considerable initiative (1)	Quite creative (1)	Average (4)
Average (2)	Average (3)	Seldom considers the future or consequences
Has little initiative (5)	Seldom is creative (3)	Never looks ahead
Never imitates	Never creates, always copies	Surprised by consequences

The important conclusion from studying the inventories, used in each of the elementary grades, was the general consistency shown. One of course immediately raises a question as to the reliability of the observations and the data recorded. In defense it can be pointed out that the anecdotes found in the Appendix show that Patricia very early in her school career formulated her observable outside personality. The anecdotes seem to suggest that after some exploration and experimentation in the first and second grades she presented year after year the same picture with little variation. This same idea holds for the ratings made on the characteristics noted above. Patricia displayed very little change. Grade One ratings indicated that she:

Grasped new ideas readily; remembered well and retained; imitated easily and well; and was quite creative.

Observers in other grades were quite unanimous in rating Patricia as follows:

Attention—dreamy or non-attentive
Understanding—understands after questions
Concentration—holds to task with occasional lapses
Memory—(no consensus)
Imitation—average
Open-mindedness—average; conforms
Initiative—little
Originality—seldom
Foresight—anticipates; average

Mental Functioning: The second check-list used by observers contained the following categories and characterizations:

Sensitivity	*Purposing*	*Planning*
Very sensitive and quick to respond	Purposeful in school and out	Plans all actions carefully and well (1)
Fairly sensitive (1)	Has many purposes and achievements	Plans fairly well
Average (6)	Average (3)	Average (6)
Seldom is aware of new stimuli	Has few purposes but holds to them (3)	Makes imperfect, inadequate plans
Responds with difficulty even when pointed out	Has many purposes but gives them up	Copies plans of others (1)
	Copies purposes (2)	Is unable to plan
	Purposeless	

Execution	*Judging*
Carries out plans efficiently, modifies when necessary	Has high standards and judges achievements accurately
Acts efficiently without planning	Has good standards and judges fairly well (2)
Follows plans fairly well (2)	Average (4)
Average (3)	Has very low standards and poor judgment
Follows plans imperfectly (1)	Has no standards and is unable to judge
Unable to follow a plan, his or others	

Generalizing	*Analytical Ability*	*Vicarious Learning*
Always profits by his experiences	Is a very good thinker, anaylses, criticizes, and diagnoses very well	Is able to enter into and profit by the experiences of others
Seldom makes the same mistake twice (2)	Is a good thinker (3)	Has some ability to profit by the experiences of others (3)
Profits considerably by experience	Average (5)	Average (5)
Average (4)	Analyzes little and imperfectly	Has little ability to enter into the experiences of others or profit by them
Profits little from his or other experiences	A poor thinker	
Repeats mistakes many times	Is unable to reason or anaylze at all	Has no ability to enter into the experiences of others
Repeats blunders over and over		

General concensus throughout all six grades showed the following dominant characterizations:

Sensitivity—average
Purposing—had few purposes but held to them
Copied purposes from others
Planning—average
Execution—average
Judging—had good standards and judged fairly well; average
Generalizing—average
Analytical ability—average
Vicarious learning—average

The rather consistent ratings of "average" throughout the various schedules are perhaps the result of observers' inabilities to select other categories. The anecdotes tended to disagree with some of these. It would seem to the writer that the comments recorded in the Appendix would suggest placement of Patricia in the classifications listed at the lower rather than the middle part of the scales. Nevertheless, there was more consistency than disagreement.

Perhaps another factor was more responsible for the average-to-low interpretations than Patricia herself. This probably was the kind of school program which was available. Ample anecdote is recorded to point out that although informal, very little creative and thought-provoking activity was offered during the time of the observations. It should be mentioned that all observations were made during the afternoon sessions. Consequently it can be rightfully inferred that the more serious and formal school activities took place in the morning. This is correct with reference to this particular school. Nevertheless, if informality is to be an afternoon contrast to morning formality, the afternoon program certainly could have been more creative, pupil-planned, motivating and exploratory.

Breadth of Intelligence: In general there are four types of intelligence: (1) abstract or academic intelligence; (2) social intelligence; (3) concrete (including mechanical) intelligence; and (4) esthetic intelligence.

This classification was helpful in analyzing the abilities of Patricia. It enabled us to point out high points and low points as we saw her with reference to these divisions. It would seem from our observation that social intelligence was her greatest asset. She had a way of making herself popular but through a very limited utilization of opportunities. She laughed, she pushed, she dramatized. Observation after observation verified this interpretation. Patricia never became the teacher's pet, she never excelled in her class work. Her work habits were bad and yet she held considerable status in her group. And, particularly to the point, she seemed to slightly improve her group relationships in spite of continuity of indifferent classroom performance.

Her next best intellectual characteristic was the "abstract" or "academic." Early impressions of Patricia convinced the writer that she had reputable academic competence. This conclusion is borne out by report cards sent home which suggested quite satisfactory achievement although almost all anecdotes seemed to imply almost the opposite—carelessness, indifference, slowness, and lateness in completing assignments. The casual reader might conclude that either her teachers greatly over-rated Patricia or the observers were entirely too critical and over-impressed by insignificant detail. To the writer it seemed that both were right. Patricia demonstrated continuously the kind of behavior recorded and yet she did quite well whenever a "show-down" was required. One must conclude that Patricia performed very well for so little effort and interest.

In mechanical and esthetic intelligence she seemed immature and naive. Her increasing ungainliness could account for lack of concrete or mechanical performance that required small-muscle utilization. Big-muscle involvement was another matter. Witness the ball-playing and gas-pump operations! It is likely however that mechanical intelligence as designated refers to the more delicate manifestations of which Patricia seemed quite bereft. Esthetic intelligence or esthetic interests also appeared quite undeveloped. Art in its true sense was lacking. Neither home nor school contributed much to her development in this sense.

2. *Mental-Growth Curve*

Patricia was given the Kuhlman-Anderson tests four times during her elementary-school career, Table III. I.Q.'s indicate approximately normal intelligence on all four testings.

Nature of Patricia's Mental-Growth Curve: The curve resulting when Patricia's mental-age scores were graphed showed the two-cycle growth phenomenon, Figure 4.

In Pat's case the break came just short of 120 months (10 years), and gave signs of sustained rapid growth at 140 months of age. In comparison with a group of

TABLE III

KUHLMAN-ANDERSON RESULTS

Grade	Year	Month	Age in Months	M.A.	I.Q.
1st	44-45	Feb.	82	80	97.5
2nd	45-46	Jan.	93	91	97.8
4th	47-48	Jan.	117	108	92.2
6th	49-50	Nov.	139	137	98.5

60 girls on whom continuous measurements were available, Patricia's curve-constants presented considerable agreement, Table IV.

As shown by Table IV, Patricia grew mentally at a slightly slower rate in both cycles and toward significant lower maxima. However, she demonstrated an earlier advent into adolescence (111.6) than was shown for the average of the sixty girls (129.4). The rate of mental growth displayed by Pat fitted the conventional description of negative acceleration but differed in that it followed two cycles of growth.[1] Stated more simply this means that between nine and twelve years of age mental development approached a maximum (plateau) but, inspired by the glandular changes accompanying the beginning of adolescence, proceeded upward on a revised pattern.

I.Q. Status: The I.Q.'s computed for Patricia should be given some comment. In her case the conventional interpretation would be that: (1) they presented little shift; or (2) that they varied slightly from an over-all average of the four, Table III. Neither observation is significant or important. We may raise a question, however, which will assume significance in view of the discussion to follow. The question relates to the reliability of the testings. If one merely wished to establish the I.Q. of a child or to determine whether there were large changes or not, four testings would be sufficient. Looking at Patricia's mental growth from the longitudinal approach, the small number of testings should be judged as inadequate.

In the first place the four give results which fit very nicely into the concept of two-cycle development, as mentioned earlier. In other words, they fit too well. The writer can not refrain from feeling very unhappy that there were no more scores available. Several more between the ages given and one or two in her current grade (7th) would have been greatly beneficial. These would have aided in establishing the validity of the curve shown (Figure 4), whereas one or more in the seventh grade would have provided evidence to strengthen or deny the claim of an adolescent cycle. And incidentally, they would have increased our accuracy

[1] So did the 60 girls mentioned but most other investigators generally report no such pattern of mental development in utilizing massed averages.

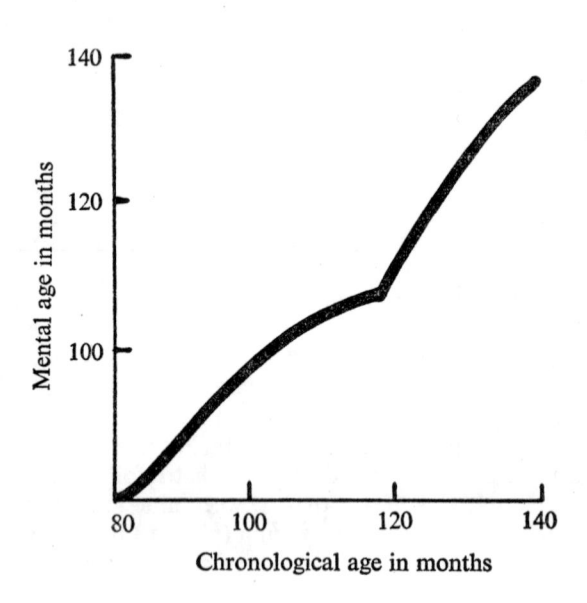

Figure 4. Mental-Age Curve

in computing the adolescent maximum. Since these data were not available it was necessary to proceed on what there was at hand.

Such variation as was found among the I.Q.'s computed for Patricia was small enough to raise no particular issue or problems. Even the conventionalist would not challenge the results, provided the testings could be certified as reliable. Her range was from 92 to 99. A range of seven points is well within average limits.

Relation to Achievement: Mental age has always been looked upon as a criterion for academic performance. When a child has a mental age of six and a half years, providing he is in the first or second grades, he is regarded as mentally mature enough to begin reading. When he has a mental age of ten years he is supposed to have the ability to do the work of the ten-year-old. In Patricia's case it appeared that her mental age qualified her to do the work of her grade. Reports from teachers indicated that she brought about the expected relationships between mental ability and school achievement.

In this particular school system no special demand was made of children on the basis of I.Q. standing. Grouping was not used except in an informal manner. Consequently the I.Q. meant little to the teachers of Patricia. Her general respect for

TABLE IV

COMPARISON OF CONSTANTS IN PATRICIA'S CURVE WITH CURVE OF CONSTANTS OF SIXTY GIRLS

	Pre-Adolescent		Adolescent	
Constants	Patricia	Norm	Patricia	Norm
Rate	.282	.270	.668	.797
Starting point	2.2	0.4	111.6	129.4
Maximum	130	153	170	219.3

Starting point represents age at which cycle begins. Maximum represents mental age in months at which the cycle matures.

authority and her rather satisfactory academic achievement sufficiently appeased them so that her intelligence-test results were given no wide-spread application.

3. *Significant Implications from the Curve*

Continuous Growth: Patricia's curve of mental growth points out that, for her, mental growth was continuous with little deviation from a very regular pattern of growth. Since it is theoretically assumed that growth proceeds in this manner only when modifying conditions are relatively constant, we may assume that she not only followed a defined pattern but that the forces which might have changed it or produced variation were rather inoperative. This is not to say that her growth was good or bad. She had no serious illnesses throughout this period. Her peer status remained relatively stable. Her home and family background seemed to show no important economic variation or shift. All children develop in a manner determined by the kind of sensitivity between ability to grow and the environment which makes growth possible. For Patricia the balance seemed to be uniform throughout her elementary-school years.

Stability of Performance: There is a question whether stability or consistency of performance is a matter of temperament, a matter of continuing balance between potentiality and environment (culture) or a combination of both. Thus when we speak of stability we are not quite sure whether we are speaking of the individual or the conditions which affect life performance. In either case, Patricia's regular pattern of growth indicated much of what we generally call "stability."

This is a little surprising in view of the picture drawn of her. In one sense she displayed consistency of behavior but on the other hand consistency for her was represented by constant shifting from apathy to interest and back again, day after

92 SCHOOL AND CHILD

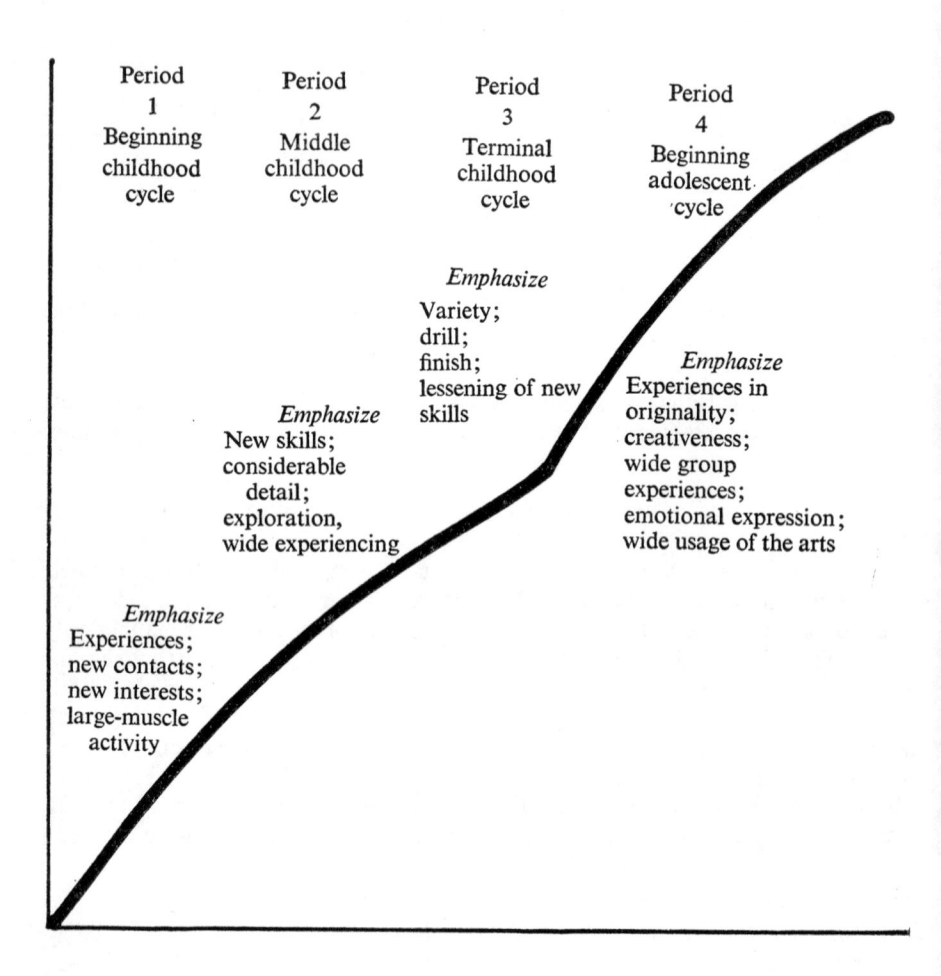

Period 1	Period 2	Period 3	Period 4
Beginning childhood cycle	Middle childhood cycle	Terminal childhood cycle	Beginning adolescent cycle

Emphasize Variety; drill; finish; lessening of new skills

Emphasize Experiences in originality; creativeness; wide group experiences; emotional expression; wide usage of the arts

Emphasize New skills; considerable detail; exploration, wide experiencing

Emphasize Experiences; new contacts; new interests; large-muscle activity

Figure 5. Suggested Emphasis for Skill and Broad Learnings in Relation to Patricia's Maturing Mental Growth.

day. Since the data are limited any final conclusion to be drawn by study of growth patterns must await analysis of other curves. This point will be dealt with in the section under "Learnings," and fully in Part Three where likenesses and differences in all her measurable growth sequences will be scrutinized in greater detail.

Relation to Learning: Certain implications in regard to learning may be formulated from a study of a child's emerging mental-growth pattern. Such an employment is probably the most important of all the many usages we have made of mental-test data. It is not surprising that it is one quite unlikely to be described in a text or in a discussion of mental-test uses. The idea is new and its utilization requires a higher degree of professional skill than will generally be employed in schools for a long time to come.

The usage of which we are thinking springs basically from the thought that an emerging curve can give a clue as to the proper rhythm of study and appropriate curriculum experiences. The data on Patricia lent themselves most strikingly for such an interpretation. Her mental-growth curve is again shown but with a background of suggestions for the kind of pacing that would have been most appropriate for her developmental capacities, Figure 5. The relationship shown applies equally well for academic and for the broader and more intangible social and personal, creative, and other real-life learnings.

There is no evidence in our files to suggest that Patricia's teachers made such usage of the information at hand. For her teachers, as for most, mental-test scores were used only for computing I.Q.'s. If the I.Q.'s obtained are compatible with current academic standardized test scores the child is not regarded as a problem. It is only when testings from the two types of tests provide contrasting results that teachers feel something ought to be done. Fortunately, as has been said before, Patricia's intelligence and academic scores were in accord on this basis and consequently she was not made a subject of questionable teacher study and discussion.

Patricia could have profited from such a pacing or rhythm of instructional offering. In spite of her rather satisfactory academic achievement she was given little motivation toward, or experiences in, "awakening" types of activities. It is amazing how well such a child can achieve with so little interest and motivation in the school program. Had such a schedule of studies as suggested in Figure 5 been paralleled with her continuously changing pattern of mental growth, there seems little question but that the impact would have provoked greater interest and motivation for achievement in broader and, as yet, unexplored areas.

SELECTED REFERENCES

B.T. Baldwin and L.I. Stecher: "Mental Growth Curves of Normal and Superior Children." *University of Iowa Studies in Child Welfare*, Vol. II, No. 1. Iowa City, 1922.

Nancy Bayley: "The Relation of Age and Tests to Consistency of Mental Growth from Birth to Eighteen Years." *American Psychologist*, II, 1947, p. 314.

M.E. Breckenridge and E.L. Vincent: *Child Development*. Saunders, Philadelphia, 1943.

S.A. Courtis: *The Measurement of Growth*. Brumfield, Ann Arbor, 1932.

W.F. Dearborn and J.W.M. Rothney: *Predicting the Child's Development*. Sci-Art, Cambridge, Mass., 1941.

F.N. Freeman and C.D. Flory: "Growth in Intellectual Ability as Measured by Repeated Tests." *Monographs of the Society for Research in Child Development*, Vol. II, No. 2. National Research Council, Washington, 1937.

Arnold Gesell: "The Appraisal of Mental Growth Careers." *Journal of Consulting Psychology*, III, 1939, pp. 73-9.

C.V. Millard: *Child Growth and Development*, pp. 57-99, 119-45. Heath, Boston, 1951.

"Physical Growth from Birth to Maturity." *Review of Educational Research*, XI, 1941, pp. 573-91; XIV, 1944, pp. 427-37; XVII, 1947, pp. 371-9.

K. Simmons: "The Brush Foundation Study of Child Growth and Development," II, "Physical Growth and Development." *Monographs of the Society for Research in Child Development*, Vol. IX, No. 1. National Research Council, Washington, 1944.

F.K. Shuttleworth: "Sexual Maturation and the Physical Growth of Girls Aged Six to Nineteen." *Monographs of the Society for Research in Child Development*, Vol. II, No. 5. National Research Council, Washington, 1937.

Helen Thompson, "Physical Growth." *Manual of Child Psychology*, Leonard Carmichael, ed. Wiley, New York, 1946.

Chapter VIII

ACADEMIC LEARNINGS

A. Available Data

ABUNDANT academic achievement data were available on Patricia. During her elementary-school career she was given seven Stanford testings covering all grades except the fifth but with two testings each in the second and the sixth grades. Complete results are shown in Table V.

TABLE V

PATRICIA'S STANFORD-TEST RESULTS

	\multicolumn{7}{c}{Month given}
Test	May	Nov.	Apr.	Oct.	Apr.	Oct.	May
Par. meaning	10	8	17	32	33	46	48
Word meaning	11	10	14	29	43	47	55
Ave. reading	10.5	9	15.5	30.5	38	46.5	51.5
Lang. usage	—	—	—	29	32	42	54
Arith. reason	—	13	17	36	40	52	52
Arith. comp.	—	14	23	30	44	48	55
Arith ave.	—	13.5	20	33	42	50	53.5
Literature	—	—	—	27	35	36	40
Social studies: I	—	—	—	31	30	42	31
Social Studies: II	—	—	—	35	32	44	67
Social Studies-Ave.	—	—	—	33	31	43	49
Science	—	—	—	24	30	30	35
Spelling	—	11	29	36	45	22	51
Total: Ave.	10.5	11.2	20	31	36.4	41.9	49
Age in months	85	91	96	102	120	138	145
Grade	1	2	2	3	4	6	6
Year	44-45	45-46	45-46	46-47	47-48	49-50	49-50

Other tests given included the Gates Reading Readiness and the Metropolitan Achievement tests when she was in the fourth grade. These were not utilized in the findings since results were similar to those shown by the Stanfords, and furthermore, they did not lend themselves to inclusion in the longitudinal achievement picture of Patricia since they differed somewhat in their statistical backgrounds.[1]

B. Reading Achievement

Patricia's scores in reading are presented below with norm comparisons, Table VI.

Conventional Evaluation: The table is arranged to make comparisons both at various grade levels and at various chronological ages. For example, the score of 10, achieved by Patricia on *Par. meaning* during May of her first-grade year, represents a grade level of 1.9. If we count September as the first month, May becomes the ninth month in this grade. Consequently a grade-level equivalent of 1.9 is equal to the norm. Likewise, using 10 achieved at this time, for illustration, we find that this score has an age equivalent of 82 months. This score, when coupled with her grade-level equivalent for interpretation, would indicate that—although grade standard was achieved—Patricia fell three months below expectations for a child of her age. We arrived at this conclusion by comparing her chronological age at this time, which was 85 months, with the age equivalent of 82. The difference is three months. Other data can be interpreted in the same manner, by subtracting Age-Equivalent Average from the Chronological Age when the test was taken.

TABLE VI

PATRICIA'S READING SCORES

Grade	Month	C.A.	Scores P.M.	Scores W.M.	Scores Ave.	Grade Equivalents P.M.	Grade Equivalents W.M.	Grade Equivalents Ave.	Age Equivalents P.M.	Age Equivalents W.M.	Age Equivalents Ave.
1	May	85	10	11	10.5	1.9	1.9	1.9	82	83	82
2	Nov.	91	8	10	9	1.7	1.9	1.8	80	82	81
2	Apr.	96	17	14	15.5	2.4	2.2	2.3	88	86	87
3	Oct.	102	32	29	30.5	3.4	3.2	3.3	101	99	100
4	Apr.	120	33	43	38	3.5	4.5	4.0	102	114	108
6	Oct.	138	46	47	46.5	4.8	4.9	4.8	117	119	118
6	May	145	48	55	51.5	5.0	5.9	5.4	120	131	126

[1] In presenting a longitudinal picture of achievement it is preferable to avoid mixing different batteries of tests.

ACADEMIC LEARNINGS 97

Referring to her curve, we see achievement starting out somewhat below the norm, approaching it at 102 months (third grade), and falling away in the fourth and fifth grades, Figure 6. Obviously, Patricia displayed her most rapid achievement and gain in the second and third grades.

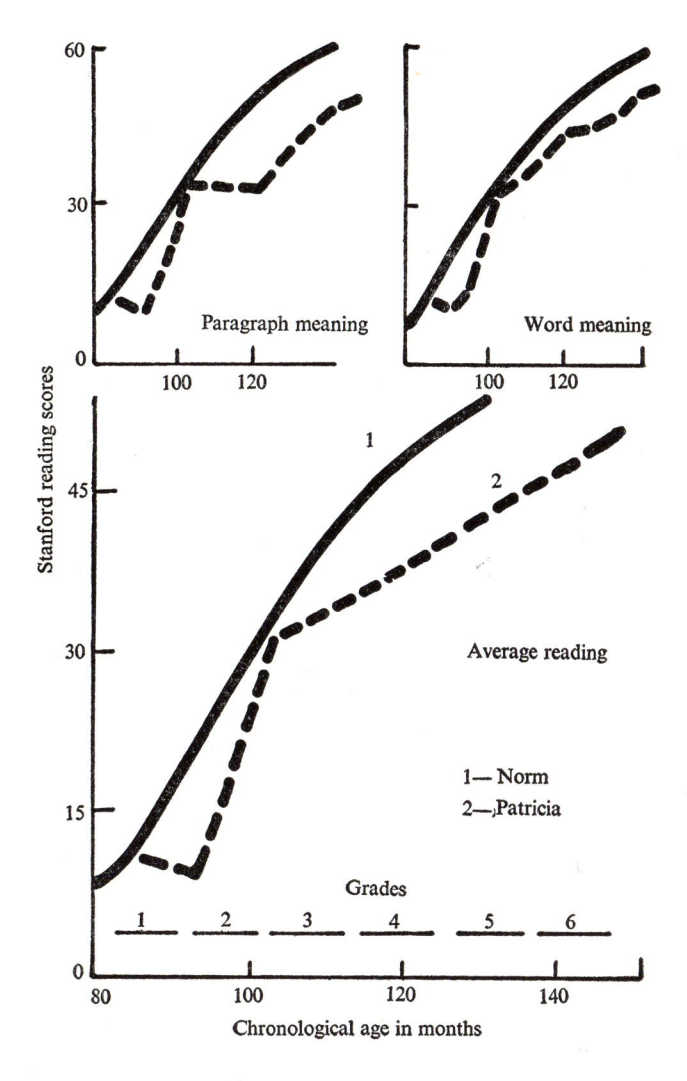

Figure 6. Comparison of Patricia's Reading Curve with Curve of Norms. [The comparison is based on score norms for chronological age rather than for grade-level or age equivalents.]

98   SCHOOL AND CHILD

Deficiencies in grade level and in months are shown for each period tested, Table VII.

TABLE VII

DEFICIENCIES BY NORM COMPARISON: AVERAGE READING

Testing (Grade)	Grade levels			Age equivalents		
	Norm	Pat	Diff. (Years)	Norm (C.A.)	Pat (R.A.)	Diff. (Months)
1 (May)	1.9	1.9	0.0	85	82	− 3.0
2 (Nov.)	2.3	1.8	−0.5	91	81	−10.0
2 (Apr.)	2.8	2.3	−0.5	96	87	− 9.0
3 (Oct.)	3.2	3.3	0.1	102	100	− 0.2
4 (Apr.)	4.8	4.0	−0.8	120	108	−12.0
6 (Oct.)	6.2	4.8	−1.4	138	118	−20.0
6 (May)	6.9	5.9	−1.0	145	126	−19.0

Table VII clearly indicates that Patricia did not read up to her appropriate grade levels. It also points out that greater discrepancy is shown when her scores are translated into reading age in months and compared with her chronological age, last column of Table VII.

Character of her Curve: Authorities recognize five stages in growth in reading. These are: (1) reading readiness, (2) the initial stage in learning to read, (3) a stage of rapid progress in fundamental reading habits and attitudes, (4) a period of wide reading that greatly extends and enriches the child's experiences, and (5) a stage of refinement which ordinarily comes during later adolescent years. To show the significance of these stages let us relate them to the increasing maturity of the child as he progresses through school. The relationship is noted below:

Period of Maturity

(1) End of babyhood cycle
(2) Beginning of pre-adolescent cycle
(3) Rapid pre-adolescent growth
(4) End of pre-adolescent with merging of adolescent cycle
(5) Advanced adolescent period

Reading Stage

(1) Reading-readiness stage
(2) Initial stage in learning to read
(3) Stage of rapid progress
(4) Period of wide and enriched reading
(5) Stage of refined reading

Most children in the kindergarten are approaching the end of the babyhood cycle. In the first grade they slowly begin a new period of development. This usually is reflected in all growth curves—height, weight, reading, etc. Beginning growth at this time is slow. Rapid progress in this cycle usually occurs in grades three, four, and five. The fifth, sixth, and sometimes the seventh grades are characterized by improved quality but not necessarily by increased scores obtained from standardized tests. The fifth stage, beginning after adolescence is under way, witnesses the development of maximum reading.

In a good many ways Patricia's developmental scheme was similar to this sequential picturization. Obviously, a standardized achievement test can not be used during the readiness period. This is the period preliminary to reading and consequently was not actually defined by Patricia's reading data. Her height curve, previously shown, may be studied in this connection. When we compare the two we find: (1) that between 65 and 75 months the height curve unveils a flattening-out period starting upward between 75 and 85 months; and (2) that shortly after 90 months the reading curve begins its marked upward ascent. The flat portion of the height curve during the kindergarten and early first-grade months suggests the idea that this was Pat's reading-readiness period.

Pat's rise in reading during the age of from 90 to 110 months paralleled very closely her growth in height. As in the instance of similarity between reading and height in the earlier school days, we again find, during these middle grade years (2, 3, 4), impressive similarity between reading and height growth in the character of the two curves.

The paucity of data between 102 and 138 months—only one testing at 120—precluded the possibility of making strictly reliable interpretations concerning the break which signaled adolescence. There can be little challenge, however, of the idea that such a break occurred sometime between 102 and 120 months. All curves yield some evidence of this phenomenon, Figure 6. Although minimized through obtaining the mean and thereby not strikingly displayed in the "Average Reading" curve, it is marked and quite conspicuous in the separate "Paragraph Meaning" and "Word Meaning" curves.

Thus the total reading-achievement progress of Patricia parallelled closely the aforementioned theoretical stages of reading, and her reading curves denote uniformity with her emerging developmental pattern as indicated by her height curve, previously shown.

General Conclusions: In some instances schools report objective test results to parents and through comparison with norms justify a particular program of instruction. Or conversely, they point out needs and weaknesses. Objective test results alone are quite insufficient for either purpose. These must be supplemented by observation of reactions of individual children to arrive at truths that have real meaning and significance.

In Patricia's case nothing like this was done. Her reading performance at all times was reported as satisfactory. Calling attention to the discrepancy between such a conclusion and the facts noted here would not have helped. As a matter of fact, her teachers should be commended for ignoring this slight discrepancy. And further they should be commended for refusing to put any particular pressure on Patricia to achieve at a higher level. This point may be validated by the following analysis.

First, the reading curve shown is the result of over-all environmental effects, including the total school program. The effect of specific activities of her teachers in reading are hidden among the total impact and are quite unrecognizable. The similarity between her reading and height curves is much more striking than the homogeneity between her reading curve and the teaching activity in a particular grade.

Secondly, her reading curve as determined by achievement-test scores followed an usually regular and precise delineation. It is unlikely that pressure would have produced significant changes.

Another consideration, and perhaps the most important, is the question of what might have happened under other circumstances. Patricia displayed very little interest in reading. As noted by one of our observers, Patricia could not name a single book except one given her on her birthday. This was not surprising. Books held an unimportant place in the school curriculum except for minimum reference and usage. There was little evidence of their presence in the school environment and there was little evidence that books held an important position as *aids* to learning. Patricia's home background was of such social status and ethnic origin as to be unable to recognize this deficiency or to compensate for it. Consequently books meant little except as something the teacher used in order to "keep" school.

Perhaps what was lacking here was a broad conception of the purpose of reading. After helping children to gain some skill in handling reading material, this goal should then become secondary to the much greater goal of utilization and enjoyment of books and other reading materials. This requires the building of room-library facilities—either the orange crate type or equipment more elaborate in design—and supplementary materials of all kinds. These include books, pamphlets, newspaper and magazine articles, bulletins, government reports, manufacturer's bulletins, and many other kinds of materials. Utilizing reading skills as means to other ends is likely to multiply many times the breadth of children's reading. Some school reading should be purely recreational. When children are encouraged to browse and read for pleasure they develop a real taste for and fondness of good books.

What would have been the effect of intensified reading activities of this kind on Patricia's test scores is pure conjecture. It would seem, in view of the theory of a strong inheritance impact on an individual's growth pattern, that activities of this kind would have had but little lasting effect.

We do believe, however, that an enriched reading program would have had tremendous "side" effects. Patricia would literally have devoured materials related to her ethnic origin. Her interest in ear-rings, for example, could have been the basis of intensive research on customs and dress among various cultures. Other opportunities came along which were ignored or surveyed merely with casual interest or unchallenging comment.

C. Arithmetic Achievement

Arithmetic scores on new Stanford tests are presented with age and grade equivalents in the following table.

TABLE VIII

PATRICIA'S ARITHMETIC SCORES

Grade	Month	C.A.	Scores			Grade equiv.			Age equiv.		
			R	C	Ave.	R	C	Ave.	R	C	Ave.
2	Nov.	91	13	14	13.5	2.1	2.2	2.1	85	86	85
2	Apr.	96	17	23	20	2.4	2.8	2.6	88	93	91
3	Oct.	102	36	30	33	3.8	3.3	3.5	105	99	102
4	Apr.	120	40	44	42	4.2	4.6	4.4	110	115	113
6	Oct.	138	52	48	50	5.5	5.0	5.2	126	120	123
6	May	145	52	55	53.5	5.5	5.9	5.7	126	131	130

Tests were given in grades two, three, four and six. Two testings were administered at over-long intervals in grades two and six. Figure 7 presents the graphical picture of the results shown in the table.

Conventional Interpretations: Tables VIII and IX have been prepared to provide a conventional interpretation of Patricia's achievement. Table VIII presents grade equivalents and age equivalents at each testing period, and conveys information on reasoning (R), computation (C), and the average of the two, called "Average Arithmetic" (Ave.). A glance at this table indicates that Patricia from May in the second grade to May in the sixth grade progressed from grade level standards of beginning second-grade (2.1, 2.2) to late fifth-grade achievement (5.5, 5.9). Obviously during this period of time she lost about one year of achievement since normal expectancy for May in the sixth grade would be 6.9.

In comparison with her chronological age, Patricia showed even greater discrepancies, Table IX. Only in October in the third grade did she come up to normal performance. From this point on her scores gradually receded from the norm. At the end of the sixth grade, achievement in arithmetic was fifteen months below that of the average child of her age.

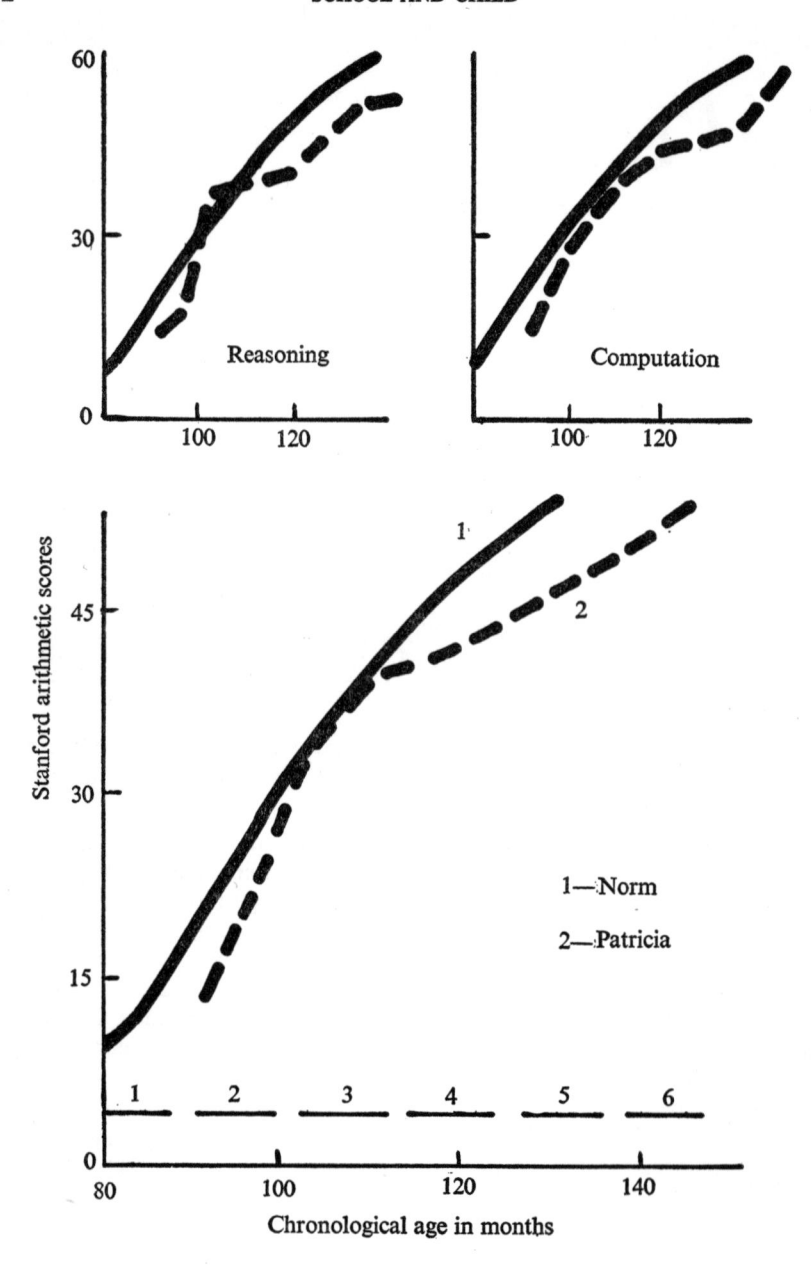

Figure 7. Comparison of Patricia's Arithmetic Curve with Curve of Norms.

TABLE IX

DEFICIENCIES BY NORM COMPARISON: AVERAGE ARITHMETIC

Testing (Grade)	Grade levels			Age equivalents		
	Norm	Pat	Diff. (Years)	Norm	Pat	Diff. (Months)
2 (Nov.)	2.3	2.1	−0.2	91	85	− 6.0
2 (Apr.)	2.8	2.6	−0.2	96	91	− 5.0
3 (Oct.)	3.2	3.5	0.3	102	102	0.0
4 (Apr.)	4.8	4.4	−0.4	120	113	− 7.0
6 (Oct.)	6.2	5.2	−1.0	138	123	−15.0
6 (May)	6.9	5.7	−1.2	145	130	−15.0

Some interest may be attached to a separate comparison of her "Computation" and "Reasoning" scores, Table VIII. In these two quite different skills Patricia demonstrated almost identical quantitative performances. The greatest discrepancy may be noticed at the late second- and the third-grade testings where six-point differences are found. The difference first favors "Computation", but in the third grade the superiority is in favor of "Reasoning". It is likely that the differences were of a chance nature and had no special significance.

Comparison of Achievement With Teachers' Reports: Patricia's teachers seemed quite pleased with her achievement. No record was ever made which indicated serious dissatisfaction nor were any special efforts made to give her special attention and assistance.

It is likely that the discrepancy between performance and norms, if noticed at all, was given little meaning since Patricia achieved and performed on school tasks about as well as most of the children in her grade.

Absence of records of teacher criticism would seem to clear with the observation records on the case. Her teachers were never reported as "nagging" about poor performance or creating tensions and pressures in the hope of improving academic performance. This attitude on their part would appear to indicate that such nervousness and tension as shown occasionally by Patricia was fostered through a strong desire for group acceptance and adequacy rather than a desire for academic prestige.

Nature of Her Achievement Curve: Patricia's arithmetic-achievement curve implies normal rather than abnormal dispositions. This conclusion is borne out by the fact of continuous growth emerging on a two-cycle pattern. The "Reasoning" curve reveals the adolescent spurt somewhat earlier than that indicated by the "Computation" curve. The graph of the average of the two portrays very smooth continuous achievement toward a definite maximum.

As in her other curves, Patricia demonstrated very regular growth. In general such a characteristic has been interpreted as a sign of consistency and stability. In Patricia's case such a conclusion might be debated. Evidence from anecdotes seems to present rather unanimous belief that Patricia was erratic, interested at one time and apathetic at another. Actually such observation might be taken as testimony for stable, consistent reactions on the thesis that Patricia naturally presented varying responses to varying situations.

It might be argued further that in one type of situation she always showed the same type of response, and that in another kind of situation she reacted uniformly also. At this point in our analysis, the latter hypothesis would seem the more tenable.

A Longitudinal Look at Arithmetic Performance: It would be impossible for the writer to proceed to another aspect of Patricia's academic performance without making further comment about the sharp differentiation from so-called "normal" performance. There are many teachers who would give several reasons for the kind of achievement curve displayed by her.

Since Patricia had her greatest gains from the late second to the fourth grades, and the least in the grades following, there are many who would attribute these differences to inequalities in teaching effectiveness, possible shift in home conditions, variation in interests, change in peer status, or to changes in any number of other affects. The conventionalist would probably give greatest weight to possible teaching differences.

The character of nearly all curves of norms leads teachers into such misinterpretations of academic data. Consequently, not much blame can be placed on them for such an error. Actually, Patricia's curve is a better representation of normal growth than the curve of norms. It demonstrates the kind of learning that takes place with a normal child under normal conditions. Patricia showed progress at the time in which she had the most rapid childhood growth. Her curve reveals the natural "rounding-off" toward a preadolescent maximum. And finally, it shows a later spurt with no additional accompanying influential factor than that of a new physiological phenomenon—the onset of adolescence.

The quality of her performance is a different matter. Arithmetic was not organized or presented in such a manner as to challenge her imagination or to meet her needs especially. It is reasonable to assume that Patricia absorbed enough to gain status, to obtain her teacher's approval, and to satisfy her parents. And further, it is also tenable that in an incidental manner her specific needs, whatever they were, were entirely satisfied. Intensified teaching, including comprehensive and diversified drill, more academic assignments, etc., might perhaps have resulted in higher scores. The answer to this question is mere conjecture. It is our belief that this could have happened only under circumstances in which: (1) higher standards were acceptable to the children themselves, (2) there was a higher economic-social-cultural level, and (3) there existed a greater community and school cultural enrichment. These of course were not the kind of conditions in which Patricia found herself. Her standard of performance was acceptable to all concerned.

D. Spelling Achievement

In the analysis of Patricia's reading and arithmetic achievement we had the opportunity to observe performance in two different aspects of each subject-matter field. In reading, "Paragraph Meaning" and "Word Meaning" scores were separately available. In arithmetic, the two aspects tested were "Computation" and "Reasoning." The two different aspects of each subject, when averaged together, provided data for a third curve. In the analyses presented, all three were given consideration.

Spelling, however, on the Stanford series, makes available only one set of data. Consequently we were more limited in our interpretations. Scores and norm comparisons are presented in the following tables with a similar graphical representation as shown in the previous academic analyses but limited as indicated above.

Comparison With Stanford Norms: Table X indicates that, with the exception of the score obtained in October of the sixth grade, Patricia presented continuous gains in grade-level and age equivalents from 1.9 to 5.4 and from 83 to 125 months, respectively. Over this period of time she began with approximately the appropriate grade level for a second-grade child but by the time she completed the sixth grade had lost a little over one whole year of normally expected progress. In respect to comparison with her chronological age she appeared even more retarded. At the sixth-grade level, when she was 145 months chronologically, she had achieved a spelling age of only 125 months.

TABLE X

PATRICIA'S SPELLING SCORES

Grade	Month	C. A.	Score	Grade equiv.	Age equiv.
2	Nov.	91	11	1.9	83
2	Apr.	96	29	3.2	99
3	Oct.	102	36	3.8	105
4	Apr.	120	45	4.7	116
6	Oct.	138	22	2.7	91
6	May	145	51	5.4	125

The picture of acceleration-retardation during her school career brings out more specifically her deficiencies as determined by Stanford norms, Table XI. It is interesting, however, to note exceptions to the implication of the comparison—that she was retarded in spelling. At the second- and third-grade testing periods Patricia acquired approximately a half year advance. Even in comparison with her chronological age she was advanced at these times. Both testings indicated a 3-month superiority.

The graph of Patricia's scores brings out these points even more clearly, Figure 8. It more glaringly depicts the fall in score at 138 months. This was unquestionably a testing error and should be given little consideration beyond mere mention. The testing at this time was either incorrectly scored or was given under improper conditions.

TABLE XI

SPELLING ACCELERATION-RETARDATION BY NORM COMPARISON

Testing (Grade)	Grade levels			Age equivalents		
	Norm	Pat	Diff. (Years)	Norm	Pat	Diff. (Months)
2 (Nov.)	2.3	1.9	−0.4	91	83	− 8.0
2 (Apr.)	2.8	3.2	0.4	96	99	3.0
3 (Oct.)	3.2	3.8	0.6	102	105	3.0
4 (Apr.)	4.8	4.7	−0.1	120	116	− 4.0
6 (Oct.)	6.2	2.7	−3.5	138	91	−47.0
6 (May)	6.9	5.4	1.5	145	125	−25.0

Character of the Curve: The score at 138 months was indeed an unfortunate circumstance. Until this point in her growth pattern, Patricia demonstrated very regular cyclic growth. The curve until this time parallels other curves and agrees with them as to rapid rises and slowing-down periods. Here, as in the other curves, we found the time of rapid progress to be located in the late second and early third grades. The time of rapid rise, with reference to chronological age, was the period from 90 to 110 months of age.

Unfortunately the faulty score at 138 months precluded any possibility of presenting convincing discussion concerning the effect of adolescence. A speculation, however, may be in order. One reasonable estimated score prediction, had the test been correctly administered, would be placed at a point exactly between the scores of the previous and the following testings. The second plausible placement would be only slightly beyond the previous result so that the gain from this point to the next would provide evidence of a second cycle. The logic for the first hypothesis is the logic of the law of averages, and the logic at the back of the second placement would rest on the generalization that pubescence must show an effect. Both are reasonable speculations. This discussion is of value only in pointing out the controversies that may arise when too little data are available.

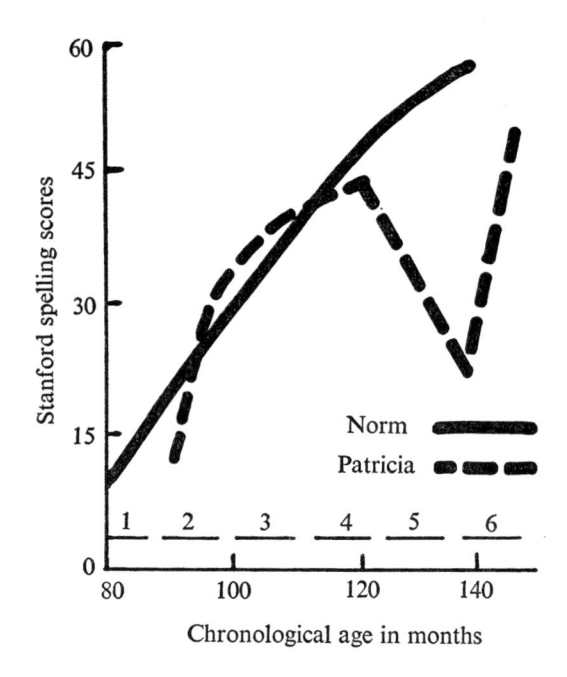

Figure 8. Comparison of Patricia's Spelling Curve With Curve of Norms.

Qualitative Analysis: We have rather deliberately set up two conflicting interpretations of Patricia's spelling performance. The tables shown in this section, and the comment provided, definitely suggest both retardation and acceleration, but with the balance weighted in favor of deceleration. Conventionally, Patricia must be considered as retarded in her spelling performance.

The total record, however, leads one to conclude that there was nothing basically wrong with Patricia's spelling. She had no particular difficulty at any time. She often received "A's" on her papers, and occasionally "spelling" was mentioned as one of her best subjects.

The mechanics of spelling used in this school depend to a great extent on the use of workbooks. As indicated in our observations, Patricia did not respond well to busy-work of this kind. She was not particularly neat and she tended to daydream when taken out of vigorous class activity. The spelling routine was too monotonous to motivate her. Patricia would have responded better to spelling games, contests, and other opportunities involving exciting group activity. This does not necessarily mean that such organization would have been desirable for all, or in Patricia's case would necessarily have produced a different design.

For Patricia, in spelling as well as in reading, a "lifting" of her achievement-growth pattern would likely have occurred only through total cultural enrichment. Unless this happens, and it isn't probable, Patricia will continue to demonstrate the kind of growth previously witnessed. She spelled well enough for her needs and she had no particular difficulty.

E. MISCELLANEOUS ACHIEVEMENTS

In addition to reading, spelling, and arithmetic, the Stanford battery provides test opportunities in social studies, science, language, and literature. It is these latter academic areas that will be given attention in this section. The subject matter groupings for presentation were made on two bases. First, Patricia was given reading, arithmetic, and spelling tests as early as the second grade. Since more data were therefore available it seemed logical to give these results consideration before discussing the others. And secondly, reading, arithmetic and spelling are conventionally known as fundamental or 3-R subjects.

Science, social studies, language and literature tests were first given Patricia in the third grade. They were repeated in April of the fourth grade, omitted during the fifth grade, and offered twice while she was in the sixth grade. Scores, grades and age-level equivalents are shown in Table XII.

TABLE XII

PATRICIA'S TEST RESULTS IN SOCIAL STUDIES, SCIENCE, LANGUAGE, AND LITERATURE

Grade	Month given	C.A.	SS	Sci.	Lan.	Lit.	SS.	Sci.	Lan.	Lit.	SS.	Sci.	Lan.	Lit.
3	Oct.	102	33	24	29	27	3.5	2.9	3.2	3.0	102	94	99	97
4	Apr.	120	31	30	32	35	3.4	3.3	3.4	3.7	100	99	101	114
6	Oct.	138	43	30	42	36	4.5	3.3	4.4	3.8	114	99	113	115
6	May	145	49	35	54	40	5.1	3.7	5.8	4.2	122	114	130	110

(Columns: Scores | Grade equiv. | Age equiv.)

Social Studies: With reference to acceleration-retardation, Patricia slightly exceeded Stanford norms at the beginning of the third grade but at each following testing time displayed greater departure than at the previous testing, Table XIII.

A more encouraging picture, offsetting a deficiency interpretation, may be found in the way in which her curve, Figure 9 (A), reveals signs of paralleling the norm. This circumstance indicated that Patricia, although remaining somewhat behind in relation to the norm, presented a rate of improvement entirely commensurate with average expectations.

TABLE XIII

SOCIAL STUDIES ACCELERATION-RETARDATION BY NORM COMPARISON

	Grade levels			Age equivalents		
Testing (Grade)	Norm	Pat	Diff. (Years)	Norm	Pat	Diff. (Months)
3 (Oct.)	3.2	3.5	0.3	102	102	0.0
4 (Apr.)	4.8	3.4	−1.4	120	100	−20.0
6 (Oct.)	6.2	4.5	−1.7	138	114	−24.0
6 (May)	6.9	5.1	−1.8	145	122	−23.0

From the growth standpoint, the curve gives interesting evidence of other effects, all of which have been mentioned previously in connection with the various curve analyses. The signs are clear enough and the conclusion is sufficiently important to repeat. First, Patricia's social-studies curve reflects not only progressive gain in this academic area, but likewise reflects her total individual pattern of growth. The data available portray the pre-adolescent levelling-off and the adolescent upsweep. Clearly, there is evidence here of a two-cycle curve. Secondly, the similarity of this curve to others previously shown adds more substantiation to the general over-all conclusion constantly hinted at in this analysis, that maturation appeared to be more dominant in affecting the pattern of the curve than the kind of teaching conditions which prevailed throughout her entire elementary-school career. The up-swing at 120 months in social studies *must* have been the result of either (1) chance, (2) teaching, or (3) maturation. When test results on a given academic area match (or parallel) data on mental growth, height, weight, as well as the other academic areas, surely the conventionalist backing the teaching-effect theory must be considerably disturbed. Our hypothesis finds maturation to be the dominating factor.

What this child really received from her social-studies activities may further be deduced from speculation and partially from reference to anecdote and observation. It was very obvious to those who knew Patricia—her teachers and observers—that she gained very little from the formalized aspects of her program. Her responses were lethargic, half-hearted, and without real interest. From further speculation it would seem that Patricia could have profited greatly from group organization, planning, busy and "in-motion" activities such as might be involved in project or unit study. If any child could benefit from a busy core or project program, Patricia would have been a likely candidate.

Science: By comparison with social studies, language, and literature, Patricia achieved most poorly. It is debatable whether this was a particular defect in the program offered by the school Patricia attended or whether low scores in science are characteristic of low-normal suburban-fringe communities. It is a matter of

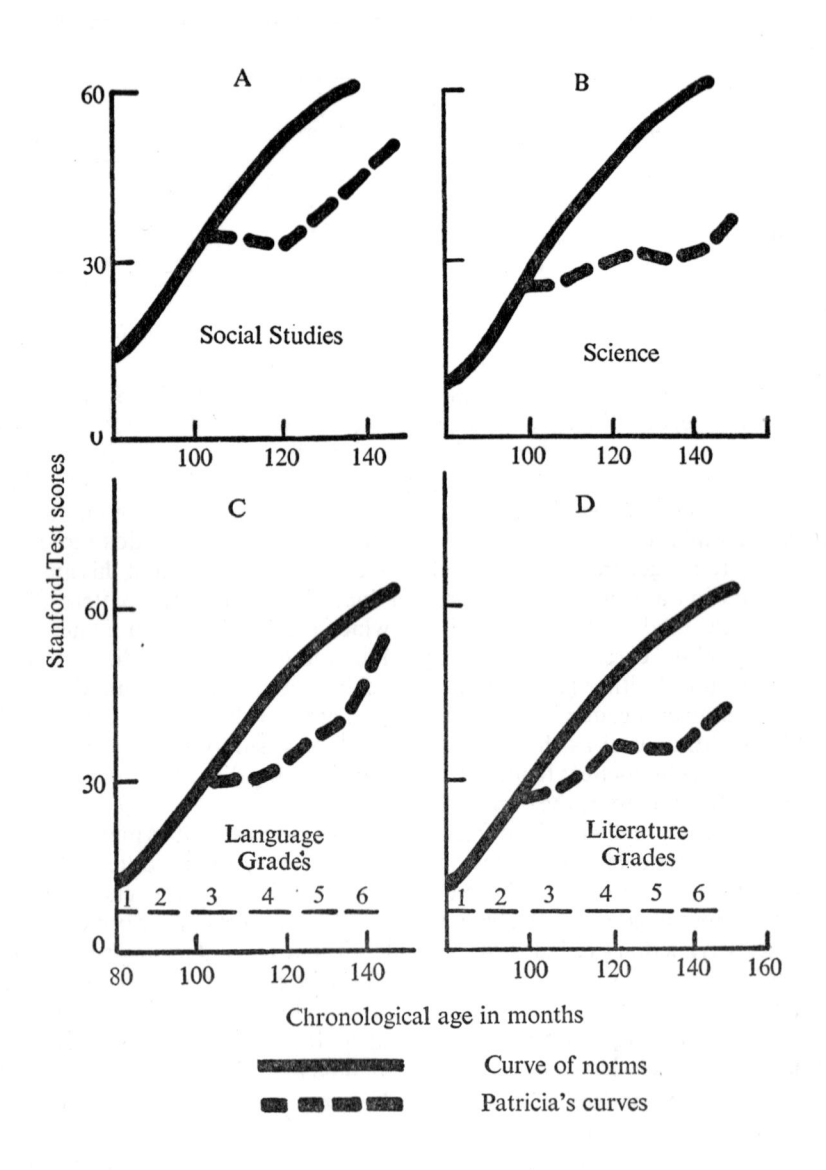

Figure 9. Graph of Achievements—Social Studies, Science, Language, Literature.

observation that this particular school gave little attention to science in either a formal or an informal way.

TABLE XIV

SCIENCE ACCELERATION-RETARDATION BY NORM COMPARISON

Testing (Grade)	Grade levels			Age equivalents		
	Norm	Pat	Diff. (Years)	Norm	Pat	Diff. (Months)
3 (Oct.)	3.2	2.9	−0.3	102	94	− 8.0
4 (Apr.)	4.8	3.3	−1.5	120	99	−21.0
6 (Oct.)	6.2	3.3	−2.9	138	99	−39.0
6 (May)	6.9	3.7	−3.2	145	114	−31.0

Patricia's science curve, Figure 9 (B), demonstrates every characteristic shown by her social-studies curve, commented upon. The most important difference may be found in the respective times at which the two begin to show the adolescent up-swing. In social studies this occurred at 120 months. In science this effect is not noticeable until the age of 138 months. There may have been chance factors which produced such a difference.

Of greater import is the added evidence of considerable consistency achieved by Patricia on a great majority of her testings. With the exception of spelling which displayed an unexpected and unexplained tremendous "dip", all other scores demonstrated more than usual consistency and steadiness in progress. This generalization is important because it may have bearing on the kind of personality and temperament possessed by this child. As stated at one point, and repeated here because of its importance, such a characteristic of stability does not match the more subjective observations on Patricia. Nevertheless, it may be the more valid conclusion.

Language: Of the four subjects reported in this section, Patricia achieved her best results in language. She progressed from a 3.2 to a 5.8 grade level, Table XII. In age equivalents this amounts to a range of 99 to 130 months, Table XII.

With reference to acceleration-retardation, Table XV, Patricia showed retardation at all times except on her first testing. Encouraging was the lessened retardation on the sixth-grade May testing.

In studying her language curve, its superiority to the others, Figure 9 (C), will immediately be noticed. The break seemingly comes at 120 months with a sharp rising adolescent cycle in the making. This part of the curve obviously is increasing at a larger rate than that shown by the curve of norms, Figure 9 (C).

Literature: Patricia's scores in literature came near to successful competition with science for a last-place position. Science, however, won out by a slight mar-

TABLE XV

LANGUAGE ACCELERATION-RETARDATION BY NORM COMPARISON

	Grade levels			Age equivalents		
Testing (Grade)	Norm	Pat	Diff. (Years)	Norm	Pat	Diff. (Months)
3 (Oct.)	3.2	3.2	0.0	102	99	− 3.0
4 (Apr.)	4.8	3.4	−1.4	120	101	−19.0
6 (Oct.)	6.2	4.4	−1.8	138	113	−25.0
6 (May)	6.9	5.8	−1.1	145	130	−15.0

gin. The relative position of these academic fields with reference to the others is certainly in agreement with the relative amounts of emphasis placed on various subject-matter areas in this particular school.

TABLE XVI

LITERATURE ACCELERATION-RETARDATION BY NORM COMPARISON

	Grade levels			Age equivalents		
Testing (Grade)	Norm	Pat	Diff. (Years)	Norm	Pat	Pat (Months)
3 (Oct.)	3.2	3.0	−0.2	102	97	− 5.0
4 (Apr.)	4.8	3.7	−1.1	120	114	− 6.0
6 (Oct.)	6.2	3.8	−1.4	138	115	−23.0
6 (May)	6.9	4.2	−2.7	145	110	−35.0

Such a conclusion would imply to some extent that more emphasis, or balanced emphasis, would have produced different results. The writer could give some affirmation to such a conclusion. Debate could arise, however, as to how and what kind of emphasis. The point of view would be maintained that book-work, recall, and drill would not materially affect the situation. What seemed to be needed here were materials surrounding the child that encouraged and motivated expansion of natural interests and challenge of imagination. Also informal reading and much more recreational and exploratory reading were badly needed. This of course would have required books at hand, books available in the school library, and a technique for utilizing them in the instructional efforts of teachers.

While science and literature are teamed in terms of discussion on instructional limitations, it may be well to point out significant similarities besides lack of achievement. Each curve starts at about the same time and shows, likewise, remarkable unanimity. Both suggest pre-adolescent cycles covering the same age range and both record a late beginning adolescent cycle. This suggests that there can be no easy denial of the maturational effect on all learning curves regardless of teaching or instructional emphasis.

F. THE TOTAL ACADEMIC PICTURE

The reader at this point should have received the impression that Patricia was a child who showed extraordinary similarity in her various academic-growth patterns. This is true, and to highlight such a conclusion it seems advisable to present all achievements within a common focus. Consequently, all seven subject-matter test results have been brought together with reference to original scores, Figure 10, and shown as average achievement in Figure 11. The alternatives of graphing by grade-level or by age-equivalents have both been dismissed at this point for several reasons. First, all scores on Stanford tests are comparable without interpolation, and secondly, interpolation (to grade or age equivalents) tends to minimize individual growth characteristics.[1]

What the Picture Shows: First, Patricia's achievement picture presents much consistency with reference to progress. In the seven curves graphed, only once did a test digress to anything more than a chance deviation from a regular pattern of progress, Figure 10. This happened in spelling where she fell to a score of 22 at the testing at 138 months. A slight deviation is found in reading at the very beginning of the curve where chance effects are to be expected since the child was just beginning a new cycle of development. The only other deviation is found in social studies in the drop from 33 to 31 between 102 and 120 months of age. In the average picture, Figure 11, progression is regular and without digression from the pattern.

Secondly, as judged by the three available testings in reading, arithmetic, and spelling, the period of most rapid growth for Patricia was the time between 90 and 102 months of age. This corresponds to second-grade placement for her year of greatest growth. This point is important since it does not agree with general conclusions concerning the elementary-school year of greatest growth. We usually consider third and fourth grades as the placement period for the most rapid academic-achievement advance. The discrepancy might be accounted for by Patricia's advanced age. Patricia, it must be remembered, was somewhat old for her grade. Her birthday coming in May gave her a considerable chronological advantage over other children going through school with her. Had she started to school a half year earlier, her second-grade high achievement might then have appeared at the third-grade level, although this arrangement would have been accompanied by certain disadvantages.

[1]All standard norms fail to recognize fully the cyclic nature of growth. This has the effect of reducing individual characteristics of growth to straight-line relationships.

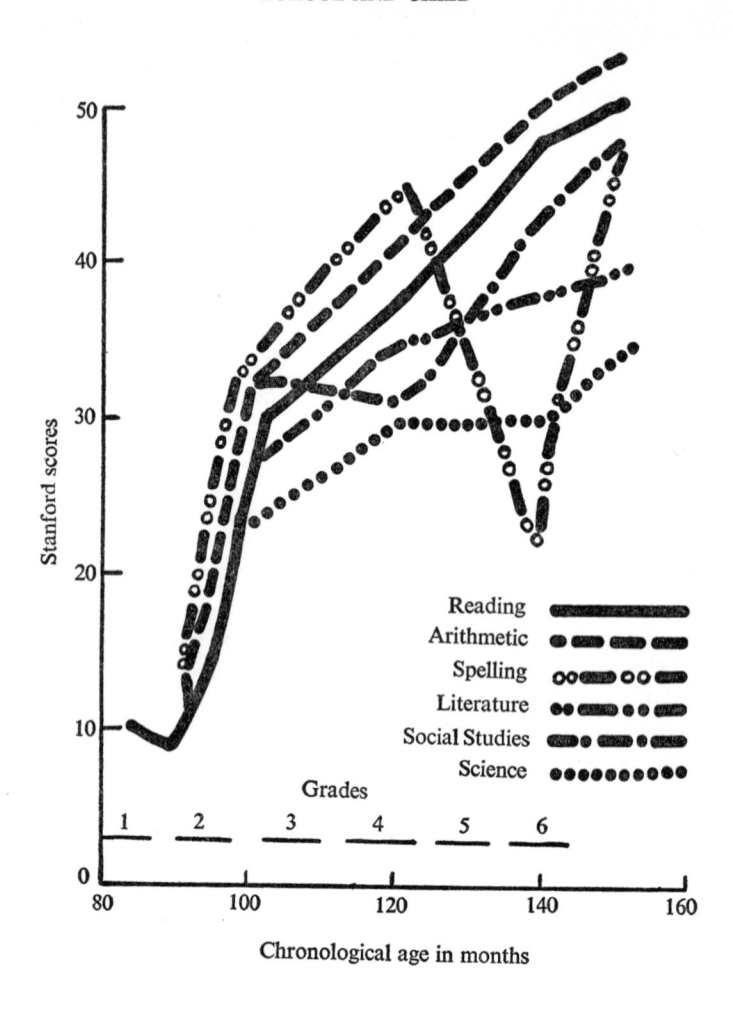

Figure 10. Patricia's Total Achievement Pattern—Stanford Tests.

Thirdly, the general picture tends to demonstrate a flattening or levelling-off in performance between 110 and 130 months, and a slight up-swing between 120 and 140 months, Figure 11. These phenomena have been discussed under each subject-matter presentation and need no further analysis here.

Fourthly, the achievement picture presented by Patricia seems to point out the absence of pressure-teaching during her elementary-school days. This conclusion is supported by evidence of continuous rather than erratic (gains and losses) growth progressions, and the consistent demonstration of cyclic growth.

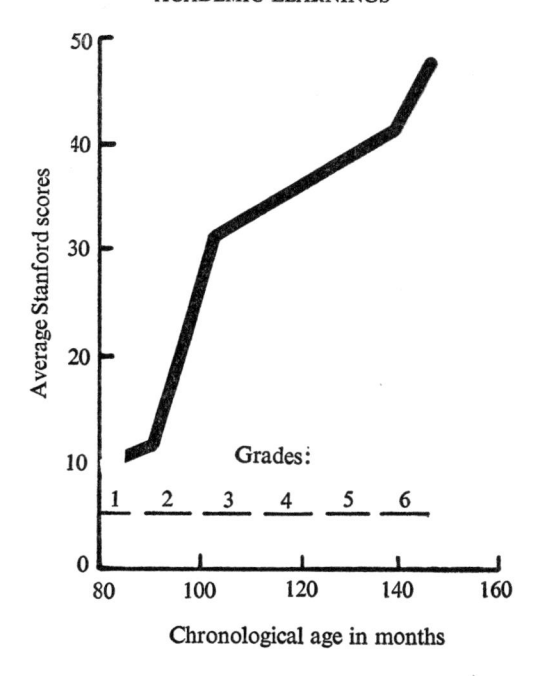

Figure 11. Patricia's Average Academic Growth—Stanford Scores.

Lastly, the achievement pattern presented challenges sharply the value of norms in interpreting academic learning. In not one aspect of her academic progress did her curve approach or bear much similarity to the hypothetical curve of norms. Fortunately, Patricia was never forced to approximate such a standard.

Selected References

S.A. Courtis: "Discipline." *Child Growth in an Era of Conflict*, C.V. Millard, ed., pp. 22-47. 15th Yearbook, Dept. of Elementary School Principals. Michigan Education Association, Lansing, 1944.

W.E. Goslin, Mary Beauchamp, and Others: *Organizing the Elementary School for Living and Learning*, pp. 7-74. Association for Supervision and Curriculum Development of the National Education Association, Washington, 1947.

A.J. Huggett and C.V. Millard: *Growth and Learning in the Elementary School*, pp. 115-257. Heath, Boston, 1947.

C.V. Millard: "The Nature and Character of Pre-adolescent Growth in Reading Achievement." *Child Development*, XI, 2, 1940, pp. 71-114.

C.V. Millard: *Child Growth and Development*, pp. 269-78. Heath, Boston, 1951.

C.V. Millard and A.J. Huggett: *An Introduction to Elementary Education*, Chapter IV. McGraw-Hill, New York, 1953.

Chapter IX

PERSONAL-SOCIAL DEVELOPMENT

A. General Personality

BEFORE discussing Patricia under this category it may be well to see what we are thinking about. The topic of personality is so broad that almost anything said concerning an individual can come under this subject. Rather than run the risk of developing over-extended discussion it seemed better to consider certain definitions and concepts and thereby to limit the presentation.

There are many definitions of personality. What we should like to establish as we write of Patricia's personal development may be outlined as *the sum total or the integration of all the capacities of the individual in action.*

This viewpoint is in agreement with the concept of the organism as a unified mechanism acting in totality. It is, of course, considerably different from the idea of the individual as an organism consisting of many parts and many abilities. Personality as we define it is the totality of individuality which, for a given person in a given situation, will represent a balance or pattern. In the pattern, certain traits assume dominance. Traits may shift, in accordance with such a concept, corresponding with the meaningfulness of a given situation. Patricia afforded a nice illustration in point. In the light, airy, rough informality of the playground she was friendly, energetic, cooperative, and somewhat of a leader. In this kind of situation her eyes lighted up and she veritably sparkled. In the formalized confined classroom she appeared dull, uninterested, and—what is more important—uninteresting. Patricia illustrated the idea that personality, although having fixed limitations for expression according to total potentialities, is seen as varied and changing in accordance with shifts in motivations in the environment at hand.

Patricia's personality was greatly affected by her social surroundings. Her basic ethnic-cultural background provided her with limitations as well as with potentialities. It gave her friendships outside of school among other girls with similar backgrounds. The school likewise gave her developmental opportunities. She was provided there with areas of operation, although limited, to which her over-all personal development reacted favorably.

It is with respect to possible future environmental surroundings that school and home may have been inadequate. If Patricia remains in a type of environment similar to that with which she is familiar, she will find that she has resources for generating and maintaining friendships. If, by chance, she moves to a higher type of social and cultural surroundings, she may find personal dissatisfactions. Up to this point in her life she had few interests, hobbies, and thoughts that would make her interesting to others with broader and more diversified backgrounds.

B. Personal Habits and Traits

This section will deal with conclusions and ratings posted by the observers who worked with Patricia. The preceding section gave a general introduction to the problem of describing personality development. This section will deal with specific traits. Comment will be provided throughout in an attempt to relate these with an over-all emerging design.

Ratings on Patricia were available in every grade. Table XVII has been prepared so that possible shifting in specific traits could easily be detected. The ratings ranged in quality from a high of 1 to a low of 5.

In the picture of Patricia presented there is some evidence of pattern and design

TABLE XVII

RATING OF SPECIFIC PERSONALITY TRAITS

General trait	Specific rating on	1	2	3	4	5	6
Attitude	Confidence	4	4	4	3	3	2
Attitude	Cooperation	3	3	3	3	2	2
Attitude	Courtesy	3	3	3	1	1	2
Attitude	Dependability	3	3	3	1	2	2
Disposition	Controlled	3	3	3	1	1	2
Disposition	Happy	3	3	4	2	3	2
Disposition	Kindness	3	3	3	2	2	2
Disposition	Optimism	3	3	3	3	–	2
Reliability	Promptness	2	1	3	1	2	2
Reliability	Obedient	2	2	3	2	1	2
Reliability	Responsible	3	3	4	2	2	3
Reliability	Effort	2	3	3	3	3	3
Personal	Dominance	3	3	3	4	3	3
Personal	Integrity	3	3	3	2	–	3
Personal	Leadership	3	4	5	5	5	3
Personal	Moral	1	1	3	1	–	2
Personal	Stable	3	3	3	2	1	3

Ratings: High ←—1—2—3—4—5—→ Low

in her developing individuality. For example, the traits listed under "attitude" and "disposition" suggest a considerable change in grades 4, 5, and 6 as compared to the ratings made in grades 1, 2, and 3. In the traits under the categories of "reliability" and "personal" there is much uniformity throughout. What Patricia was with reference to the latter seemed satisfactory to observers in the early grades and was seen in about the same light in the later grades.

In contrast, in "attitude" and "disposition," Patricia bloomed in the upper elementary years. She became more self-confident, less shy, and being less shy gave overt evidences of "courteousness." Her "dependability" also was recognized. With respect to "disposition" she often gave signs of "happiness," "kindness to others," and "general optimism."

How These Add To Our Understanding: The general observations recorded, added to other data, tend to confirm the idea that certain aspects of personality were growing and developing normally. What we have in mind are those aspects of personality which relate to social well-being. The natural charm of Patricia unfolded to a considerable degree. She continuously gained confidence in herself. She cooperated more cheerfully, and she was courteous and quite understanding of others. The general consistency of the ratings, in implying steady growth of desirable traits, indicated considerable stability and balance in her total personality matrix.

The limitation of this kind of evaluation manifests itself less by the kind of instrument used than by the kind of situation in which it is used. The school setting which provides a wide range of behavior is much more conducive for studying personality than a setting in which behavior is restrained or limited to specific learning opportunities. Thus the ratings recorded must be supplemented by information related with the instructional opportunity offered when the child is observed. Records indicated considerable uniformity among Patricia's teachers throughout these years. The type of climate provided might at best be described as varying between strictly dominated teacher-control to friendly autocracy. In this kind of climate Patricia was seen as a child somewhat suppressed in the first and second grades, shifting to a mild type of unrestraint in action but firmly anchored to compliance with teacher demand in fundamental pupil-teacher relationships. We can illustrate this by pointing out that Patricia, although slow in handing in work or getting out her books, was never tardy in responding to teacher dictate. When she was told to sit still, she sat still. When the teacher asked her to pass the books, she did so. She was never too noisy, too rough, never showed real anger or dislike, but took full opportunity to express herself through minor behavior deviations.

Throughout the course of an afternoon under such a climate Patricia was enervated at one moment and then made listless and desultory. Listlessness and lack of interest represented no infraction of rules. Therefore she sprawled and stole glances through the window while keeping one eye on the teacher. Under the circumstances this seemed a normal procedure and in no way damaging to our argument of stability and consistency of behavior in a given situation.

Another possible weakness of this kind of personality rating in a confined situation is that there can be little opportunity to observe wide emotional expressions of behavior. Observer anecdotes, however, pointed out that Patricia "got mad" after school. In school it was not permitted and Patricia acted accordingly. Consequently, it is likely that she was never seen in overt conflict. Inner conflict undoubtedly occurred often. When the individual maintains reasonable control, inner conflict is difficult to observe. This raises a question and poses a problem for those who expect to study personality in the formal school situation. The child can be one person in school and another person out of school.

C. Character and Ideals

Integration: It is of interest to note that observers rather generally were unable to identify Patricia's behavior with the following personality characterizations:

(a) *Well integrated:* strong purposes both in and out of school. Life has a dominant unity for her;

(b) *Somewhat integrated:* many purposes but not too well coordinated;

(c) *Average:* (no description provided);

(d) *Poorly integrated:* conflicting purposes; little thinking or planning;

(e) *Not integrated:* no plan; child merely responds to whatever stimulus is present;

(f) *Disintegrated:* child torn between conflicting pulls which he is unable to integrate or control.

In all grades, obersvers in dealing with the above listing either checked or wrote in comments under the heading of "average." But such other comments as the following were elicited:

2nd grade: "She does what she has to most of the time and does it well."

3rd grade: "Does not seem to think too much about the future; indifferent."

4th grade: "Patricia is pushed by her parent's desires. She normally is a little below average."

Inability of observers to match Patricia with some of the more important characterizations suggests again the difficulty of evaluating behavior in the typical school scene. This is undoubtedly true. But, on the other hand, these descriptions are perhaps quite inappropriate at this stage of development. And, in addition, it is quite likely that inappropriateness of the scale may have been magnified by a classroom proceeding which obscured the expression of child purpose, goal, and aim. During the many hours that Patricia was under observation, almost no time was spent by her in the selection of goals, laying plans, evaluating results, etc. Thus the record itself, used in the classroom setting, must parallel both pupil behavior and range of classroom opportunity.

Ideals and Standards: Another schedule produced better results. Data on Patricia with respect to ideals and standards are reported below. These were taken from year-to-year listings with the characteristic recorded which was checked as she progressed from grade to grade. The numbers in parentheses represent the grade in which the characteristic was noted.

About Self

(a) Ambitions from grade 1 to grade 6
  (1) Is quite ambitious; (2) not particularly; (3) average; (4) Pat takes things as they come; (5) not very; (6) not too clear but on latest inventory she stated that she would like to become a teacher.
(b) Care of self and possessions from grade 1 to grade 6
  (1) Very careful; (2) she is too young to worry about her appearance; (3) fairly neat; (4) very careful; (5) average; (6) sometimes messy but mkaes a conscious effort to improve.
(c) Self-control of emotion from grade 1 to grade 6
  (1) She shows her feelings by gestures; (2) she is not emotional; (3) good; (4) very good; (5) very good; (6) usually even-tempered.

About Self and Authority

(a) Laws, rules, etc., from grade 1 to grade 6
  (1) Obeys the rules laid down for her; (2) has a healthy regard for rules and truth; (3) obeys most of the time; (4) respect for them; (5) respect; (6) cooperates willingly.
(b) Attitudes toward others from grade 1 to grade 6
  (1) She is not particularly interested in the other children; (2) (no comment); (3) usually respectful; (4) holds great respect for them, especially teachers; (5) respect; (6) respects authority and older people.
(c) Truthfulness from grade 1 to grade 6
  (1) Is very truthful, never cheats; (2) (no comment); (3) usually tells the truth but will deceive when she feels she has to; (4) truthful as far as we can tell; (5) (no comment); (6) conscience stricken at times when she is not truthful.

About Responsibilities

(a) Those she accepts, from grade 1 to grade 6
  (1) Readily accepts responsibilities; (2) Pat takes little on herself except care of her own materials; (3) care of her own things; (4) doesn't accept them willingly; (5) some resistance; (6) seems willing to do her share.
(b) Those put on her, from grade 1 to grade 6
  (1) Accepts them readily; (2) all without too much grumbling; (3) usually accepts although on a few occasions made no move at all; (4) I believe that Patricia is a responsible person; (5) accepts them; (6) accepts them and generally carries them out.

About Work

(a) Curricular and home, from grade 1 to grade 6
  (1) Enjoys working in the school room and helps keep the table clean and neat; (2) lazy, doesn't care if work is done or not; (3) average; (4) does her share; (5) does her share; (6) speaks with pride of work in store.
(b) Play, Fun, and good times, from grade 1 to grade 6
  (1) Doesn't go out of her way to have a good time; (2) more the better; (3) energetic with a group outside her grade; (4) likes to play with a small circle of friends; (5) enjoys all; (6) loves to have a good time, to have fun, and to join in all play groups.

About Others

(a) Superiors, from grade 1 to grade 6
(1) Obeys them without question; (2) (no comment); (3) courteous; (4) very much respect; (5) much respect; (6) respectful, courteous, and considerate.
(b) Friends, from grade 1 to grade 6
(1) Does not seem to have many; (2) especially friendly with two girls in another room with same ethnic background; (3) about three or four girls around her, asks them for help and gives it to them on request; (4) friendly with those she knows well; (5) sometimes cold; (6) cooperative and affectionate.

About Care of Things

(a) Own, from grade 1 to grade 6
(1) Takes good care of her things; (2) desk drawer is untidy—otherwise is neat; (3) neat; (4) a good sense of value; (5) good; (6) not always tidy.
(b) Others, from grade 1 to grade 6
(1) takes good care of other children's things; (2) treats with care; (3) careful; (4) excellent; (5) excellent; (6) very considerate.

The comments recorded give some insight into Patricia's personality. They show her as a child not too careful about her appearance and somewhat indigent in her school housekeeping. She was generally honest, truthful, and discharged responsibility without much protest or rebellious tendencies.

A careful study of possible shifting of attitudes or character aspects showed very little change from the first to the sixth grade. What little there was can be described as a somewhat increasing negligence toward specific subject-matter assignments, a slight increase in personality affections of boisterousness and horse-play, and considerable increase in those aspects of personality related with social affability.

Patricia undoubtedly was bouncing with energy. She got little opportunity to display it but within the area of minimum-maximum teacher leeway made the most of her opportunities.

Other characteristics—as neatness, care of self, possessions, etc.—reflected home attitudes. Her home and parent's store were run in a somewhat relaxed and indifferent fashion but with full respect given to basic fundamental requirements. They were not neat nor were they plain dirty. Thus the home background seemed to be a very strong factor in molding Patricia's growing-personality pattern.

The school contributed in a sense. It gave Patricia the opportunity to become what she seemed destined to become anyway. Stated differently, it provided her with no frustrations in realizing personal and ethnic potentialities nor did it encourage expansion on what she had at the beginning.

Miscellaneous Traits: Yearly ratings on miscellaneous personality traits were of the kind that would be obtained on most children showing no extreme behavior reactions, Table XVIII. They described a child that adjusted well to the kind of climate prescribed by a teacher—no rebellion, general acceptance, no ser-

TABLE XVIII

MISCELLANEOUS PERSONALITY TRAITS

Positive	1	2	3	4	5	6	Negative
Honest	1	2	2	1	1	1	Steals, cheats
Truthful	1	2	2	1	1	1	Lies, deceives
Courageous	2	2	2	1	2	2	Cowardly
Loyal	2	3	3	2	2	2	Treacherous
Generous	2	3	3	1	1	1	Stingy
Happy	2	2	2	1	1	1	Happy
Kind	2	2	2	2	1	1	Mean
Thrifty	2	2	2	1	1	2	Spendthrift
Reasonable	2	2	2	2	2	2	Self-willed
Considerate	2	3	2	1	1	1	Inconsiderate
Unselfish	2	3	3	2	2	1	Selfish
Dependable	2	3	3	1	2	2	Irresponsible
Appreciative	2	2	2	1	2	1	Ungrateful
Self-reliant	1	2	3	2	2	2	Dependent
Stable	2	2	3	2	2	1	Erratic
Cooperative	2	2	2	1	1	1	Uncooperative
Humble	2	1	1	2	2	2	Conceited
Tranquil	2	2	2	1	1	2	Easily Upset
Reverent	2	1	1	2	2	1	Disrespectful
Communicative	2	2	2	1	2	2	Too talky
Friendly	3	2	2	2	2	1	Reserved

Grade Level Rating

Rating Code
1—High; toward positive end
2—Average; like other children
3—Low; toward negative end

ious achievement problems. They also indicated that this child was not one that was outstanding in a positive way. Patricia did not assume responsible leadership roles. Nor did she impress one with evidences of strong loyalties to children or to her teachers. She was not particularly plastic but on the contrary a little self-willed. She was not recognized as especially dependable nor was she clearly irresponsible. Self-reliance, affability, extroversion were only average.

In looking at the table to determine whether ratings showed any kind of improvement pattern, a thin thread of evidence may be found. These combine in such a way as to reveal some design. The characteristics referred to in which there seems to be a progression from "2" or "3" to "1" may be found in "honesty", "truthfulness", "generosity," "happiness", "kindness", "considerateness", and "cooperation."

Improved ratings in "honesty" and "truthfulness" do not necessarily represent improvement. What is shown here probably means increased opportunity to judge the child in situations in which these characteristics became more clear-cut and observable. The early elementary grades in the conventional school give small opportunity to appraise honesty and truthfulness. Children at this age are more receptive to teacher suggestion; their activities are more controlled, and the children themselves present but little group organization and dynamics in which honesty and truthfulness can be isolated. Judgments as to honesty and truthfulness in the schoolroom are usually made from a study of the child in teacher-pupil relations. If the child accepts teacher domination the observer can do nothing more than to rate him as average. This was probably the situation in Patricia's early ratings. Her later ratings of 1 in "honesty" and "truthfulness" are more significant. In grades four, five, and six the average child tends to rebel if unhappy, or at least to experiment with behavior to the limit of the scope of freedom allowed by the teacher. Consequently situations arise in which the child is tempted to lie to the teacher, or to cheat on tests or on paper work. The ratings of 1 freed Patricia from this kind of suspicion. For many children a high rating (teacher approval) might indicate increasing humility, decreasing peer status, or an attempt to gain teacher favor as a compensation for loss of status with playmates. Other ratings ("generosity", "happiness", "kindness", etc.) would imply that Patricia was equally honest and truthful in her social reactions—games, and general peer relations.

Most encouraging, and brought out more clearly here than in other schedules, are the improved ratings on "generosity", "kindness", "considerateness" and "cooperation." It seems plausible to believe that there was some reliability expressed in the judgments made. Personal observation of Patricia's behavior over a six-year period tended to corroborate this generalization. She seemed to develop from a meek, obscure, shy little girl into a friendly, cooperative person with sufficient poise and assurance to assert herself mildly within the group. She did not challenge those with leadership roles but liked to align herself close to those who were so recognized.

D. Emotional Characteristics

In attempting to discover whether Patricia had undergone adequate emotional development we are operating under limitations generally faced by those working in the schools. No device available today lends itself adequately to the calculation of extent of emotional maturity.

The materials that we had at hand on Patricia were two in kind. One was the objective data resolved into a number of growth patterns shown in previous chapters. The other was a series of ratings filed by observers throughout each year of her elementary-school career.

The use of longitudinal growth patterns of various kinds, obtained from objecive data, represents a new approach to the study of emotional behavior. The hypothesis back of this usage is based upon the idea that consistent, marked deviation in any growth pattern without a clearly defined trend up or down indicates an emotional effect—the greater the variation, the greater the effect. The idea may be illustrated in the following figure. The A part of the figure delineates a wholesome effect of an emotional state on a specific growth process. Part B of the figure postulates what happens to the growth pattern when the child is undergoing emotional stress or strain. The pattern displayed in B, incidentally, assumes that the testing itself is not a part of the emotional syndrome. This of course could explain irregular peformance. Such an incidental effect, however, can be minimized in a child-study program conducted under proper conditions.

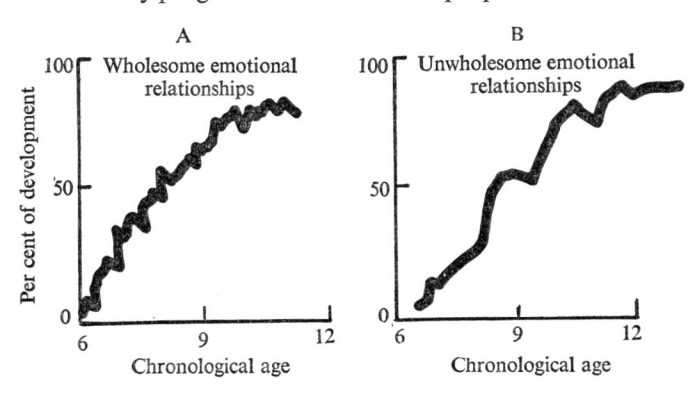

Figure 12. Wholesome and Unwholesome Emotional Relationships in the Developmental Pattern.

Data have previously been shown on physical, mental, and academic aspects of Patricia's development. In nearly all instances, and particularly in academic areas which are more likely to respond to emotional effects, Patricia exhibited patterns of growth which resembled Part A much more closely than Part B, Figure 12. This was true of all academic growth curves with the exception of spelling. The reader will notice one slight difference in the comparison of these, Figures 6 to 11 inclusive, with the hypothetical curves shown in Figure 12. The illustrations in Figure 12 picture only the single-cycle development to age twelve. Patricia presented the beginning of a second cycle which is indicative of physiological rather than emotional change.

Patricia's mental curve also pictures growth with little or no variation from the normal second cycle in the pattern. Height and weight curves respond more readily to other influences so that variation in them can give but little clue to the effect of emotions.

From the evidence we are justified in concluding that Patricia enjoyed considerable emotional stability. To the extent that the hypothesis is valid we may say that Patricia had acquired abundant balance.

Miscellaneous Characteristics: There are many symptoms of emotional feelings that are observable. Feelings of pleasure and displeasure, excitement, joy, sorrow, etc., all are demonstrated at times in the classroom. From our raters a long list of characteristics was recorded.

Two approaches can be made to the handling of these data. All could be tabu-

FREQUENCY OF CHARACTERISTICS SHOWN (TOTAL NUMBER OF OBSERVERS—7)

1. *Happy*—1[1]
2. Romantic
3. Optimistic
4. Courageous
5. *Pleasant*—3
6. Confident
7. *Self-reliant*—1
8. Cheerful
9. *Sense of humor*—2
10. Frank, open
11. *Kind, thoughtful*—2
12. *Ambitious*—1
13. *Sympathetic*—2
14. *Generous*—2
15. Forgiving
16. Dreamy
17. Refined
18. *Nice*—1
19. *Obedient*—4
20. Mischievous
21. *Good*—2
22. Troubled
23. Distressed
24. Pessimistic
25. Cynical
26. Antagonistic
27. Blustering
28. Boisterous
29. Sullen
30. *Moody*—2
31. Depressed
32. Cheerless
33. Mean
34. *Rough*—2
35. Obscene
36. Profane
37. Resentful
38. Jealous
39. *Envious*—2
40. Self-willed
41. *Coarse*—1
42. Disobedient
43. Viscious
44. Evil-minded
45. Bad
46. Fearful
47. Nervous
48. Irritable
49. Easily angered
50. Afraid
51. *Timid*—3
52. Shy
53. *Self-conscious*—5
54. *Sensitive*—2
55. Fickle
56. Weak
57. Holds grudge
58. Noisy
59. *Self-controlled*—2
60. *Even-tempered*—4
61. *High-tempered*—1
62. Hot-tempered
63. Sentimental
64. Silly
65. Giggly
66. *Clowning*—1
67. Placid
68. Phlegmatic
69. Stubborn
70. Dull
71. Stupid
72. *Uninteresting*—1
73. Repulsive
74. *Laughs easily*—1
75. *Smiles frequently*—4
76. *Stolid, unemotional*—2
77. *Frowns, scowls*—1
78. Cries easily
79. Temper tantrums
80. Grouchy
81. Complains
82. Objects
83. Tattles
84. Criticizes
85. Bossy
86. Dominating
87. Aggressive
88. Persistent
89. Possessive
90. Leader
91. *Independent*—1
92. Self-assured
93. *Sincere*—1
94. *Docile*—2
95. *Easily influenced*—1
96. Secretive
97. *Follower*—2
98. Submissive
99. Sub-servient
100. Superiority complex
101. Strong ego
102. Conceited
103. Seeks spot-light
104. Demands attention
105. *Sensitive to thoughts of others*—4
106. *Indifferent to others*—1
107. Unaware of others
108. Self-willed
109. *Reserved, aloof*—3
110. Humble
111. *Inferiority complex*—3

Numerals represent frequency rather than grade where the characteristic was noted.

PERSONAL-SOCIAL DEVELOPMENT 127

lated together to see if certain characteristics seemed dominant throughout. The second approach afforded would be a tabulation of characteristics grade by grade to determine change. Both will be utilized in the discussion to follow.

Over-all Picture: Significant unanimity of opinion was shown by the observers throughout all grades. Three or more raters, of the seven employed, judged Patricia to be "pleasant," "obedient," "timid", "self-conscious," "even-tempered," "smiling frequently," "reserved and aloof," and showing an "inferiority complex."

Grade-to-Grade Picture: A review of the characteristics noted according to the grade in which they were recorded will add little meaning and significance but may bring up reinforcement for conclusions already made. They will also give some clues as to possible shifts in behavior:

Grade 1	*Grade 2*	*Grade 3*
Pleasant	Obedient	Obedient
Self-reliant	Good	Good
Ambitious	Moody	Moody
Good	Self-conscious	Timid
Cynical	Sensitive	Self-conscious
Self-conscious	Even-tempered	Sensitive
Self-controlled	Uninteresting	Even-tempered
Frowns, scowls	Smiles frequently	Smiles frequently
Independent	Indifferent to others	Easily influenced
Sensitive to others' thoughts of her	Reserved, aloof	Sensitive to others' thoughts of her
Reserve, aloof	Inferiority complex	Reserved, aloof
Inferiority complex		Inferiority complex

Grade 4	*Grade 5*	*Grade 6*
Pleasant	Pleasant	Happy
Sense of humor	Sense of humor	Pleasant
Kind, thoughtful	Kind, thoughtful	Self-reliant
Sympathetic	Sympathetic	Sense of humor
Generous	Generous	Kind, thoughtful
Obedient	Obedient	Nice
Rough	Rough	Self-conscious
Envious	Envious	Even-tempered
Coarse	Timid	Clowning
Timid	Self-conscious	Laughs easily
Self-conscious	Self-controlled	Smiles frequently
Even-tempered	Even-tempered	Independent
High-tempered	Smiles frequently	Sincere
Smiles frequently	Stolid, unemotional	Sensitive to others' thoughts of her
Stolid, unemotional	Docile	
Docile	Natural follower	
Natural follower	Sensitive to others' thoughts of her	
Sensitive to others' thoughts of her		

Several conclusions can be drawn from these groupings or delineations presented by Patricia in these various grades:

1. These was significant uniformity of design in grades 1, 2, 3 and in grades 4, 5, 6;

2. The fourth grade represented a time of observable shift from the characteristics previously noted to quite a new listing;

3. The developmental matrix of Patricia seemed to be very wholesome in the type of shift shown.

Character of Shift in the Developmental Matrix: In grades 1, 2, and 3 Patricia was judged to be a child somewhat pleasant but rather meek and obedient. All raters labeled her as self-conscious and all three noted that she was reserved and aloof. Undoubtedly such general characterization led all three to add that she seemed to have an "inferiority complex."

Grades 4, 5, and 6 were years in which no observer suggested an "inferiority complex" although all three, as in the first three grades, concluded that she was self-conscious and sensitive to the opinions of other children.

An outstanding emergence in the upper elementary grades was her "pleasantness," "thoughtfulness," "generosity" and "cooperation." This conclusion is in agreement with generalizations previously drawn and tends to substantiate the analysis of her general personality. It seems rather significant that observation with so little direction showed considerable agreement with more elaborate anecdotal recordings.

General Analysis: To say that a child demonstrates a certain characteristic is of minimum value in understanding him or in interpreting the kind of experiences that were his lot.

Needed is a list of conclusions and generalizations concerning this child. At first glance it would seen that the instruments used were too simple and naive for this purpose. There are more advanced and more complicated measuring stratagems for disclosing personal and emotional traits. They are superior to the type of schedule used with Patricia when neither is supported by other types of observation and measurement. In the study program used here, however, there was continuity of observation which approached this child as a complete individual. She was always seen in relation to other children and in a total reaction pattern. At no time were observations limited to an interview or to a situation which ruled out concern for affective factors. More complicated psychological tests and inventories might have added something to the picture derived. It would seem they might at best have contributed corroboration of what we have already concluded. There was not so much a significant lack of more complicated schedules for obtaining statistically reliable but piece-meal pictures of personality, as a need for devices to observe the individual more clearly in a developmental sequence. Since these were not available it was necessary to proceed as well as we could with the material available. From these the following conclusions may be drawn which will be elaborated in the following section.

(a) Patricia's emotional tone did not seem to inhibit or frustrate growth in various school achievements.

(b) Emotional behavior appeared normal with respect to self-control, self-discipline, etc.

(c) Emotional behavior was judged to mature in parallel with her development.

(d) Emotional behavior seemed to indicate adequate balance between ego-inspired and group-inspired reactions.

(e) Observational records and inventories failed to point out that emotional reactions were aroused in creative situations in the school.

(f) Observational records and inventories failed to point out activities that tended to sharpen and to challenge development of desirable emotional states.

(g) Emotional development was encouraged only through miscellaneous and incidental group processes—no personal challenge.

(h) Records showed no positive attempt to develop broad sympathy for and understanding of others.

(a) *Relation to School Achievement:* The emotional behavior shown by children in the classroom is quite as important as their achievement in reading, their spelling performance, and their scores on intelligence tests. In a way it is even more important because it can color and influence learning. Children find any number of ways of behaving and acting under emotional stress and strain. Temper tantrums, fighting, and aggressive action are common manifestations. With respect to Patricia there was little evidence of such behavior. Her several school achievements demonstrated steady and consistent growth. Moodiness, depressive behavior, or elation and over-stimulation following in a progression could affect performance. As pointed out previously such behavior could produce marked deviation in school achievements. Her various growth patterns which submitted to objective appraisal showed no evidence of flight from normal progression.

(b) *Self-Control Normal:* Patricia at times showed the beginnings of aggression —pushing, fighting, bossing others, etc. These, however, were short-lived and did not persist beyond the third-grade level. These methods of attracting attention and contesting for peer status were abandoned after some exploratory action in the first and second grades.

The ability of a child to exercise self-control and self-discipline gives certain clues to emotional affects. Patricia very early in her school life presented an inclination to respond to teacher-imposed boundaries on expressive behavior without loss of personality equilibrium and without feeling restrained or bottled-up. In playground and after-school relationships, where teacher restraint was not present, she indicated ability to get along with others. She projected herself only in a limited way unless chosen or delegated to a specialized role. Any parent could be proud of Patricia in the kind of restraint displayed.

(c) *Maturation of Emotional Behavior:* Patricia's growing self-control, her recession from attention getting to restrained group roles, her growing cooperation and friendliness all indicated emotional maturation along with total organismic maturation. This is not to say that specific emotional aspects of her behavior could be charted and shown in a developmental pattern as was done with her achievement and general physiological growth. We are merely saying that at various stages of her developmental pattern old emotional affectations were dropped and new ones were assumed which were more compatible with that specific stage of maturity. New manifestations were well within the limits of conventionality and took no unusual exploratory pathways. Patricia constantly did the thing that was expected of her.

(d) *Balance Between Ego-Inspired and Group-Inspired Reactions:* The concluding statement above might imply that Patricia grew continuously from a highly ego-centered individual to an individual that took all cues for response from the group with which she associated. This is not the implication intended. The picture of Patricia drawn by the observers is that of a child in the early grades with a high potential for egocentric behavior. She was first seen as withdrawn, overly obedient, meek, sulky at times, and—when infringed upon by children in a mild way—as aggressive and combative. In later years she maintained enough of the aggressive aspects of her personality to star in strenuous games and to clown considerably, but continuously reflecting increased friendliness, sympathy and cooperation. Thus she was not entirely meek, although doing little in the way of seeking leadership roles, but maintained what seemed to be a desirable balance between personal and group demands.

(e) *Relation of Development to School Activities:* Emotion means much more than a mere behavior accompaniment to the process of self-adjustment. Emotion can produce a desirable affective state accompanying highly challenging and highly stimulating learning situations.

Patricia appeared to be a child with untapped potentialities in this respect. While her whole picture in school showed a kind of phlegmatism there was nevertheless the suspicion that fine affective qualities existed within her of which she was entirely unaware. In relation to general emotional maturity these were aspects in which growth had not even begun. Emotion of the kind to which we are referring is in reality nothing more than emotional tone or satisfaction derived from enriching, creative experiences. Development of this kind requires broad opportunities of participation, exploration, experiencing and appreciation in artistic and aesthetic activities. Little of this kind of opportunity was available to her.

(f) *Dearth of Activities Motivating Desirable Emotional States:* Emotion also may be described as the feeling which goes beyond the general mild level of pleasantness or unpleasantness involving sensory perceptions and visceral change. This implies that emotion represents a complex interaction between the child's physical-social environment and his organic being. Undoubtedly some such affects were brought out in the experiences of Patricia in and out of school. Unfortunately there was little evidence that such experiences were school-planned and part of the curriculum. There undoubtedly existed a great void of offerings such as listening to musical compositions with possible associated meanings, and opportunities to participate in self-motivated, self-planned tasks in the general social-studies areas.

These are all considered good for a child in that they have a tonic effect on physiological processes in particular and result in an over-all well-being in general.

(g) *Emotional-Maturity Incidental:* If Patricia lacked planned opportunities of this genus one must conclude that such emotional maturity as occurred was the result of unplanned or incidental experiences related to, but not a part of, the formal program. Fortunately, the social nature of the school organization contributed considerably without any planning on the part of teachers. Her teachers in general were sympathetic and understanding in that they wanted the best and provided enough of a permissive climate to encourage incidentally some development even in formalized experiences.

(h) *Sympathy, Cooperation, etc.:* These were also incidental. Patricia's case supplies evidence that teachers should, in their planning, give more attention to emotional behavior.

No other personality display requires more of an intelligent understanding and handling of a child than emotional expression. Insight into the part played by attitudes and emotions should be reflected in instructional planning. Knowledge of the possibilities for enriching the growing child's life by wholesome affective experience should challenge all teachers to reconsider their instructional programs. Emotion should not necessarily be regarded as something to be feared and repressed but rather as a basic organismic need demanding some kind of outlet and expression.

E. Social Development

Definition of Personal-Social Behavior: This term may be used to describe an individual's activity in relation to a group which furnishes the basis for social living and motivates adjustment processes accordingly.

Regardless of the type of quality of schooling or training offered, the total environment furnishes some kind of motivation for personal-social development. Where heritage is poor and the conditions for enrichment are also poor, the child's chance for adequate development is small. Where both are good, or where one is good, the chances are accordingly improved.

General Data Available: General data available for an analysis of Patricia's over-all personal-social development included:

a. Status inventory (all grades);
b. Anecdote and observation (all grades);
c. Sociometric grouping (6th grade).

Status Inventory: A status inventory was used in each of the six grades. The inventory consisted of check-list items, with frequency of possible ratings ranging from zero to seven, as follows:

1. *Makes advances to others*—1
2. Makes friends easily
3. Socially minded
4. A good mixer
5. *Well-liked by class*—2
6. Has respect of class
7. *Likes to share with others*—2
8. *Has good times with others*—2
9. *Cooperative*—6
10. Extrovert
11. *Friendly with all*—2
12. *Friendly with few*—1
13. *Has a few chums*—1
14. Haughty, cold
15. Wide interests and many friends
16. *Responds to advances*—2
17. *Makes friends with difficulty*—6
18. *Individualistic*—4
19. *Has few friends*—5
20. Disliked by class
21. *Avoided by class*—3
22. Ridiculed by class
23. Persecuted by class
24. Uncooperative
25. Introvert
26. Friendly with many
27. Friendly with none
28. *Exclusive, few friends*—2
29. *Lonely, would like friends*—4
30. *Narrow interests and few friends*—3

Putting the above patch-work together into a whole aids in bringing out a reproduction that is somewhere between that of an independent, reserved child and one that is friendly, cooperative, and quite generally well-liked. When we break down the concensus into ratings at various grade levels we find less of the dual personal-social traits suggested by the previous listing. Ratings and comments by grades are as follows:

Grade 1: Makes friends with difficulty; individualist, has few friends; has narrow interests; exclusive; *cooperative.*

I think perhaps she has an inferiority complex due to her Syrian background. However the other children don't seem to treat her differently.

Summary: Tendency toward isolation.

Grade 2: Makes friends with difficulty; individualist, has few friends; exclusive, lonely, has narrow interests; *makes advances to others; cooperative.*

Patricia tries to act so very busy and grown-up. I really think that she would like the children to pay more attention to her. She doesn't stand out. Any attention paid her will make her eyes sparkle and dance.

Summary: Attempting to break away from an isolated position.

Grade 3: Makes friends with difficulty; has few friends; avoided by class; lonely, would like to have friends; *cooperative.*

Pat seems to stand by herself. She stands around near a group that is having fun but makes no attempt to enter into the fun. Seems easily put to anger when shoved around. She doesn't walk away from aggression but pitches in and takes her own part.

Summary: Aggression a part of friendship development, is trying for better status.

Grade 4: Makes friends with difficulty; avoided by class; lonely, would like to have more friends; *has a few chums; friendly with select few; cooperative.*

Since last year Pat has acquired friends in her own room. She plays with them, works with them in the classroom, and seems proud to think that she can go over and talk to them without feeling embarrassed. She is a sweet girl, but I don't believe that most of the children really know and understand her.

Summary: Great progress in establishing satisfactory group status.

Grade 5: Avoided by class; has narrow interests and few friends; lonely, would like to have friends.

In a class friendship sociogram, Patricia was chosen once. She chose, in return, the girl who chose her. No one else selected her.

According to her teacher Pat is well liked by many of her classmates, but her special friends are girls from another room.

Summary: A continuing status struggle.

Grade 6: Makes friends with difficulty; individualist; *responds to advances by others; well-liked by class; likes to share with others; has good times with others; cooperative.*

Summary: Social status in this grade represents peak achievement.

Sociometric Status (Sixth Grade). One of the recent techniques devised for analyzing group action is the sociogram. The one shown on p. 134 adds little to the picture of Patricia but contributes a description of the social involvement of the group of which Patricia was a member.

The group itself was one in which there were no important dominating sub-groups but rather several groupings which included nearly all children in the room. Patricia, however, was on the fringe of what might be thought of as a minor group.

The kind of organization shown, with no strong sub-groups, might be judged as indicating a well-integrated roomful of children. To some extent other observations obtained from continuous contact with these children would support this hypothesis. At no grade level were we able to detect persistent, power-gathering cliques. Teachers attempted in the main to work with children in large groups. Consequently there was little opportunity for children to gather in small clusters whose selection might have been the result of like interest and background.

The kind of gathering presented here tends to agree with observation records regarding instructional organization. Aside from some grouping in the teaching of reading based on estimated ability, classroom instruction was organized on the whole-group level. The pattern followed definite time sequences given over to various subject-matter offerings in which reading, reciting, attention to workbooks, etc., took up most of the time. Projects or large-unit activities which tend to bring children together around an interest or allow for choices on the basis of friendships were almost entirely lacking. Recess and after-school activities provided the major available opportunities of this kind.

Small-group activity was thus discouraged. Children at times were allowed to work with "friends" but only a minimum of small-group interaction was allowed.

Instructional organization which fails to encourage sub-group dynamics can be both helpful and harmful to an individual child. Patricia provided a good illustration of such a dichotomy. In the way of advantages, this type of organization protects the child from striving to become a member of a preferred dominant sub-group and thereby saves him from possible conflict in meeting its demands. And secondly, it tends to eliminate the possibility of isolate status. All children

Patricia

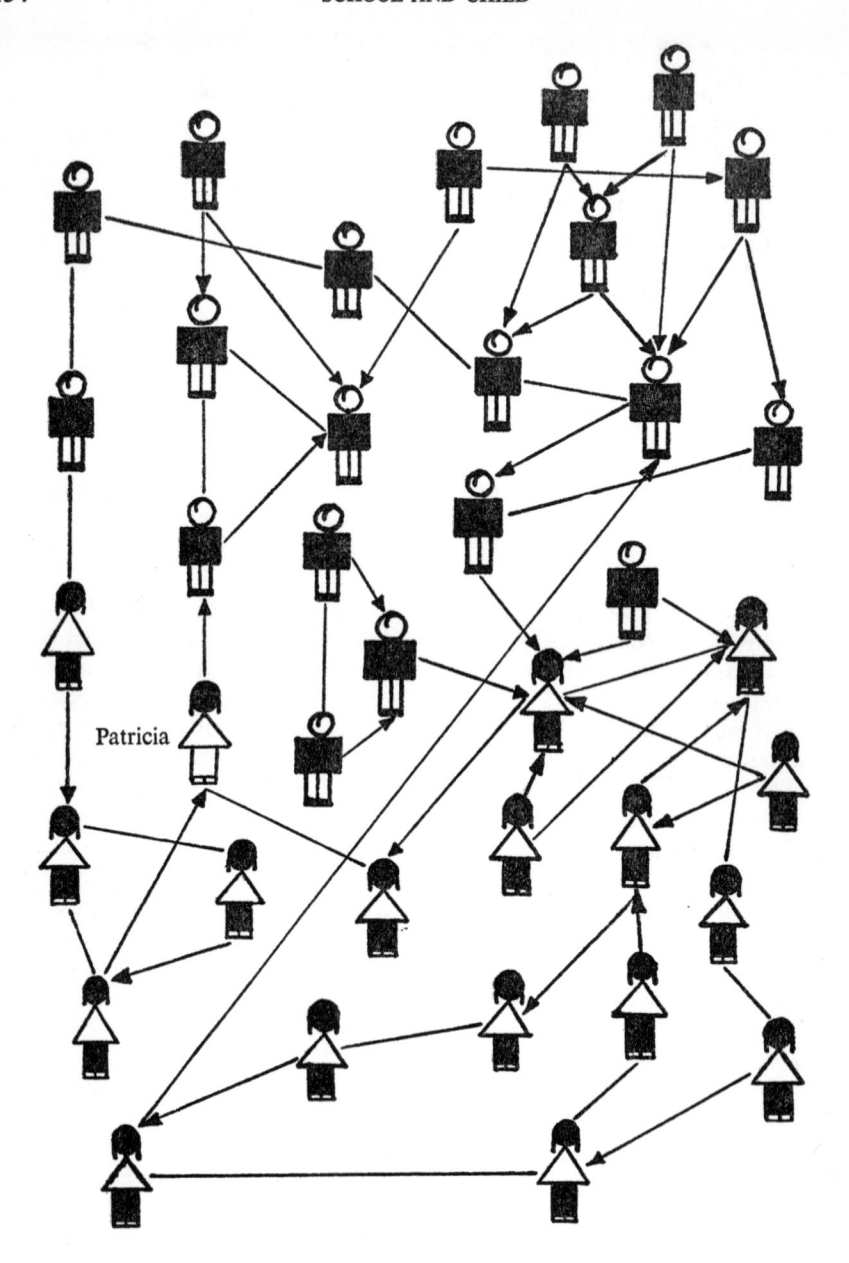

Figure 13. Sociometric Rating.

under these conditions get some sort of opportunity for attention and broad contact. At least each child has a minimum relationship with many children.

The defections inherent in whole-room class organization are two in number. Children fail to experience the social benefits which strong sub-groupings provide. Secondly, such organization usually fails to offer strong motivating curriculum challenges. With respect to the first point we are inclined to speculate as to what would have been the effect of strong sub-group organization on Patricia's social development. Would she have been less acceptable? Or would she have acquired the characteristics that would have given her a feeling of belongingness?

Patricia even in the loose cliques as found in her room came to borders of the popular groupings. Consequently one may assume that more intense pressures conceivably could have brought her closer to the center of at least one group cluster. Up-grading with reference to strong common interests might have been beneficial to all concerned, even including Patricia. Her struggle for status under such conditions might have resulted in a richer personality. On the other hand perhaps her role under any conditions would be that of a person with but mild stimulation from group action and interaction.

General Longitudinal Interpretation: There can be little question, in face of the evidence provided, that Patricia had not established much belongingness throughout her elementary-school years. In the pre-school years she apparently satisfied this need in relations with her family. Family history indicated that she was wanted, loved, and important for family unity. We know little of early childhood days, but in kindergarten and first-grade years she successfully explored contacts with other children. During this time she was somewhat aggressive but shy, and occasionally friendly. As she gradually found greater security among her playmates her negative characteristics began to disappear. She discovered that among a few children she was quite important. This was satisfactory to Patricia and from such a base she discovered the kind of contributions—in fun, play, superiority in games—that she could make. The total affect of her individual-group relations contributed to minimum satisfactory personal-social development.

From the third grade on Patricia gave evidence of having established confidential relationships with at least one child. This child usually accepted Patricia without compromise. For her these relationships were very important. Patricia in making but little group impact had a special need for a "mutual-pair" relationship. This she seemed to have achieved. When seen in company with one of these children (a different one in different years) she appeared very natural, uninhibited and in a good many ways demonstrated true social qualities.

Among many children in the upper elementary grades peer loyalty begins to threaten home and parental relationships. This is due to the fact that the child more and more turns to group standards as a criterion for behavior and less and less to home and parental guidance and regulation. Family security and identification becomes secondary to the need for belonging to a desired group. When acceptance requires behavior of a different kind than that approved by parents the child finds his loyalties in conflict with each other. It is of considerable interest that this condition did not appear in Patricia's life. It is true of course that crises of this kind become serious during junior and early senior high-school years. Nevertheless for some children peer-family conflict has its beginnings in the late elementary-school grades. For a child of Patricia's maturity one might speculate that this would happen. Evidence however gave no indication of conflict between playmate and parental demand. Two factors may be cited as deterrents in her case. Patricia seemed to belong to a family grouping in which rule and regulation were at a minimum. She worked around the store, had no specific bed time, and was given spending money as needed. This points out that sufficient family laxity was afforded so that shifts within the pattern of behavior demanded by her peers were well within the limits of family acceptability. Patricia's ethnic background was brought into play here. It is possible that this factor rather than parental understanding made harmony possible. The ethnic culture of this child was significant in her upbringing. It seemed to be the desire of her family to maintain certain old-country customs at home—diet, continuous contact with others of similar background, dress, language, etc. This was important for them and made important in Patricia's life. Other things were less important. Everyone was busy and had his own work to do. There was little time for regulation and enforcement of regulation. And also there was the effect of this level of society. Less attention is paid to children and they are given more freedom than children in higher economic brackets.

The second factor is the absence among her age groups of strong gang clusters. Neither school nor community gave evidence of strong pre-adolescent or early adolescent cleavages. Perhaps the community was more responsible for this deficiency (good or bad) than the school. Or perhaps it is impossible to form strong sub-groups in school which cannot be carried over into out-of-school life. In this respect the community was not a true community. It afforded certain opportunities for adult contact within its own confines but lack of many cultural and institutional facilities left only the school as the meeting place for children. But, as is customary in most instances, the school almost exclusively offered its after-school facilities to adolescents and adults.

General Factors: Propinquity of playmates is one of the important factors governing a child's personal-social development.

Patricia began her early elementary years holding family security, maintaining friendships with girls of her own ethnic background but at the expense of friendships within her own room. This suggested some insecurity in the first years. However by the time she reached the third grade (her most important) she had dropped these contacts and substituted friendships with girls of her own grade and age. A late start in developing these contacts may explain her borderline relationships to key groups within her room at the sixth-grade level. Up to this point she had been able to achieve little in the way of group involvement. Or, supporting another hypothesis, perhaps Patricia had gone as far as she could in her present development. Upper elementary-grade status is said to depend on ability in games, cleanliness, courtesy, classroom behavior, and friendliness with playmates. Patricia seemed to have capitalized on her motor dexterity as shown in games, her special personality traits for clowning, but was still lacking in courtesy and friendliness although having shown great growth during the time studied.

Specific Factors: Up to this point little has been said about Patricia's increasing awkwardness due to excessive weight. At the outset it should be added that she progressed remarkably in her social development for a child obviously becoming more and more obese and ungainly. Fortunately, in the early grades, other children did not pay much attention to this. In the middle grades her additional weight gave her status on the playground. She could push harder than the other children. She could throw and hit the ball farther than the other girls. It gave her a sort of masculinity of which she took full advantage. Even the boys were interested in her athletic prowess. Patricia, herself, at about the fourth-grade level began to show some concern about her size. Motor coordination was not quite what it was formerly and she became breathless and tired. Very obviously in the fifth and the sixth grades there was some sex consciousness. She confided in our observers and asked questions about reducing and about diet. She began to show some concern about her status which up to this point had seemed satisfactory. Undoubtedly Patricia was beginning to look ahead and to vision her problem as an adolescent.

F. The Effect of the School

The theory that development is amenable to outer as well as inner influences leads us naturally into an appraisal of the potency of the school in motivating Patricia's personal-social development. Forces act in totality in this respect although for limited portions of time special factors may produce specific deviations in the over-all pattern. In general however there is more pattern than deviation. Thus the school is part of the total force rather than a specific factor influencing development. Yet the school can assume varying roles in the total affective influence. In some communities, the home and the community play dominant roles. In other communities, the school can assume this role. Unfortunately, in situations where direction and dominance can best come from the school it is unable to accept the challenge. A weak community usually means a weak school and a strong community bespeaks a strong school program.

Patricia, like other children in this community, had to get along with considerable deficiencies in affective motivating conditions for enriched personal-social development. It is true that she didn't know what she had missed. Basic personality needs were met. Satisfying contacts were provided. She was active and interested in what went on around her. It might appear that everything necessary had been done for her.

Some Limitations: There were certain limitations in the school influence which might not have been present under other circumstances. Mention of Patricia's Syrian background always caused her embarrassment. Her teachers and others seemed to take the attitude that she should talk about it and not be ashamed. There is little evidence of encouragement to talk about it because she should be proud. In other words, she had handed on to her the idea of acceptance of a somewhat inferior heritage by the process of slight praise. No strong intercultural study formed the framework of such encouragement as was given her.

A somewhat similar limitation may be found in the feeble efforts of the school to improve community living. Perhaps efforts in this direction by such communities are always feeble. Perhaps uniformity or near uniformity of class groupings results in lack of standards, or results in merely copying in its plans what some other community has achieved. Another factor prevented this particular community from developing its own resources. This was not due to lack of community pride but mainly from its lack of financial status and its propinquity to its metropolitan neighbor. Since it could not afford to do much for itself it leaned too heavily on its neighbor's resources.

In its direct influence on Patricia the school might be called delinquent or not fully effective because up to this point it had left her "unawakened." This point has been made before. Patricia seemed to have possibilities, beyond any of those explored, particularly in the creative arts. The community itself was probably more responsible for this limitation than the teachers and the school administration, since there was little community interest in adult education, improvement of community life, or in other projects that might have resulted in community drive and action.

Schools sometimes encourage room or inter-room projects resulting in the beginnings of strong interests and hobbies. Patricia's school experience was quite deficient in this respect. Teachers and parents alike were content to measure effectiveness in over-all achievement in the 3-R's.

To what extent can schools afford to experiment with activities for which there is no demand? If educators instigate creative curricula on the basis of teacher or expert judgment they run the risk of criticism for using empirical judgments in curriculum planning. They then stand in as precarious a position as the "essentialists"—as a matter of fact they do become essentialists, but with a new listing of "essentials." The only safe solution lies in taking the position that the student-needs approach, if followed, leads to an incorporation of many essentials.

Such speculation raises two vital questions. The answer to these in instructional applications are important to boys and girls. First, how far should the school go in exploring children's needs which immediate environmental impact fails to bring to the surface? Experiences in creative arts were not an obvious need in terms of Patricia's individual and group demands.

Secondly, the question may be raised as to how far the school should go in its efforts to centralize community interests around community problems. The answer, probably acceptable, is that the school certainly should take certain steps in this direction.

G. An Evaluation

The theory that personal-social development is subject to modification enables teachers to play important roles as they come into contact with the child. Personal-social characteristics of the individual grow and develop under many kinds of circumstances. Whatever the circumstances, the individual develops new patterns and discards some of the old, all of which eventually brings him into adult levels of behavior. It is likely that the effect of modifying factors becomes less influential as the individual matures. This is not in particular the result of maturation. It is more likely due to the fact that as the individual finds adequate satisfaction in his adjustment pattern he rejects new challenges. Thus the role of the teacher shifts according to the maturity of the individual. The child in the early years needs enrivonmental enrichment in order to accumulate a great variety of experiences. As he matures he tends to select from these the experiences that produce the greatest satisfactions. Teachers in his later years should attempt to broaden those that are satisfying and thereby give less attention to exploratory experiences except as these parallel new stages of maturity.

Concept of Individuality: As the child makes choices and seeks further satisfactions, individuality emerges. Within specific ranges of deviation an over-all core or pattern of behavior asserts itself. Patricia gave evidence of this type of development. Her personal-social reactions were beginning to show a kind of uniformity in all types of situations in which she was to be found. Individuality, thus, may be defined as a pattern of action in which variability of response in a specific situation, and breadth and scope of response in many situations, are entirely characteristic. Patricia provided an excellent illustration of this concept. It was possible to predict her performance in a good many kinds of specific situations.

There is a further aspect of this concept. Individuality is high-lighted not alone by the core or summation of dominant traits but very importantly by the individual's potentiality for modification. It seems altogether possible that Patricia ranked high in this respect. One factor will play an important part in negating possible future development. That factor is Patricia's excessive weight. Regardless of opportunity or the lack of it, Patricia will be affected by this weight factor. As she advances into adolescence and becomes more stimulated by the need for peer status it may prove to be the one handicap that will cause her to be shunned by other boys and girls. If she accepts an isolated position under such circumstances it is likely that she will be utterly unresponsive to new situations and experiences. On the other hand, if this handicap could be removed and her other personal attributes thereby permitted to emerge, she is likely to respond favorably to satisfying personal and social challenges.

Role of the Teacher in Modification: The role played by Patricia's teachers in her personal-social development to date has been that of similar roles played by teachers almost universally. Hardly any teacher does more than develop permissive circumstances. This is to say that at best they try to allow further development of whatever they see as good. They try to block frustrating and negative factors. If they see a certain talent in the child they try to encourage it. If they see desirable personality aspects emerging they do everything possible to bring about full maturity of them. Describing the situation in another way we may say that the teacher encourages the effect of factors already operative in producing a design of emerging behavior which seems desirable and good.

It would appear that Patricia's teachers went this far in aiding her. In comparison with the practices of many others, the accomplishment of Patricia's teachers was no meagre achievement. Personal-social development for many children needs but little more than organization of children in a classroom with a teacher who has sufficient understanding not to be in the way, thus allowing group and individual action to take their course. This does not imply approval of chaos. It merely means that a helping hand here and there will do much.

But there are steps beyond the permissive concept of group climate which may be taken. We shall attempt to discuss some of these and to point out ways and means by which Patricia's development in the forthcoming school years may be enhanced.

Limitations in Opportunity: One of the opportunities missed by her was experience in varied group organization. Teachers have given too little attention to the possibility within the typical classroom of experimenting with group dynamics. Children are brought together usually on the basis of ability, interest, or on the basis of groupings formed through outside-school motivations. Children who read at the same level of ability are brought together. Children who have like interests come together on the playground. For most children such groupings are satisfactory. They are deficient in that there are always a few children who are left out and ignored. It would seem logical that throughout a given school year each child should have the opportunity to have something more than casual contact with every child in the room.

Children often find themselves in certain sub-groups through coincidence or chance. They accept status accordingly and participate without much motivation or interest. Such children welcome an opportunity to make new contacts and to have a friendly adult break the ice for them, so to speak, in new exploratory alliances. The teacher who attempts to break up strong group cleavages more or less permanently, however, is following an ill-advised practice. Temporary groupings, deliberately assigned, can serve this purpose. Children need teacher assistance in this type of group organization. Some children are afraid of losing status with friends already made if they experiment on their own in the making of new friendships. Leadership among children is frequently aggressive and punitive. When a child seems to reject the gang, even by trying to be kind to others, he is likely to suffer criticism from some one of his earlier friends.

Patricia experienced throughout her entire elementary-school career a rather limited contact with children in her various rooms. Her friendships were few and her opportunities limited through lack of teacher direction and planning. Another opportunity not afforded Patricia was participation in group organization built around interesting and stimulating activities. She worked with other children in planning assembly programs, parties, and entertainment for mothers on special occasions. These however harbored limited experience in that they called on only those abilities in the group that were already characteristic and somewhat developed. Patricia and her friends were not encouraged to venture far into the unknown or unexpected. They learned what to expect from each other and from their teachers and increasingly were discouraged in explorations. This is to imply that teachers should not allow group patterns to become too solidified. All children need experience in group interaction salted and seasoned by interesting challenges and demands. Because Patricia did not have much of this kind of background she developed certain personal-social limitations. She had but little insight into the capabilities of other children as individuals. Performance of other children was judged as "good" or "bad." If one of her playmates was a star performer on the playground this child was recognized as "good." If he was a "bad" performer he got no encouragement whatever. She expected only specific reactions. If she did not like or accept group viewpoint she withdrew or day-dreamed. She seemed to be growing toward an individuality which will never try to change or modify group judgments. She was not seen as a participant in any kind of group interaction where challenge was recognized as a natural part of its function. Patricia's home life, life with children outside of school, and teacher-pupil reaction and experience were all consistent in this respect. Patricia reached this stage of maturity lacking skills for enjoyable group activity. Apart from her ability in ball playing and her somewhat accepted skills as a clown, she had little experience in happy group "plot and plan." Repeating an earlier prediction, it seems that Patricia is quite unprepared for the social challenge which must come in a junior high school where new status and prestige must be achieved. Her skills were on the immature side and of little value in meeting social requirements at a higher level of maturity. Those skills she had require participants and an audience. She had little to lean on in the way of personalized skills. She read little. She did not draw or paint. She had no musical skills.

Throughout Patricia's school career she saw no official recognition of merit except in terms of teacher approval and reward. Consequently she received little aid in gaining a sense of personal worth. Perhaps even more important is the broad conclusion that she saw little value in other individuals except when their contributions brought attention to them. Broad group social sensitivity was quite lacking.

Importance of Social Development Not Recognized: Patricia is judged to be a product of the typical school in which social development is recognized at best as a secondary or supplementary educational objective.

Teachers are quite cognizant of their responsibility for social development when the child first enters school and aid him to make satisfactorily the first adjustment to school life. They are quite negligent of the implication that by the time the child reaches twelve years of age the peer world definitely surpasses the family world in its importance. Consequently, little is done in a planned way to ease the adjustment process so that the child is definitely aided in making this transition.

It is impossible to be too critical of Patricia's teachers since simple devices for evaluating individual-group relationships were then generally unknown and only today are experimentally employed. These are aspects of personal-social evaluation which should be mentioned merely to point out progress in this area.

Use of Sociometry: One of these devices is the sociometric chart by which is it possible to determine groupings, and, by administering the device over a period of time, the strength of cleavages and the extent of improvement of status of individual children. This technique was not called into play until Patricia's last year. It served however to provide a standard by which future measures of Patricia's status may be determined. At this point it is almost needless to say that mere measurement does nothing more than present a comparative picture of status achieved. The obvious implication points toward some needed teacher-manipulated group dynamics as a means of improving status of children in between evaluation periods. And it will be unnecessary to add that this technique also provides a means for evaluating teacher effort in this direction.

The Value of Grouping: Patricia attended a school in which there were several sections of each grade. Placement of children in these sections followed no highly purposive plan. The writer recalls no observation of procedure in which section placement in a given home room followed a diagnostic or correctional scheme with reference to personal-social development. This of course is a situation that is quite unusual. Incidents are many that testify to the familiarity of school administrators, generally, with section placement based on ability or achievement levels. Lately, the plan of continuing children together through the elementary grades is becoming popular. This plan has advantages over the other plan judged from certain considerations of child development. Where teachers are also continued, the teacher-pupil relation remains intact. The argument for validity of this practice is the opportunity offered the teacher for gaining an increasing knowledge of the children under her tutelage. The conventional plan along with "ability groupings" ignores this relational aspect and is established primarily to facilitate achievement of the "skill" subjects.

From the standpoint of personal-social development, ability grouping has minimum validity. The second plan considerably disregards inferred efficiency in the learning situation, and if followed blindly also has certain deficiencies. First, there is nothing sacred in the idea of holding children in the same groups throughout their school career. Secondly, where children come together through coincidence, group cleavages form which isolate some children while assigning star roles to others. Perpetuation of these cleavages, as is the tendency where they remain together year after year, is frustrating to creative group contacts and serves to perpetuate whatever patterns are established first. The idea registered here is that attention should be given to the possible advantages of transfer of certain children according to their personal-social needs. Sociometric evaluations provide the means for determining desirable placement at the beginning of each school year and throughout the year as the occasion demands. Teachers need, however, to support the sociometric picture by intelligent observation and speculation and at best with a thorough understanding of the children involved and some reliability of prediction of results when transfer is made.

More Projects for Human Understandings: One of the greatest deficiencies in the modern elementary-school curriculum is the lack of procedure for developing in children respect for the individual and respect for the group.

The first is given attention in the very recent new materials which attempt to help children to understand themselves and other children. Such materials are based on such general themes as "growing up," "understanding ourselves", and "getting along together."

There is no reason to infer that the personal problems of children can't be as rightfully regarded as the subject of curriculum activity as such subject matter as physiology, hygiene, health, etc. Actually it appears that this kind of approach is supplanting the past academic handling of the latter-mentioned subject-matter area.

Patricia showed the effects of this kind of subject-matter delinquency. In this respect however her situation was not unique among others going through school with her. It is to be hoped that this new trend in teaching will catch up with Patricia in her junior high-school years. She seemed to be a child that would be greatly responsive to this kind of instructional motivation.

Selected References

L. K. Frank and Others: "Personality Development in Adolescent Girls." *Monographs of the Society for Research in Child Development*, Vol. XVI, Serial No. 53. National Research Council, Washington, 1951.

W. A. Gruelich and Others: "A Handbook of Methods for the Study of Adolescent Children." *Monographs of the Society for Research in Child Development*, Vol. III, Serial No. 15, No. 2, pp. 365-88. National Research Council, Washington, 1938.

Eugene Lerner and L. B. Murphy: "Methods for the Study of Personality in Young Children." *Monographs of the Society for Research in Child Development*, Vol. VI, Serial No. 30, No. 4, pp. 253-87. National Research Council, Washington, 1951.

J. W. Macfarlane: "Studies in Child Guidance, 1. Methodology of Data Collection and Organization." *Monographs of the Society for Research in Child Development*, Vol. III, Serial No. 19, No. 6, pp. 42-98. National Research Council, Washington, 1938.

J. W. Macfarlane: "Study of Personality Development." *Child Behavior and Development*, R.G. Barker, J.S. Kounin, H.F. Wright, eds., pp. 307-28. McGraw-Hill, New York, 1943.

Lois H. Meek: *The Personal-Social Development of Boys and Girls*, pp. 15-148. Progressive Education Association, New York, 1940.

C. V. Millard: *Child Growth and Development*, pp. 207-52. Heath, Boston, 1951.

R. N. Sanford and Others: "Physique, Personality and Scholarship." *Monographs of the Society for Research in Child Development*, Vol. VIII, Serial No. 34, No. 1, pp. 125-326. National Research Council, Washington, 1943.

Caroline M. Tryon: "Evaluations of Adolescent Personality by Adolescents." *Monographs of the Society for Research in Child Development*, Vol. IV, Serial No. 23, No. 4, pp. 1-13. National Research Council, Washington, 1939.

Chapter X

PERSONAL ADJUSTMENT

A. Adjustment Profile

IN THE STUDY of Patricia no standardized questionnaires nor tests relating to mental hygiene, such as adjustment inventories, were used. Only a very limited checklist was filled out each year by laboratory observers. This device or profile seems to have been designed to give a status picture of the child. In its broad general categories, it suggests a likeness to an adjustment inventory but lacks discriminative features. Nevertheless it provided some assistance for diagnosis.

General conclusions may be drawn from the various ratings. First, one is impressed by the similarity between the profiles presented and the over-all theme or pattern of behavior shown by this child and revealed in the previous sections. In general, Patricia had a few friends, was fairly well poised, somewhat calm and self-controlled, was generally alert, responsible, happy, and well-behaved. These few phrases, although sketchy, summarize the general adjustment description.

Secondly, the pictures presented describe a reaction design earmarked by considerable consistency. This is not to say that this child was necessarily stable at all times but that the stability-instability ratio as shown by her was consistently maintained as she passed from one grade to another. Patricia's observers rated her almost identically. In each of all six grades she received the same rating under "emotional control," "nervousness," "alertness," "assumption of responsibility," "state of happiness," and "conduct." She disclosed only a single deviation from unanimity of opinion in "social attitudes," "responsibility," and "interest."

And thirdly, some conclusions may be derived from the position given Patricia in the various ratings. To the writer, Patricia appeared to be a child who came into school with traits generally related to acceptable behavior and continued the demonstration of these throughout her elementary-school grades. A conclusion so obviously lacking description of dramatic and colorful behavior may seem to the reader to characterize a child who was painfully common and uninteresting.

PERSONAL ADJUSTMENT SCALE
Showing grades in which characteristic was noted

I. SOCIAL ATTITUDE

(a) Makes friends easily	(b) Few friends	(c) Unfriendly	(d) Shunned
6	1, 2, 3, 4, 5		

II. EMOTIONAL CONTROL

(a) Well poised	(b) Easily irritated	(c) Frequent outbursts	(d) Fearful; depressed
1, 2, 3, 4, 5, 6			

III. NERVOUSNESS

(a) Calm; self-controlled	(b) Uneasy; bites fingernails	(c) Stammers; Nervous; hyperactive	(d) Nervous; mentally upset
1, 2, 3, 4, 5, 6			

IV. DAYDREAMING

(a) Responsive, alert	(b) Generally alert	(c) Seldom alert	(d) Withdrawal; phantasy
	1, 2, 3, 4, 5, 6		

V. RESPONSIBILITY

(a) Responsible	(b) Frequently irresponsible	(c) Assumes responsibility	(d) Irresponsible
1, 2, 3, 5, 6	3		

VI. INTEREST

(a) Spontaneous interest	(b) Intermittent interest	(c) Interested only in play	(d) Slight or no interest
1	2, 3, 4, 5, 6		

VII. HAPPINESS

(a) Happy	(b) Frequently unhappy	(c) Moody	(d) Morose
1, 2, 3, 4, 5, 6			

VIII. CONDUCT

(a) Well behaved	(b) Among other children	(c) Impudent; quarrelsome	(d) Cruel, bullies
1, 2, 3, 4, 5, 6			

B. A Definition of Mental Hygiene

Good mental hygiene is the personal condition which results when all factors for growth are favorable for reasonable achievement of potentials. Physical, mental, emotional, and all other aspects of development are involved. Thus the factors underlying behavior may be inner or outer. They may affect behavior either through involvement related to one aspect of development or to another depending upon the individual concerned. Or in the same individual two or more aspects may be involved simultaneously.

Stated in simpler terms, good mental hygiene occurs when all aspects of development are given proper encouragement and facilitation for progressing toward maximum levels in accordance with the motivation and objectives of the individual concerned. Poor mental hygiene occurs when such influences are not present or when favorable growth factors fail to parallel individual goals. Such a definition assumes a normal inheritance, normal environmental encouragement, and normal life objectives. Some children may reach their potentials and still not achieve a satisfactory objective.

Let us use as an illustration an unusually short child. Shortness of stature may be his congenital heritage. He may achieve his growth potential in this phase of his development, but because other children are taller he may feel inferior and finally insecure and rebellious. He then demonstrates in subsequent behavior an unsatisfactory mental-hygiene condition. Treatment for him involves not an "enriching" of environment but aid in solving the problem of adjusting to his limitations. Patricia had limitations that gave her trouble. One was her ethnic background and the other was her heavy type of body build augmented by excess weight. As a result of these she showed some insecurity, lack of broad group acceptance, and a tendency toward withdrawal. One can scarcely question the need in her case for a special kind of guidance and help pointed directly toward the development of attitudes and adjustments which did not fail to recognize her limitations and which attempted to turn the ethnic factor into a kind of social advantage.

C. Behavior Mechanisms

Mental conflict in some form or another is a universal experience in the life of everyone. As the individual faces the problems of everyday living, he is constantly finding situations that call for two or more conflicting responses. Personal satisfactions urge one path to be followed; ideas of right or wrong may press in the other direction. Arriving at a solution or compromise is a common event in all behavior.

A characteristic of the human is that he can make only occasionally a clear-cut decision. Due to necessity one finds the need for developing stereotyped ways of behaving in the face of conflicting forces. These are called behavior mechanisms. Some of these devices or stratagems are harmless; others are harmful. The most normal of all individuals employ them but in a manner leading to stability. Because they enable individuals to side-step the full force of reality, they are helpful.

Patricia was a child who utilized these behavior mechanisms to a normal extent and without any evidences of succumbing to the unreality which they offered in the extreme.

Compartmentalization: The individual who shifts attitudes according to the situation or difficulty involved illustrates "compartmentalized" behavior. Patricia was judged almost completely devoid of this classification of personal adjustment. In school, on the playground, at parties, and in the home, she showed an essence of freedom from this method of adjustment. She was cooperative in school to about the same extent that she was cooperative at home and she appeared to be honest and truthful in a great variety of situations.

Compensation: One of the most frequently cited illustrations of compensation concerns the child who doesn't do well in school and consequently bullies other children on the playground. Although Patricia didn't perform extremely well in the usual school subjects she gave negligible signs of bullying. Nor did her size or ethnic difference lead her to any extremes. The only indication of compensation shown by her was in her interest in playing ball and in other games calling for unusual activity. It is a question whether this interest was real or whether it was motivated by a desire to perform in a manner which she could not accomplish in the classroom or in her social activities. In any event her behavior was quite normal. She utilized playground skill in making contacts with other children which she succeeded in carrying over into the classroom and into her outside-school friendships. It is unlikely that she would have achieved this position without her wholesome, friendly, dominating, superior playground activity. In this sense the amount of compensation used by her was desirable and good. It provided satisfaction which did not require effort and ability beyond her capacity. Her efforts were rewarded by some indication of total group approval.

Daydreaming: Here we face a locked door in our search for evidence as to the "hows" and "whys" of Patricia's behavior. Throughout each year she presented evidence of being a daydreamer. Not a day passed, when Patricia was under observation, that she did not sit for some time looking into space or staring out of the window. Due to the sedentary nature of her school program it was impossible to determine whether she was travelling the road of phantasy in her thoughts or merely relaxing during periods of boredom.

The evidence favors the latter viewpoint. She snapped back quickly. In a second without hesitation or confused moments she mobilized all of her necessary resources toward a challenging stimulus. Patricia was occasionally questioned about her thoughts. She returned answers that were only half serious, or answered rationally that she was thinking about the "trip the children were going to take the next day," etc.—or other equally non-revealing remarks.

The conventional school lacking challenging alternatives to a sometimes boresome single-track curriculum, or lacking opportunity to offer something interesting when children are tired of working on spelling or arithmetic or when work is completed on these, is likely to encourage a listless daydreaming attitude. Children who have slight difficulty with assignments may choose to defer them or to ignore time limits when their interests are not challenged, but when they are dismissed from school show no evidence of this kind of indigence. Patricia definitely gave the impression of being this kind of child.

Displacement: Boys and girls who rebel against home restrictions but are afraid to do anything about them frequently turn their feelings against their teachers and other persons in authority. Patricia showed almost nothing of this kind of behavior. If she presented any significant reactions of this type it was to be found in the exaggerated attention given one of the observers and the rather unusual friendliness offered all observers from the fourth grade through the sixth. It was at this time too that she seemed to have abandoned, at least slightly, her readiness to follow teacher mandate "to the letter." Here we found some indication of rejection of teacher and parental attention and a desire to form adult alliances but with persons younger than teachers or parents. There was also some evidence of a mild rebellion toward teacher attitude that failed to recognize the needs of increased child maturity.

Distortion or Sour-Grapes Attitudes: Patricia expressed very few alibis for failure to achieve distinguished status. She probably expressed, however, this type of behavior mechanism by often refusing to try something in which she was not competent. Receding rather than aggressive behavior characterized her attitudes toward activities in which she was unskilled.

Identification: During her first years in school Patricia presented strong identifications with her parental ethnic background. At about the fourth-grade level she abandoned identification with her particular cultural eccentricities and sought closer alliance with the customs and habits of the other children. In doing this she had no particular problem of choice in reference to one group or another since the children in this school, products in the main of only slightly differentiated economic levels, showed no strong group preferences.

Thus Patricia presented a normal composite in reference to this adjustment characteristic. At no time did she pitch her efforts beyond her reach or otherwise attempt identification indicative of even mild mental confusion. Her problem was merely that of easing the transition from home to group loyalties.

Negativism: Patricia at all times in her pre-adolescent developmental period was free from extreme negativism. She was never indifferent to group motivations and frequently sought opportunities for cooperative expression. Significantly enough, her school career was marked by gradual increase in desire for the kind of activity that precludes a trend toward negativism.

Projection: Two of the most common examples of garden-variety projection are tattling on other children or complaining about a teacher as a cause of failure.

Patricia at no time was observed exercising this kind of attitude. Since projective behavior shows lack of security or dislike in following one pattern rather than another, the absence of such suggests a future uncomplicated at least by this kind of motivation.

Rationalization: Another sign of Patricia's normalcy in adjusting to problems arising throughout her elementary-school years was lack of rationalization. Patricia often said that her arithmetic was "hard" or that she didn't like handwriting but she did not say that her teacher was at fault or that the teacher didn't like her. She would say, "I am not good in that", or, 'Wasn't I awful." She would not say that, "I slipped when I started to hit the ball," or "You should have seen me yesterday when we were playing."

Regression: Regression is an immature response to frustrating circumstances. Throwing a tantrum is a common illustration. Bullying other children is another. Patricia displayed little of this type of action. In one aspect of her general behavior, however, she exercised this particular device in a mild way. The illustration in point was her clowning in a large group gathering. For Patricia, attention-drawing behavior was beneficial since it gave her a certain degree of status with other children.

Sublimation: As in most other behavior manifestations, Patricia utilized sublimation to a seemingly proper degree. She accepted standards of behavior of home and school without feeling embittered. She established and accepted goals which were not far above her performance level. In every observable way she conformed to about the right degree without sacrificing dominant personality traits.

D. SUMMATION AND INTERPRETATION

School people dealing with a child through longitudinal study basically want to know if the child's behavior is helpful to him, and if it is or is not, what his chances are for satisfactory adjustment in the future. To some extent our records on Patricia gave an indication of "what she was" and "how she had progressed." Dare we predict what she will be in the future?

The conventional scientist probably would abstain or withdraw from this assignment. It might be that he could justify his attitude, particularly if he recognized no responsibility for the child. Teachers can shy away from this task less successfully. If teachers are to work with children in a constructive beneficial manner they need to make certain assumptions about a child before providing him with reconstruction experiences as might be found in a remedial environment.

Consequently, in order to present a form of procedure that may have some value to teachers interested in this phase of analysis, an attempt will be made to raise pertinent questions and to provide tentative answers.

1. *General Behavior Pattern*

The first question to be asked is concerned with the quality of her behavior. Was she normal or abnormal? Was her mental outlook right for her? In looking back to her earlier school days and comparing them with her later elementary-school years we found that our impressions of Patricia changed very little. Her friendliness, cheerful smile, and ability to respond to a teacher's suggestion seemed as dominant in the sixth grade in her over-all personality traits as they appeared in her first kindergarten contacts.

However, some slight changes came about in her personality pattern as it matured over this span of years. These have been mentioned. Perhaps the reader will recall that they consisted mainly of a desirably increasing aggressiveness during the third and fourth grades in her contact with other children, accompanied by less dependence on teacher direction in pursuing school assignments. Her adjustment was good. Her ability to accept failure, her modesty in acknowledging success on the playground, and enough independence of teacher and classmates speak well for future mental health.

2. *Behavior and Personality*

Patricia was a rather short and stocky child. Aside from a marked feminine countenance she showed few personality traits that were particularly feminine. Slight masculinity rather than strong femininity characterized her activities both in the classroom and on the playground. Like boys rather than girls, she easily became bored with classroom affairs. She looked out of the window, stretched out in her seat, sighed and yawned. On the playground she again exhibited masculine traits. She ran more vigorously than most girls, wore a baseball cap like a boy, and was not afraid to get dirty.

Such behavior is compensatory for inability to be otherwise. She did not have the clothes, the background, or the figure to be dainty or coy. Boys of her own age accepted her as a pal or a good choice among the girls for games or sports. They did not, however, send her valentines or love notes. Nevertheless, her general behavior was fitting for a girl of her personality. Her slight masculinity was an asset rather than a liability. It gave her come contacts with boys and through games she acquired enough confidence to make her acceptable to the total group.

3. *Behavior and Goal*

In dealing with the elementary-school child from the kindergarten through the sixth grade, it is probably necessary to identify two sets of goals which most children strive to achieve positively or negatively. One set might be structured for the early elementary grades and the second for the later or pre-adolescent grades. The danger in the attempt to establish a division may be found in the implication that there exists somewhere near the midpoint of this span of years a distinct "break" or shift in behavior. No such viewpoint is to be condoned. These years constitute a period of growth quite unbroken. There is, however, in the growth curve of the elementary-school child a point at which goals take on new meanings which relate them quite as much to the period ahead as to the period behind.

The early goals may be described as: (1) gaining home and teacher favor; (2) experimentation in personal achievements; and (3) strengthening established security and belongingness.

The more mature, or pre-adolescent, goals that seem to direct the behavior of most children are: (1) gaining confidence and independence; (2) achieving sexual identification; and (3) preparing for the problems of adolescence.

The early goals need little discussion at this point since they formed the framework for much of our previous discussion. More elaboration upon the second group is pertinent since there is an obvious void in the literature on these points.

The adolescent period has often been characterized as stormy, full of conflict, and described as a time in which the child often finds himself in outright conflict with home and school ties. It isn't often that the parent or teacher of the elementary-school child is told that the pre-adolescent period too is characterized by strong resistant behavior and the need to gain some aspects of independence. The pre-adolescent years are particularly noted as the time for the first sustained drive for individuality, not only in actions but also to some extent in thinking. Success or failure on the part of the child to achieve this, greatly affected by the degree of parent and teacher willingness to see it happen, determines to a great extent the difficulty or ease of adjustment during adolescence.

In the period immediately preceding adolescence, or more specifically during the period when adolescence has actually begun but is not yet obvious, the child shows certain behavior reactions indicating instability and in some ways a breakup of old patterns. There is frequently a return to earlier forms of gratification and a general disintegration of personality with reference to old standards and ways of acting. According to Blos behavior of this kind is the result of efforts of children to free themselves of adult domination.

For the teacher this has a significant meaning. There can be little question but that curricula must recognize the urgent need of the child at this time for experiences that lead to independence of thinking and action. According to Benedict one of our greatest problems is adjusting the child to an adult society which requires initiative, authority, and self-reliance when the only experience he has had previously is within a framework of obedience, submissiveness, and dependence on adults.

The second goal required by our culture and one accepted by most children is the goal of achieving sexual identification. During pre-adolescent years it is particularly necessary for the child to begin to realize his sex. This is not to say merely that the boy must learn to know he is a boy and the girl to know she is a girl. The problem is that of continuing this recognition to the point where the child is ready to accept the responsibilities of his role. At the pre-adolescent stage first steps must be taken. At this time the child must develop skill in winning a satisfying role among children of his own sex. If this is not achieved, his task will be even more difficult during the next (adolescent) period of development. This responsibility is a natural assignment for this age group since extra-sex problems do not present urgent and critical issues at this time.

Our last point regarding the cultural goals of the pre-adolescent is somewhat in the nature of repetition of the previous point as well as a summarized statement of both the first and second goals. The idea that the fifth- and sixth-grade child is both an adolescent and a young child, with behavior characteristics of both stages, is somewhat new. It is, however, of great importance and when recognized by parents, teachers, and administrators gives new insight into the kind of instructional program that should be offered. Such a program, briefly, should include the following learning opportunities: (1) growth in independence while maintaining home and parental security; (2) improved ability to judge conduct with reference to its effect on others as the result of gang participation and identification; (3) recognition and acceptance of the sex role in relation to both boys and girls.

Patricia's early school years—the kindergarten and the first, second, and third grades—were years in which she demonstrated as well as any child the over-all cultural goals for this age-group. After a somewhat slow start she gained both teacher and parent approval through school achievement; she strengthened security and belongingness in so doing, and she experimented rather successfully with new contacts on the playground and in extra-class activities.

Her fourth-grade experiences and behavior brought forth a rather sharp breakaway from the previous uniform pattern. On preceding pages we have called this an increase in aggressiveness, lessened submissiveness, and increased independence in school and playground behavior.

With reference to our listing of pre-adolescent goals a similar amount of achievement was noted. The amount of independence acquired by Patricia along with retention of home approval and teacher favor speaks very favorably for continued progress in this direction. Whether she attained satisfactory status in a sex role is more questionable. Instead of clear-cut and strong identification with mixed and girl groups, Patricia only achieved moderate identification and acceptance with all groups—classmates, girls, boys, and girl-boy groupings. Except for one factor she should make continued progress: she showed a drift toward obesity which, if not blocked, will tend to make her more and more isolated. It is possible that it will prevent her from continuing in the role which she has played with fair success.

4. *Recommended Treatment*

To maintain the status already achieved by Patricia one may judge that her most outstanding need is a continuation of the type of environmental conditioning to which she is already accustomed. Removal to an entirely different type of community would offer new group cliques and problems. Consequently, adjustment under such conditions would likely be troublesome.

Regardless of environment, Patricia must adjust to new cultural demands at adolescent ages. She will be under pressure from her family to gain social status at a more mature level, and she will need to satisfy parents in terms of boy-girl relationships. It is likely that the kind of family from which she came will encourage early marriage as a successful culmination of social maturity. Such goals may prove difficult for her. If she continues to grow physically in a way that will make her unattractive to boys she is likely to encounter family disapproval to an extent never felt before. Such a conflict naturally will affect her mental status and level of adjustment.

Another point previously made but deserving repetition here is our estimate that Patricia was capable of much broader response to cultural and educational stimuli than she had ever experienced. The feeling persists, as a result of our continuous observation of her, that she had latent creative impulses which had not been challenged or stirred. Her educational environment is likely to continue with this omission. However, some teacher may have the skill and the insight to experiment with Patricia in new avenues of expression, but the hopeless consideration is that she has developed an attitude toward such experiences as unworthy and "no fun." Since her success to this point of maturity has come from activities of a non-creative type it is not likely that Patricia will abandon the old for new contrasting types of experiences without significant motivations.

SELECTED REFERENCES

L. A. Averill: "Case Studies in the School." *Mental Hygiene*, Vol. 25, 1941, pp. 43-57.

Ruth Benedict: "Continuities and Discontinuities in Cultural Conditioning." *Psychiatry*, 1938, pp. 161-7.

A. W. Blair and W.H. Burton: *Growth and Development of the Pre-Adolescent*, pp. 23-102. Appleton-Century-Crofts, New York, 1951.

Peter Blos: *The Adolescent Personality*, pp. 309-19. Appleton-Century, New York, 1941.

Arnold Gesell and Catherine S. Amatruda: *Developmental Diagnosis*, pp. 3-14, 365. Hoeber, New York, 1952.

C. V. Millard: *Child Growth and Development*, pp. 446-95. Heath, Boston, 1951.

Fritz Redl: "Deviations Tending Toward Delinquency." *Child Growth in an Era of Conflict*, C.V. Millard, ed., pp. 48-85. 15th Yearbook, Department of Elementary School Principals, Lansing. Michigan Education Association, Lansing, 1944.

Hilda Taba: "School Culture and Group Life." *Journal of Educational Sociology*, Vol. 21, 1948, pp. 497-560.

G. C. Thompson: *Child Psychology*, pp. 175-206. Mifflin, Boston, 1952.

L.P. Thorpe: *The Psychology of Mental Health*, pp. 509-86. Ronald Press, New York, 1950.

Helen G. Trager and Marian R. Yarrow: *They Learn What They Live*, pp. 293-344. Harper, New York, 1952.

W.F. Vaughn: *Personal and Social Adjustment*, pp. 78-106. Odyssey Press, New York, 1952.

PART THREE

Growth Inter-relationships

Introduction

PART ONE OF this book placed emphasis on age-grade expectations of the elementary-school child accompanied by observations on what might be called forgiveably a "typical" child. The main theme was a portrayal of the change that accompanies growing-up in a non-selective environment. Although this child was like no other child, she demonstrated certain universalities of behavior—perhaps only one, that change which accompanies growth follows no straight-line gradient from one cycle of development to another. Perhaps the greatest oversimplified concept relating to growth is the thought that there exists a constant ratio between environmental effect and developmental manifestation. Improved behavior or, better perhaps, achievement of potential maturity is something more than the result of ever-widened areas of action. What was attempted in Part One can be called a description of behavior from one age level to the next, presented so as to show the finer relationships between growth and experience.

Part Two, although attaining a somewhat more elaborate description of child development as it was observed in school, should be evaluated in relation to the hypotheses which analysis of observed behavior brought to light. These suggest rich areas for experiment and observation. Validation of any one of them would result in renewed research vigor on the part of behavior investigators. Although child-development findings have gone far beyond their applications there exists at present a plateau in research creativeness. Sinking deeper and deeper into statistical ruts leading to nothing more than blind alleys in the way of new findings, child development is now ready to profit from following some new leads.

Part Three keeps in mind the hypotheses suggested earlier and adds somewhat to a better understanding of them. Its importance, however, may be found in the contribution which it offers in the way of experimentation with a new and generally unknown method of analysis. While doing so it adds documentation to generalizations previously noted. It thereby offers greater validity and authority to those interpretations which it supports.

Part Three consists of only two chapters. Chapter XI deals with data previously recorded but releases its findings on a higher level of analysis than is generally the case. It is presented in the belief that here is a new approach to case study and a method by which the principles of child development can be more universally clarified and agreed upon. Chapter XII will review previously listed principles of growth and development with illustration of each from the data recorded throughout the volume, but with particular usage of the material of Chapter XI. It will conclude with a discussion of breaches in the material and deficiencies in methods for collecting adequate data for interpreting the total child in his school enrivonment.

Chapter XI

DEVELOPMENTAL PATTERNS

A. The Problem

THE READER may raise the question, with some justification, as to what remains to be discussed regarding Patricia. Many phases of her development have been pictured. Physical growth, mental growth, and academic learnings have been portrayed. The relation of the school to all these has been noted. A speculation as to the quality of future performance has been recorded. The most important breaches in our expostulation of this child relate to some deficiency in the relative comparisons of various types of development shown—physical, mental, academic, etc.—and a highly specific pin-pointing of common developmental designs along with a mathematical interpretation of certain growth inter-relationships. Closing the first breach will consist mainly of reducing all scores, previously recorded and shown in Part Two, to common measurements so that physical, mental, and academic measures can be evaluated in relation to each other. Closing the second breach will involve a more complicated procedure, first, because it is more painstaking and, secondly, because it requires a more refined handling of growth data.

Most of the approaches to child study have been made from detailed and systematic study of only certain phases of the child's total development. With but few exceptions not more than two or three aspects have been investigated together with the utilization of data collected over a considerable period of time. With reference to the total child, most of the research has been additive rather than integrative. Studies of physical growth, mental growth, and of achievement are of this type. To a certain degree, our exposition of Patricia can be criticized on such a basis.

There is therefore a need for a new type of study in which the picture of inter-relationships of many phases of development may be unveiled. There is no question among investigators as to the intimate inter-relations of many aspects of the total organism's activity in the child's environment. Nor is there much question as to the significance of the over-all effect of a single conditioning environmental factor. Disease, malnutrition, educational opportunity, cultural backgrounds, emotional disturbances, injury, and shock are not limited in their effects to a single kind of growth. Each of these, individually or in combination, influences total development. It should therefore be obvious that performance measures, aptitude scores, mental tests, physical measures, etc., all reflect something more than the single growth under consideration at the time.

It shall be the purpose of this chapter to present an analysis of Patricia from this kind of approach. It is believed that to the extent our effort is successful some of the breaches mentioned will be mended.

B. Growth Analysis

One of the most popular methods for evaluating growth inter-relationships was designed by Prof. Olson. Careful longitudinal studies of achievement in relation to other aspects of development have been carried on by him for years at the University of Michigan. Dr. Olson has given attention specifically to the inter-relation of such aspects of development as achievement, height, weight, teeth and carpal growth, grip, and mental age. In order to provide a basis for comparison, he translates all measures into age equivalents. All growths may thereby be graphed together and evaluations made. He maintains that the curve which results from graphing an average of all measurements provides a picture, which may be accepted as a norm, for appraising *any one* aspect of development. He has given the name "organismic age" to the average so obtained.

This method is simple, readily understood, and quickly applicable when measurements are available. There is considerable logic in his idea that the expression of measurements in terms of age gives a maturity meaning and time significance to the data, and permits comparisons of one kind of growth with another or with the summation of the total series.

It is possible to utilize the general idea of the Olson technique but with variation in accord with the limitations of available data. Following this plan, the measurements on Patricia dictated such variation. Grip, carpal, and teeth records were not collected regularly. Measurements available, as the reader now knows, were on height, weight, mental growth and academic progress. These are shown, translated to growth ages, in Table XIX and Figure 14.

In our previous interpretation of Patricia's physical, mental, and academic achievement many generalizations were drawn which are quite similar to those that we propose to record here. Obviously, translation of different kinds of scores to a common unit will not greatly add to interpretative possibilities. Our only justification for repetition is to bring more sharply into focus some of the pictures already presented, particularly as our generalizations referred to growth relationships. The data presented in Table XIX and Figure 14 will be handled under the following specifications:

TABLE XIX

GROWTH-AGE EQUIVALENTS

Chronological age in months	Areas of measurement on Patricia							
	Ht.	Wt.[1]	M.A.	Read.	Soc. Sc.	La. Art.	Arith.	Ave. Achievement[2]
65	80.5	87.0	....	....	....	....	....	....
69	82.0	94.0	....	....	....	....	....	....
73	83.7	100.0	....	....	....	....	....	....
77	86.5	106.0	....	....	....	....	....	....
81	87.0	107.0	....	....	....	....	....	....
82	....	....	80.0	....	....	....	....	....
85	88.0	110.0	....	82.0	....	....	....	82.0
89	96.0	116.0	....	....	....	....	....	....
91	....	....	....	81.0	....	....	85.0	83.0
93	100.0	122.0	91.0	....	....	....	....	....
96	....	....	....	87.0	....	....	91.0	91.0
97	104.5	129.0	....	....	....	....	....	....
101	108.0	136.0	....	....	....	....	....	....
102	....	....	....	100.0	102.0	98.0	102.0	100.0
105	110.5	143.0	....	....	....	....	....	....
109	115.0	150.0	....	....	....	....	....	....
113	122.0	152.0	....	....	....	....	....	....
117	127.0	163.0	108.0	....	....	....	....	....
120	....	....	....	108.0	100.0	102.5	113.0	105.0
121	131.0	172.0[1]	....	....	....	....	....	....
125	138.0	173.0[1]	....	....	....	....	....	....
127	....	....	121.0	....	....	....	....	....
129	142.0	181.0[1]	....	....	....	....	....	....
131	147.0	192.0[1]	....	....	....	....	....	....
137	151.0	200.0[1]	....	....	....	....	....	....
138	....	....	....	118.0	114.0	109.0	123.0	113.0
139	....	....	137.0	....	....	....	....	....
141	156.0	209.0[1]	....	....	....	....	....	....
143	164.0	218.0[1]	....	....	....	....	....	....
145	....	....	....	126.0	122.0	120.0	130.0	122.0

[1] Upper limits of weight established by graphical interpretation.
[2] Scores first averaged and then translated to growth ages.

162   SCHOOL AND CHILD

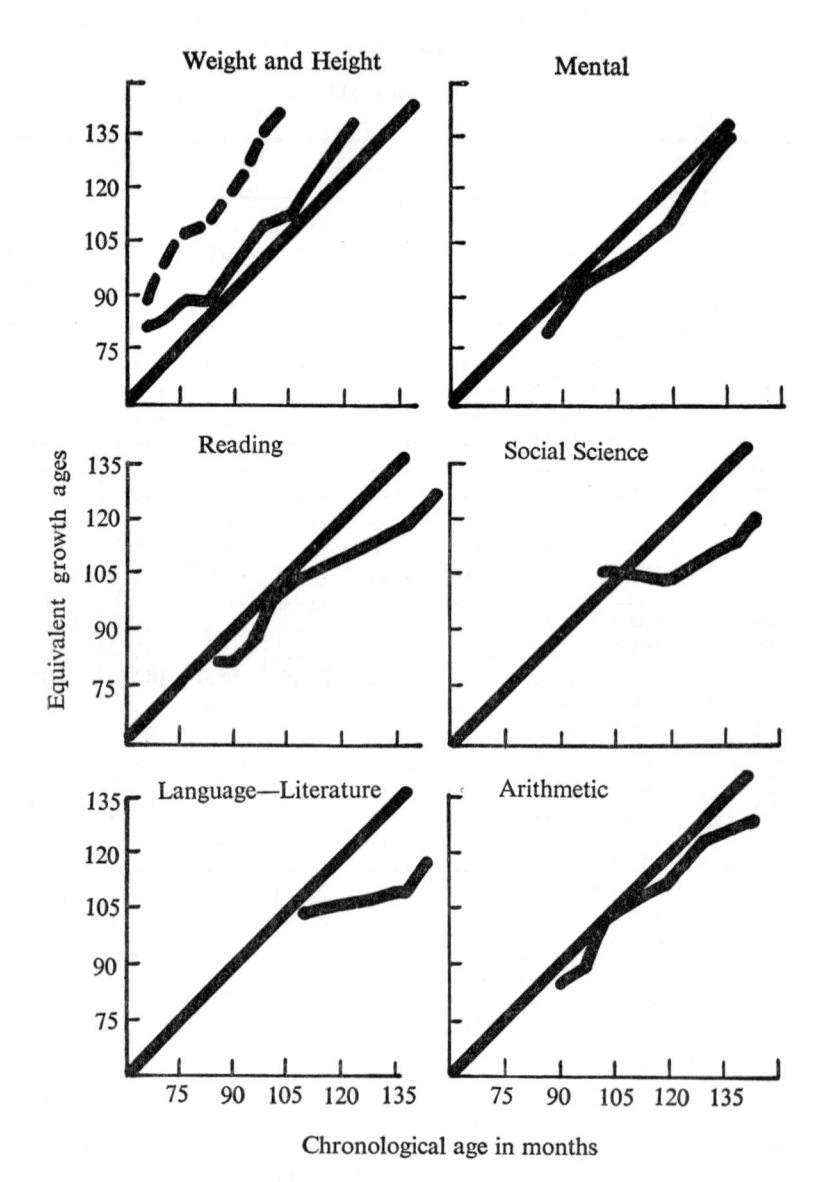

Figure 14. Growth Analysis: Patricia

(a) Range of various measures;
(b) Uniqueness of total pattern—likenesses and differences among various aspects of development;
(c) General interpretation of data in relation to organismic needs of the child;
(d) Prediction of future performance on the basis of past efforts.

1. *Range of Various Measures*

All curves show similar variation from the straight-line 1-to-1 ratio between chronological and growth age. At times they approach the straight-line and at other times they fall away. Weight growth, although exhibiting a certain amount of similarity in shifts in rate, is of course far above normal limits, even for Patricia. Beyond 120 months of age, for example, there were no available equivalent ages for a child of her weight. Taking all curves into consideration, the range of growth ages at any one chronological point is considerable. It is likely that these were greater for Patricia than they would be for most children.

2. *Uniqueness of Total Pattern*

It is impossible to define specifically likenesses and differences in the growth patterns of a child when limited to the graphical or norm-comparison approach. At this stage of analysis it can only be said that Patricia's growth curves, although reflecting certain universalities, also strongly hint at a definite individuality. The mental, social-science, and arithmetic curves all demonstrate an abrupt change at 120 months of age. This phenomenon of course is individualistic but it also suggests an occurrence that is somewhat universal—the beginnings of pubescence at approximately this age. Reading and language arts, interestingly similar and individualistic, do not present the adolescent shift until quite some time later—at approximately 138 months. Height and weight curves demonstrate universality in the presence of a babyhood (or early-childhood) cycle, but show individuality in their rather late termination. Deferred early-childhood maturation often results in a late reading curve, as was displayed by Patricia.

3. *Interpretation in Relation to Growth Needs*

Many readers will doubt the validity of interpreting growth needs from the graphic picture provided by objective measures. A longitudinal series, however, offers opportunities, to say the least, over and beyond the kind of possibilities in what is familiarly known as a "profile." Interpretative possibilities may be found in the kind of longitudinal picture presented. By "kind" we are referring to the picture shown which hints at likenesses and differences in starting points in various cycles, finishing points, rates, and maxima toward which growths seem to be progressing. Analysis can be based on the degree to which various growths parallel each other along with other manifestations of relationships. A matched set of growth patterns hypothesizes one set of conditions. A mismatched series suggests other behavior backgrounds.

In Patricia's case the picture can be described as follows:

(a) She showed very little fluctuation in her various growth curves. All of them proceeded directly toward an obvious maximum. Breaks, indicating changes in rate, appeared but there was little evidence of unsteady growth in between breaks.

(b) There was unusual similarity in timing with reference to leveling-off points and in changes of rate; in almost all instances, when one curve proceeded at an angle away from the straight-line, the other curves were found to do likewise. And last, all curves between 120 and 138 months began new rates which tended to parallel the straight-line ratio.

A conclusion from facts under (a) may be made regarding Patricia's stability of development. Putting the matter another way, it may be said that she was learning steadily and consistently with very little variation as to gains and losses. It is generally assumed that this kind of pattern characterizes a child whose growth needs are being satisfied, whose adjustment is adequate, and whose future in these respects looks favorable. Patricia's entire school history supports this thesis quite consistently.

Similarity of growth patterns as portrayed by her also offer analytical opportunities. The facts presented under (b) above may be amended as follows:

Patricia's curves portrayed distinct growth cycles—the end of the early-childhood cycle, the emergence of the pre-adolescent, and the beginning of the adolescent.

Patricia was retarded in her development as shown by these data in that she began and ended the early-childhood and childhood (pre-adolescent) phase somewhat later than other children.

The clear-cut evidence of an early-childhood cycle extending up to approximately eighty months is quite infrequent. Patricia entered the kindergarten at 65 months of age and did not reach 82 months until May of the first grade. Fortunately she was not pressed to read in the early first-grade months. When she did begin at an age appropriate for her grade level, she was, nevertheless, retarded for her age. This one growth factor—retardation in beginning pre-adolescent development—is the explanation for lag in academic achievement. Patricia progressed normally but always behind. Had she been started in school six months or a year later her scores likely would not have been different with respect to her age but would have been higher with reference to grade. It is only second-guessing to point out that had this been done the effect might have resulted in a challenge accompanying her throughout her entire elementary-school career. But, to be realistic, Patricia's excessive weight would have countermanded the suggestion even under the most elastic school conditions. Additional age-grade retardation would have magnified size self-consciousness which she constantly demonstrated. A small child under the same conditions, and like Patricia in other respects, undoubtedly would have profited from mandatory retardation in a situation where grades and teacher awards provide the main motive for achievement. What was really lacking for her was not more appropriate grade placement but rather enriched curriculum opportunity.

4. *Prediction of Future Performance*

Our last point deals with a prognosis as to Patricia's future. Some comment and speculation have already been reported. Observation and objective data relating to personal-social-cultural relations have induced us to predict successful secondary-school behavior and adjustment. Occasional displays of some lack of security in personal relations are likely to continue. The main serious threat is her trend toward obesity which, as pointed out previously, could easily render meaningless and inadequate those skills which she utilized fairly successfully in the elementary grades in gaining status and group belongingness.

The nature of Patricia's emerging adolescent-growth pattern bespeaks an ally in the continuance of satisfactory adjustment. Academic and mental growth curves both were projecting upward along with considerable similarity in timing. Physical adolescence as shown, by height and weight curves, Figure 3, was well underway. Physiological, mental, and academic maturations were progressing in a manner as to suggest aid and assistance to each other. This kind of pattern—running parallel to growth drives—is regarded as characteristically integrative and one that is believed to assist a child in gaining success and peer acknowledgement.

It should also be said that there is the possibility, in this cycle of development, of reduction of retardation between Patricia and other children. Patricia has passed the time when the gap is greatest between her and other girls in respect to organismic and developmental needs. As the more mature girls in her class approach the full bloom of adolescence with its accompanying slowing down of maturation, Patricia is rapidly catching up.

C. A New Method for Studying Inter-relationships

Up to the present, Courtis alone has devised a method for exact study of growth inter-relationships. Starting with the Gompertz curve he designed a technique whereby it is possible to resolve a natural-growth curve into its various components or what he calls "*constants*". The names given to these, respectively, were maximum, rate, and incipiency or what might roughly be called a correction, in the equation, for growths which do not begin at the zero point. Starting with log-logs of actual measures, a system of units was derived which preserves the straight-line design of log-log values but eliminates the awkwardness involved in their handling. The name "*isochron*" was given to this unit. By definition it represents one per cent of the total time required to reach maturity in a given cycle of growth. Since the equation reduces the picture of growth to a straight-line basis, it is assumed that equal growths are made for each unit of equal time. Courtis has used this method extensively with a multiplicity of types of growth data. In predicting maxima, in pointing out and defining cyclic changes, and in studying the effect of factors influencing growth, he has achieved amazingly accurate results.

The Courtis technique appears to offer the most complete and exact method for studying growth inter-relationships. It is superior to the inspectional method and to the technique of norm comparison because it can be applied to any series of performance measures without necessarily reducing data to a common unit such as growth age, the procedure followed in the previous section in this chapter.

1. *The Problem of Obtaining the True Picture of Growth*

No single test measure can be said to be entirely reliable except by coincidence. Nor can two test measures or three, for that matter, be validly claimed as representing true performance for a child in a given situation. A series of measures, over a period of time, may, however, be said to define limits within which true performance falls. The Courtis method provides a technique whereby judgments may be reinforced concerning the true pattern of growth.

In this section we shall utilize the data previously shown and, by working out equations for each growth pattern, determine the growth potential. The purpose of this attempt will be to bring clarification, substantiation, or possible negation of our previously stated generalizations concerning the presence, and inter-relationships, of various cycles in different curves.

2. *Differences in the Equations*

The equations showed a varied picture of development. To be clear on the matter let us summarize as follows:

(a) Weight: A *three*-cycle curve covering the periods from birth to adolescence;

(b) Height: A *three*-cycle surve covering the periods from birth to adolescence;

(c) Mental: A *two*-cycle curve covering the periods from birth to adolescence (had intelligence test scores been available during the kindergarten and first grade years it is possible that a *three*-cycle curve would have resulted);

(d) Academic: *Two*-cycle curves covering pre-adolescent and adolescent periods (it should be pointed out that the academic and the mental-age curves do not parallel each other since mental age begins at birth, and reading, arithmetic, etc., do not begin until after the child starts school).

3. *The Fit of the Equations to the Actual Measures*

It should be understandable to even the reader who is totally lacking in technical training that a mathematical equation used to depict growth will show a completely smooth design with no variations or fluctuations since it is an estimate of what growth would have been under perfectly controlled conditions. The untrained reader will also understand that measurements on humans are never taken under perfectly controlled conditions. The child may be ill or scared, or he may cheat, etc. Consequently it is important to determine how much the actual measures deviate from the estimated measures. Or, to put it another way, with reference to the reliability of the technique for describing actual growth, how close can we come to predicting or determining a growth design under school conditions?

Patricia provided a beautiful illustration of close matching between real and estimated performance. Because she deviated but little between theoretical and observed growth, we say that she was stable, was predictable, and then we go a step further and say that she was well adjusted.

But our main interest at this point is in the "matching" rather than in the conclusions therefrom. Figure 15 clearly indicates that from a total of 70 measurements, 44, or 62.8 per cent, showed less than 1.2 months deviation from the "perfect" growth curves depicted by the equations. The mean error was 2.4 with a standard deviation of 1.84.

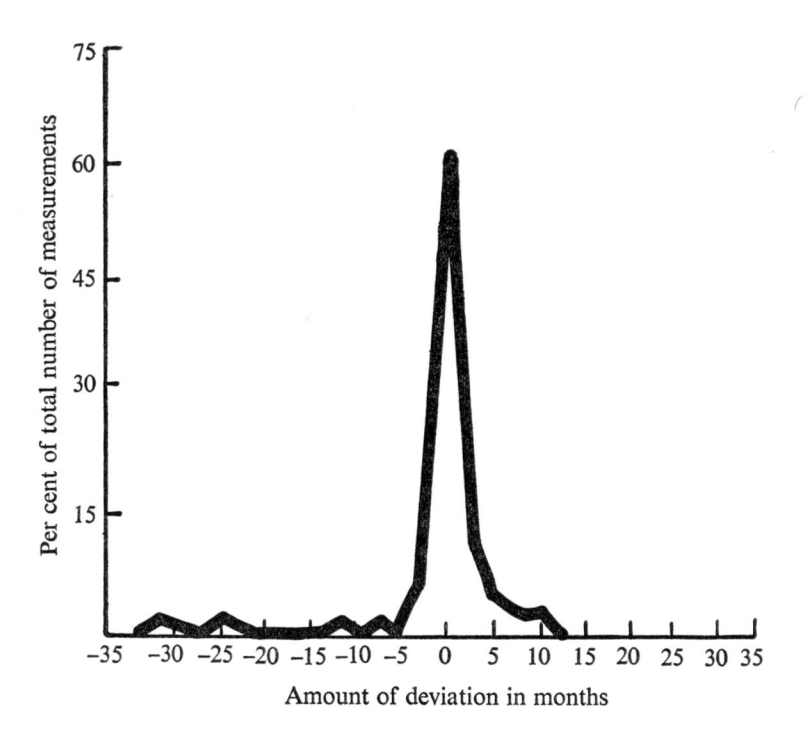

Figure 15. A Graph of Amount of Deviation of Equation Curves From Curves of Actual Performance Measures

D. Findings From the Data

1. Time Considerations

Starting Points: One of the most interesting and most significant of all "time" considerations in the growth pattern of a child is the age at which a given cycle begins. Table XX, below, presents starting points (1% of development) of various

TABLE XX

AGE IN MONTHS OF BEGINNING POINTS OF VARIOUS CYCLES

Developmental aspects	Cycles of growth		
	Early childhood (infancy)	Late childhood (pre-adolescence)	Adolescence
Weight	2.3	79.8	114.7
Height	–6.2	77.6	116.8
Mental	2.2	...	111.6
Academic	...	82.1	128.1
Average	2.0	79.2	117.8

cycles of height, weight, mental development, and academic achievement. These computations were made on the basis of equations derived from actual scores rather than from age equivalents, with the exception of mental development.

There are several interesting conclusions which may be drawn from these data.

Early Childhood: Although no height, weight, or mental-age measures were taken before this child entered school, those available resulted in equations which designated beginning points of growth (1%) close to the time of birth—an average of two months.

[In reality height and weight should show beginning points at nine months (–9.0) before birth. Our weight equation indicated a beginning point of –6.2.]

Late Childhood (Pre-Adolescence): All equations indicated pre-adolescent (late-childhood) beginning points within a plus or minus three months of an average of 79.2. Such unanimity is remarkable, as far as we know, and probably suggests a well-integrated start in school from a "whole-child" consideration.

Of some interest is the fact that the academic beginning point showed a slight delay in comparison with other starting points, -82.1 for academic to 77.6 and 79.8 for physical development. Such a relationship between physiological and academic development might plausibly be considered perfect. Whether this demonstration in Patricia was a coincidence or representative of a law of nature manifesting itself is unknown at present, since there are no other published data of this kind in existence.[1]

---

[1] Some similar materials in C. V. Millard's *Child Growth and Development in the Elementary School Years*. Heath, Boston, 1951.

Adolescence: Again, a lag is shown by the academic adolescent beginning point in comparison with physiological and mental beginning points. Height, weight, and mental beginning points show striking uniformity, with no one deviating more than three months from an average of all three. The average of all four, shown in the table, is approximately ten months from the most extreme—the academic, but within 3.1 months deviation of the other three—height, weight, and mental.

Maturity Points (99%): Certain other information pertaining to relationships between cycles in given aspects of development come to the surface when maturity points in cycles are computed and compared with the beginning points of the cycle following. Table XXI presents such information. Unlike the previous table in which much uniformity in various aspects of growth design were presented, this table displays considerable variation from the "average" except for time of maturity of various adolescent cycles, column A under 'Adolescence'. In this instance uniformity is as prevalent as was found under "starting points" shown in the previous table.

TABLE XXI

COMPARISON OF AGE IN MONTHS AT COMPLETION (99%) OF VARIOUS CYCLES WITH AGE IN MONTHS OF BEGINNING OF NEXT CYCLE

Developmental aspects	Cycles of development					
	Early childhood		Late childhood		Adolescence	
	A-1	B-1	A-2	B-2	A-3	B-3
Weight	94.8	79.8	177.5	114.7	195.8	....
Height	150.3	77.6	209.6	116.8	188.3	....
Mental	....	..	219.5	111.6	203.3	....
Academic	....	..	121.1	128.1	198.7	....
Average	122.5	78.7	181.9	117.8	196.5	....

A represents age at which cycle matures.
B represents age at which next cycle begins.

Certain other data are enlightening with respect to comparison of finishing points in one cycle (Column A) with age at beginning points (Column B) of the cycle following.

A study of the table shows for example, Columns A-1 and B-1, that the average second cycle starts at 78.7 months, although the first cycle equation does not indicate maturity until the child is 122.5 months old. A similar discrepancy exists as shown by the averages of A-2 and B-2. Here we find that, although this child in this cycle is progressing to a maturity at 181.9 months, the cycle is interrupted at 117.8 months. The only exception to "interruption" of one cycle by another is found in the case of the data shown under A-2 and B-2 for the "academic" relationships. Here, as illustrated by the 121.1 and 128.1 differences, the adolescent curve does not start until the child is a few months beyond the maturity mark of 121.1 months.

Probably the most perplexing questions arise when we compare the A-2 and A-3 columns. Utilizing the "average" we find that the maturity date for the late-childhood or pre-adolescent cycle, A-2, is within fifteen months of the maturity date of the adolescent cycle, A-3. Utilizing other data separately—height, weight, mental and academic—we find in two instances—height and mental—that the maturity point suggested by the A-2 column is greater than that suggested by the adolescent cycle and recorded under A-3.

2. Inter-Relationships

The relationships of physical and mental development to learning have been constant areas of investigation over a long stretch of time. Data available on this child provide a new approach to the problem. Stated specifically, the problem in this instance is one of determining the amount of maturity of physical and mental growth necessary for the beginning of academic learning. This particular problem has a relationship to so-called reading readiness, etc., and when solved gives a logic to the concept of readiness, thereby withdrawing it from the vague, unrealistic category in which most reading experts have placed it. To say that a child will read when he has approximately 70 per cent of his total height, 35 per cent of his weight, 40 per cent of his mental development, is much more authoritative than statements that the child will learn when "he has adequate *experiences* and *sufficient* physiological maturity". In relation to three other children with widely divergent I.Q.'s, Patricia shows similarities as indicated in the following table.[1] For her a greater percentage of height and mental development was shown before she reached a one per cent growth in academic achievement. With reference to percentage-of-weight growth she fell within the average deviation of the other three children.

TABLE XXII

GROWTH RELATIONS IN COMPARISON TO OTHER CHILDREN

Growth relationships	Patricia	Other children
Pct. of Height Growth at beginning (82.1 months) of average learning curve	75.9	66.8 A.D. 2.7
Pct. of Weight Growth at beginning (82.1) of average learning curve	33.8	35.3 A.D. 1.9
Pct. of Mental Growth at beginning (82.1) of average learning curve	47.1	36.9 A.D. 1.3

[1] C. V. Millard, *Op. cit.*, p. 50.

More revealing and perhaps even more easily understood are certain other data. These must be pooled and brought together before they would be obvious to the casual reader.

First, there is the matter of cyclic growth. It has been pointed out that in height and weight Patricia demonstrated three cycles of growth. One of these was called the Early-Childhood Cycle which began at birth and ran up into the first-grade year. As indicated in Table XX this cycle was interrupted by the late-childhood cycle (pre-adolescent) at 79.8 months for weight and at 77.6 months for height.

Secondly, Table XX points out that the academic curve started (1%) at 82.1 months.

The conclusion of course would be that the learning curve began approximately three months after the second or pre-adolescent cycle had started. How this relationship would manifest itself in other children is obviously unanswered at this time. It seems plausible, however, to suggest that reading (or learning) readiness is a matter of maturity—the beginning of a new cycle of growth—and is only incidentally affected by specialized experiences.

3. *Per-cents of Development at Various Chronological Ages*

The question of inter-relations of the various developmental phases raises curiosity as to the per-cents of development at different chronological ages. Utilizing the "score" equations, the amount of growth was computed at intervals of 10 months, and divided by the sum of the cyclic maxima. This procedure required computations for three cycles in dealing with height and weight, and two-cycle computations for mental and academic achievement. The result of the arithmetical divisions noted above was called the "per-cent of total growth" at that age. Table XXIII, following, presents these computations. At ten months of age, for example, Patricia had 13.8 per cent of her total height, 1.3 per cent of her total maximum weight, and 1.8 per cent of the maximum mental age toward which she was growing. A better impression of the relative progress of the various growths may be had from presenting these data in graphical form, Figure 16. Such a presentation high-lights differences in the maturational progress of various growths.

TABLE XXIII

PER-CENTS OF DEVELOPMENT OF VARIOUS GROWTHS AT TEN-MONTH INTERVALS[1]

Chronological age	Aspects measured			
	Height	Weight	Mental	Academic
10	13.8	1.3	1.8	....
20	30.1	4.2	4.6	....
30	46.3	9.0	9.2	....
40	58.3	15.0	15.5	....
50	66.2	20.8	23.0	....
60	70.9	25.9	30.9	....
70	73.7	29.9	38.7	....
80	75.6	33.1	45.7	.06
90	77.5	36.9	51.9	13.0
100	80.3	38.6	57.1	38.8
110	83.6	48.9	61.4	48.4
120	87.0	56.1	66.4	50.6
130	90.5	66.8	72.3	52.2
140	93.8	78.8	81.2	60.8
150	96.2	87.9	87.7	77.2

[1] Computed from "Score" equations.

E. THE OVER-ALL ORGANISMIC DESIGN

Olson with his "organismic age" curve, and Gesell with his graphical picture of the child's development give some credence to the idea that total development can reliably be pictured. However, if various growths proceed in a developmental pattern as described in Figure 16, there can be some question as to the justification of reducing these to a single curve representative of all four growths. Such a method, suitably worked out, does, however, provide an opportunity to appraise total development and to note likenesses and differences with the curves of other children.

Our purpose here in participating in this practice is to demonstrate a utilization of growth-age equivalents as originally proposed by Olson, and to raise the question as to the need for refining the single-cycle development curve popularized by Gesell, which generally has gone unchallenged.

In the procedure to be followed it was necessary to reduce all data to age equivalents. Consequently the "Age Equivalent" equations were selected and worked through for values from 10 to 150 months of age. These are shown in Table XXIV. It will be noticed that height- and weight-growth ages are much greater than

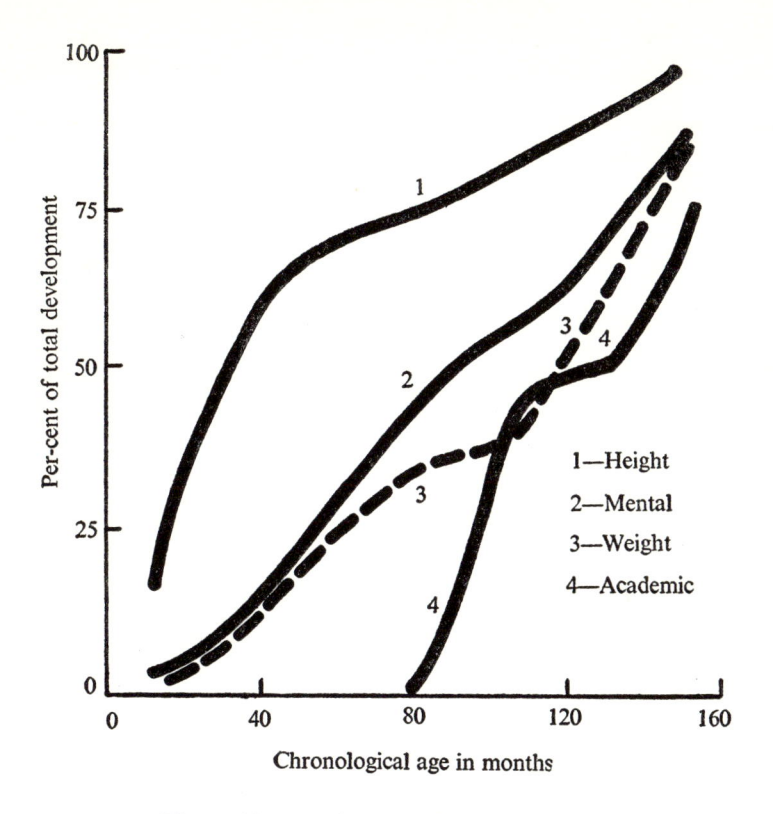

Figure 16. Maturity Curves of Various Growths

1—Height
2—Mental
3—Weight
4—Academic

the others and result in an "average" also greater at each age level than either the mental or the academic values.

Regardless of the undue influence of height and weight, the "average" data retain a proper developmental design when presented in graphical form, Figure 17. The curve is characterized by a three-cycle display with an abrupt ending to the early-childhood cycle. This is caused by the fact that the academic age at 80 months is low enough to produce a slight lessening in the average from what it was at 70 months where academic data were not available. The second and third cycles merge with less interruption in the over-all maturational picture.

Another way of handling the data is to organize them in terms of percentages of development. Such a method tends to rule out the gross effects of any extreme growth and reduces the ensuing curve to a kind of picture that is less misleading in making interpretations or in comparing one child with another. Table XXIV carries in the last column a listing of percentages of development of the average

TABLE XXIV

GROWTH-AGE SCORES AT VARIOUS CHRONOLOGICAL AGES
(Computed from age-equivalent equations)

Chronological age	Growth ages					Pct. of[1] (average) development
	Height	Weight	Mental	Academic	Average of all	
10	9.1	3.2	3.2	....	5.2	2.6
20	22.0	11.8	7.9	....	13.9	7.2
30	38.2	25.7	15.8	....	26.6	13.3
40	53.6	44.5	26.5	....	41.5	21.1
50	66.2	64.0	39.2	....	56.5	29.4
60	75.7	81.2	52.6	....	69.8	36.4
70	82.6	95.2	65.8	....	81.2	42.4
80	89.0	103.7	77.7	54.2	81.1	44.5
90	97.1	117.5	88.3	81.0	95.9	52.6
100	107.8	134.8	97.1	95.4	108.8	59.7
110	119.6	151.1	104.5	102.1	119.3	65.4
120	130.8	169.1	113.0	105.0	129.4	71.0
130	143.5	190.1	123.0	106.8	140.8	77.2
140	159.4	206.8	138.3	115.6	155.0	85.7
150	173.1	217.2	149.1	127.3	166.7	91.4
Maxima	194	228	170	137	182.2	....

[1] Pct. of development computed by dividing the average value by the average maximum.

growth age, at ten-point intervals, to the average of the various maxima. A graphical representation of these data is shown in the following figure and was used in preparing the curve introducing the various chapters in Part One.

Here is presented a somewhat smoother picture of all growths merged together. Such a representation reflects the true characteristics of growth—its cyclic manifestations, a slow beginning in each cycle followed respectively by rapid growths and a slowing down to a definite maximum.

This portrayal is undoubtedly the best that can be produced in describing the total development of the child. It is highly individualistic with respect to beginning and end points of cycles. It has undoubtedly some aspects of universality, but this can be verified only by further study of this kind on the basis of case analyses in which the type of technique illustrated here is applied. The most significant contribution of this presentation is, generally speaking, the design that it gives to the developmental process. In this respect it differs greatly from those presented by other authors, but it finds validation and reliability in the concepts

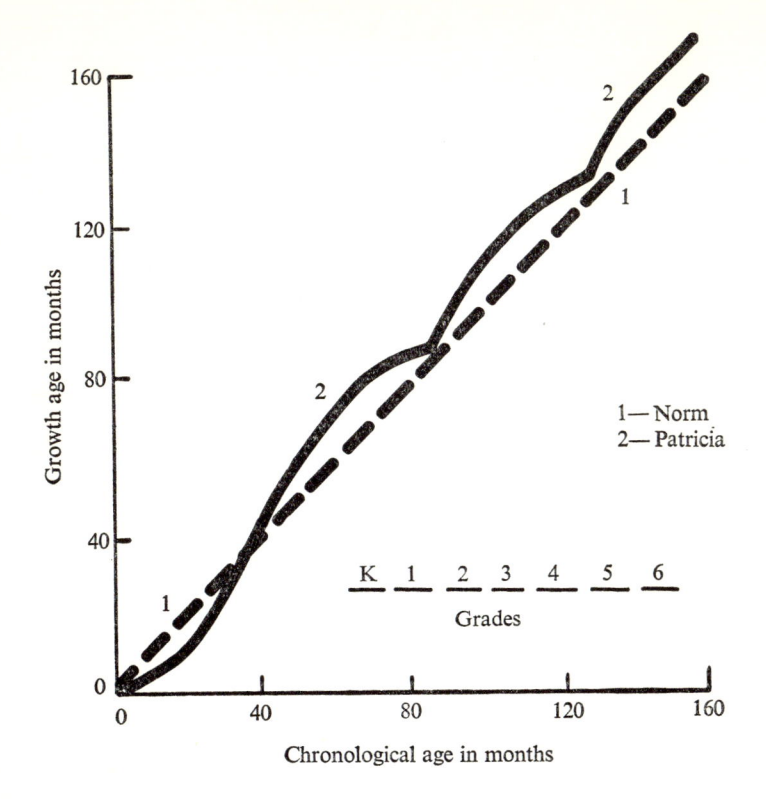

Figure 17. Organismic-Growth Age Curve

and generalizations which are universally supported as to the inter-relations and dependence of one growth upon another in the developmental pattern. Here may be found a merging of concept compatible with statistical method, along with supporting data for refinement of concept and generalization as to how children grow and develop.

Selected References

S.A. Courtis: "Maturation Units for the Measurement of Growth." *School and Society*, Vol. 30, 1929, pp. 683-90.

W.F. Dearborn and J.M.W. Rothney: *Predicting the Child's Development*, pp. 213-37. Sci-Art, Cambridge, Mass., 1941.

Arnold Gesell and Frances L. Ilg: *Child Development*, pp. 60, 88, 131, 159, 188, 212. Harper, New York, 1949.

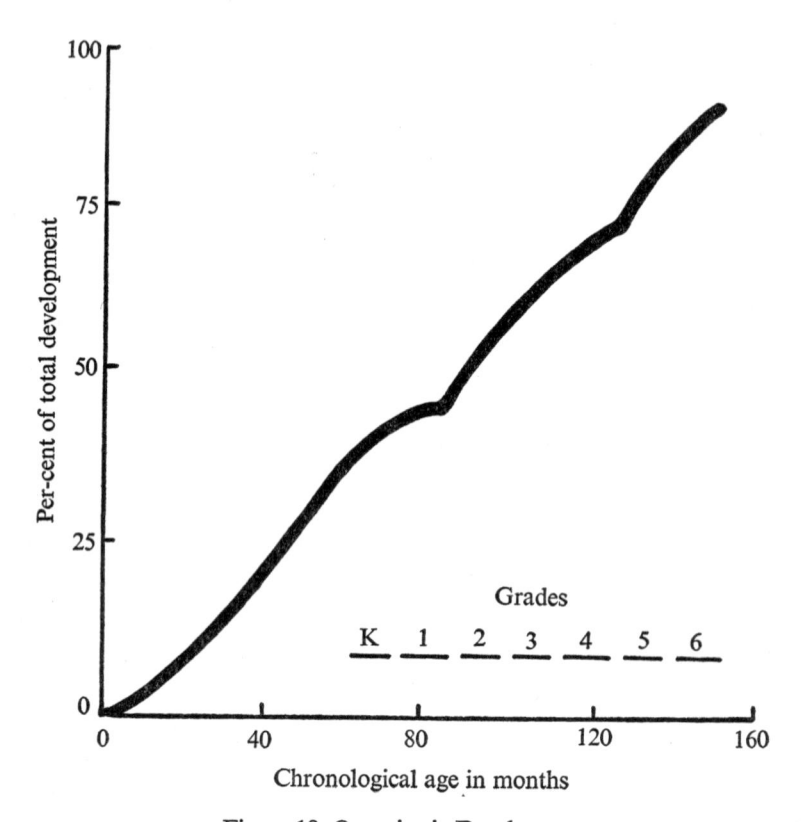

Figure 18. Organismic Development

C.V. Millard: "The Nature and Character of Pre-adolescent Growth in Reading Achievement." *Child Development*, Vol. XI, 2, 1940, pp. 71-114.

C.V. Millard: *Child Growth and Development in the Elementary-School Years*, pp. 30-54. Heath, Boston, 1951.

T.J. Nally and A.R. DeLong: "An Appraisal of a Method of Predicting Growth." Child Development Laboratory, Series II, No. 1. Michigan State College, East Lansing, 1953.

W.C. Olson: *Child Development*, pp. 163-91. Heath, Boston, 1951.

Chapter XII

DEVELOPMENTAL DESIGN—SOURCE FOR THE DISCOVERY OF PRINCIPLES OF GROWTH AND DEVELOPMENT

A. Procedures in Child Study

1. Introduction—General Purposes of Child Study

a. SIGNIFICANCE OF CHILD STUDY

THE STORY of Patricia as it has been revealed in the preceding pages indicates that the process of child study is much more meaningful and far-reaching than the mere activity of testing or measuring children. Test and measurement devices are likely to be directed only toward the determination of quantitative observations. Child study in its broader implications is characterized by efforts to evaluate the child's attitudes, his character and personality, and his ability to get along socially with others. It is also most fundamentally concerned with the child's stage of maturity and the relation of these to his environment. And lastly, it has a responsibility for doing something with the data collected. In this concept child study is much more than an academic or purely scientific or objective fact-finding activity. When all possible data are collected and assembled, generalizations must be made, hypotheses formulated, and corrective programs initiated. Child study in the broader sense does not stop even here. A remedial or corrective program initiated by diagnosis demands re-study and re-evaluation, new generalizations, new approaches, and as long as the child is available, the same cycle of activity over and over.

b. PURPOSE OF CHILD STUDY IN THE SCHOOLS

The most important purpose of child study is to improve skills for guiding and aiding children to a richer and fuller life. Realization of such a purpose demands collection and interpretation of data on individuals and on social groupings. Ideally, it requires information related to all aspects of child behavior.

A second purpose is to make available factual and scientific data for determining whether the school, along with the environmental setting in which it is found, is making its greatest possible contribution. Stated another way, information obtained on the child is used to determine whether the school is doing most efficiently what it professes to do. Although information pertaining to the child may be used in many ways to improve his situation, correction and follow-up should be directed primarily toward enriching the environmental effects. All growth and development proceeds smoothly and harmoniously when the organism is placed in favorable surroundings.

2. *Current Child-Study Approaches*

a. DESCRIPTION OF STATUS

In handling the data on Patricia considerable attention was given to status appraisal—comparison of this child with others *at a given time*. Very little in the way of profile evaluation was utilized. This is the kind of status appraisal that compares an individual on several sub-points in relation to a norm.

Most standardized tests provide an opportunity for individual profile presentation. Where a battery of several tests is used it is possible to plot scores on the sheet and connect the points forming a line which will fall above or below the norm as the case may be.

The advantage of an analytical procedure of this kind may be found in its facility of handling and the ease by which an interpretation can be made. In view of considerable risk of error in a single testing, and in view of the fact that such an analysis shows nothing of the progress of the child, this kind of technique, although very popular, must be given a low rating as an instrument for child study.

There are many evaluation devices of this kind. By using the generally accepted classifications of percentiles, standard deviations, or quartiles, it is possible to plot deviations of individual intelligence, achievement, aptitude, personality traits, behavior ratings, etc., in relation to a standard. A line drawn at a fiftieth percentile or zero point usually represents normal performance. A line drawn between the points on the scale representing the child's several performance scores provides a comparison with the norm in terms of acceleration-deceleration units.

b. THE LONGITUDINAL APPROACH

Both the Olson and the Courtis methods have been used in this book as tools for longitudinal study and need no further description. In a rather broad sense the utilization of these methods permits comparison of performance with the child's own norm. Such handling of objective measures provides an opportunity to make broad over-all comparisons of growth and consequently diminishes the necessity of piece-meal analysis which utilizes norms and highly questionable statistical interpretations.

In general the longitudinal approach provides an opportunity to make generalizations regarding growth and learning with much more reliability than is possible through the use of age-grade norms. The longitudinal approach likewise promises better returns in evaluating factors affecting growth. The Harvard Studies, the Iowa Studies, and many others reported in the Monographs of the Society for Research in Child Development often employ this method of investigation. Undoubtedly the future will see greatly increased activity on the part of teachers in the use of this procedure as they receive improved technical and professional training.

3. *Specific Study Devices*

Those carrying out a child-study program must not lose sight of the fundamental concept of child development. Any child represents a completeness, a one-ness, perhaps better described as a wholeness of growth and development. Within himself each individual is a complete organic unit. He functions in all his life's activities as a unit. When observers talk about physical growth, mental growth, intellectual growth, etc., they are referring to only one aspect of this unity. Mental growth, for example, cannot take place without accompanying physical growth, emotional growth, or social growth. All of these unfold and mature together. Consequently no single growth can be fully appraised without giving consideration to all others. Likewise, when one talks about reading scores, physical measures, intelligence measures, he cannot with any scientific substantiation deal with one to the exclusion of the others.

Child life moves through several developmental periods. When the child is born one cycle of development comes to an end most dramatically, and a new one begins. Throughout the several periods of development many changes occur which reflect themselves in changed velocities of growth. All the while however there is a uniform reflection of the total developmental pattern. One growth cannot show a change in velocity without some kind of accompanying change in some other phase of development. And likewise the kind of growth that goes along uniformly in one cycle of development has a relationship with the kind of growth that is to come in a later cycle. Although current research is at best at a somewhat elementary stage in arriving at methods for predicting the velocity of growth that will take place from one cycle to another, a certain fundamental unity underlies the total pattern from birth to maturity.

The facts on growth have significant implications for the student of child development. The child must be studied in relation to what he was and to what he will become. And further, because of the individuality of growth, it must be remembered that each aspect of development and each cycle under consideration is not only important as data in themselves revealing something about the child, but is also significant in interpreting other growth manifestations not at the moment under consideration. This means, for example, that data showing emotional maladjustment should lead the investigator to a consideration of physiological growth curves, the placement of the individual in agreement with them and their regularity or irregularity of progress. And as a further illustration, it may be pointed out that the character of a height curve can provide assistance in interpreting the reading or mental-growth curve of a child. Employing concepts as these, it should be obvious that classifications of study techniques and categories of child-study activity are justified only on the basis of convenience.

a. RATING SCALES

Aptitude tests, personality measures, and social-economic status measures are only a few examples of the devices now available. Most measures of this type limit themselves to defining status, either that of the child's environment or of certain aspects of his personality.

Aptitude tests show great possibilities. However, they should be used with caution, particularly when they are based on the theory of a constant potentiality. There exists no completely valid evidence that growth and development themselves are not factors producing shifts in the pattern. The errors made in the use of intelligence tests provide an illustration of the disrepute that follows broad utilization on a faulty premise. At present it is debatable whether aptitude tests measure special abilities or whether they measure the result of previous conditioning and experiences of the child. Only further experimentation will answer this question. Generally speaking, aptitude tests have not been developed to be administered early in the child's life and to be repeated at later time sequences for the purpose of determining the maturity or experience effect on a trait or skill. If potentiality of this kind is something that responds in a developmental fashion to experience and maturity, tests must be devised to demonstrate such a relationship.

This whole group of tests at the present time cannot be employed in the usual longitudinal manner or used effectively in determining maturities. Nevertheless, they have some value in supplementing longitudinal approaches. For example, although they cannot depict growth, they can aid in defining the conditions under which growth takes place. For this purpose they have significance and may be used from time to time, often enough that a testing may be available at the time a shift takes place in the growth pattern. To be specific, economic change depicted and verified by a social-economic status measure could be used as evidence to explain a deviation in a growth pattern that was something more than a natural developmental manifestation.

b. CHECK LISTS

One may question whether this classification is any different from the one just discussed. The reasoning back of the separation is that attention thereby can be centered on such relatively new instruments as the "time-sampling device." This instrument provides the observer with an opportunity to record how frequently in a given unit of time a certain type of behavior may occur in a specifically defined situation.

Such techniques, relatively new and not too generally used, offer possibilities for growth treatment to the extent that diminishing scores or frequencies of "undesirable" actions indicate increasing maturity;—or, conversely, to the extent that positive aspects of behavior can be observed longitudinally their increase can be assumed to reflect a growth effect.

C. ACHIEVEMENT AND INTELLIGENCE TESTS

The best known and the most widely used measuring instruments are achievement and intelligence tests. Achievement tests have been developed for a wide range of subject-matter classifications—reading, spelling, arithmetic, language, English, science and a host of other categories.

Many of these, including a number of intelligence tests, lend themselves to cumulative treatment. They may be administered repeatedly at convenient and *appropriate* times as different but equivalent forms, and the ensuing scores plotted as curves.

For those interested in longitudinal testing an important point may be made. Caution should be exercised in the selection of tests in relation to the need for repetition over a period of several years. Only those should be selected which are represented by several forms, and when found satisfactory, should be used throughout the school career of the child during those ages for which they were devised. Graphs of cumulative-testing data produce the most authentic pictures of growth when the data have been obtained from the same battery of tests throughout a given growth period. In other words, unless special circumstances dictate, reading tests should not be changed every year or two. Obviously, only those tests should be selected which have sufficient equivalent appropriate forms so as to provide adequate rotation. The point of the suggestion is to the effect that a shift from one battery of tests to another obviates the possibility of accurate graphic representation due to differences in difficulty of the tests, items used, etc.

In spite of many criticisms the standardized intelligence test has value in a child-study program. Most of its criticisms are pointed at its misuses. Others may validly be pointed toward the hypothesis upon which they are constructed, namely, that intelligence is constant and unchanging, or they may be pointed toward the neglect of the fact in their construction that mental age unveils itself through a multi-cyclic pattern of growth. Much, also, has been made of the fact that interpretation generally is dependent upon a "status" analysis. In spite of all these criticisms the data collected are helpful when properly used. The approach taken with the data on Patricia hints at a more authentic and more powerful avenue of analysis.

Perhaps a word is pertinent regarding the comparative advantages and disadvantages of the individual versus the group intelligence test. It is fairly accurate to say that the advantage, generally cited for the individual testing, springs from the differences in training of persons respectively using the two types of tests—the individual and the group. Trained testers are more likely to be found among those employing the individual intelligence test whereas almost any teacher feels that he can administer the group test if he follows directions carefully. If this is true it would appear that the teacher rather than the test gives the individual test its granted greater prestige. It must be admitted however that with trained testers in both situations the individual test still has advantages. The conditions under which it is given are much easier to control and the results thereby obtained tend to be more reliable. Another advantage, and one that is really significant in a school situation in which breadth of study is desired, is the interview opportunity offered. It cannot be denied that the individual mental test provides a setting for a general interview and for noting individual personality reactions.

Group testing is quite satisfactory when the time for frequent individual testing is not available. It would not be bad policy, nor does the suggestion conflict with advice previously given, to insert occasionally an individual testing in a group sequence. Intelligence tests seem to be more uniform in their construction than achievement tests. As a result, individual and group tests can be more satisfactorily intermingled than can two different achievement tests in the same specific area of measurement.

d. PHYSIOLOGICAL MEASUREMENTS

Health and physical growth information are obviously necessary in a child-study program. Physiological data are not only valuable for appraising this particular aspect but are of assistance in providing essential data for analyses of other aspects of development. In this connection height and weight measurements render an important service. As testimony we cite the cycle break in the height and weight curves of Patricia which were closely pursued by the rise of her academic-learning curve.

Less readily available but of similar significance are data on the eruption of teeth, grip strength, carpal growth, and motor growth. Information of these kinds is necessary for ascertaining growth inter-relationships involving the physiological patterns and for obtaining general developmental signs.[1]

e. MISCELLANEOUS MEASURES

Other scales and inventories are on the market for use in child-study programs which do not readily lend themselves to classification under the categories previously mentioned. These include techniques for evaluating interests, for determining adjustment status, appreciations, attitudes, social and economic background and status, belongingness, and sensitivity to social, moral and ideological problems. Scales of these types are constructed for securing supplementary data on current status and to a considerable degree as aids in appraising deviations in the over-all development of the child. In the main they lack potentialities for cumulative testing and thereby are sterile by themselves for use in appraising

[1] Carpal, grip and teeth-eruption data would have greatly strengthened the validity of the maturity picture shown by Patricia.

f. JOURNAL RECORDS

A productive device for use in a child-study program is the Journal Record. The Journal represents the best possible subjective instrument for supplementing and clarifying objective information. A test score out-of-line in a graphical representation may be explained by information obtained from Journal data. In addition, the Journal furnishes valuable data in its own right. It can be used to set up hypotheses concerning, for example, the impact of the child's personality on others. Such usage represents a value not found in any other technique. Since Journals may be used cumulatively they provide a running story of a given child's behavior. Four different approaches in techniques of writing have been identified:[1]

1. *Evaluative statements:* Anecdotes that evaluate or judge the behavior of the child as good or bad, desirable or undesirable, acceptable or unacceptable................
2. *Interpretative statements:* Anecdotes that account for or explain the child's behavior, usually on the basis of a single fact or thesis.............................
3. *Generalized statements:* Anecdotes that describe certain behavior in general terms, as shown frequently, or as characterizing the child..................................
4. *Specific or concrete descriptive statements:* Anecdotes that tell exactly what the child did or said, that describe concretely the situation in which the action or comment occurred and that tell clearly what other persons also did or said....................

Regardless of the approach taken, Journal Records furnish a variety of descriptions about children in specific and diverse home and school situations. Putting these together in order to bring to light a pattern of behavior is often difficult. Nevertheless, if well done, the pieces of the puzzle are often at hand and thereby furnish the opportunity for significant interpretation. When such is the result, Journals contribute greatly toward understanding the basic personality pattern of a child. Personality characteristics often remain obscured with nothing but symptoms presenting themselves to the observer. A continuing barrage of Journal Records as the child matures often succeeds in unearthing the real personality. In the case of Patricia this goal was not achieved to a high degree since Journals were obtained primarily in a restricted academic situation.

g. CASE STUDY

In its increased attention to individual children and by its utilization of the longitudinal approach, education is giving renewed attention to the case-study method. Case study has been used in a variety of settings. Probably one of the first professional training agencies to employ this technique was the school of law. Here it supplemented a method of instruction utilizing a series or number of "cases" as problem material for the purpose of identifying general principles. It

---

[1]Prescott, Daniel A., and Others: *Helping Teachers Understand Children*, pp. 32-5. American Council on Education, Washington, 1945.

received similar usage in the school of medicine and recently has been adopted by some schools of business and commerce.

Case study as applied by social workers requires diagnostic, therapeutic or remedial work carried on to bring about better relationships between the individual and his environment. Case study so employed requires a comprehensive, exhaustive appraisal. It is this latter concept that generally has appealed to teachers and others working in the schools. This viewpoint requires a paralleling of "case work" with "case study." While the child is being observed something must be done with him, and while something is being done with him, he must be observed. A case study then does not necessarily constitute the last word.[1] At best it is an estimation of progress with all documentations thereto attached. As applied in school, the teacher will be giving advice, proposing and trying out "treatments", etc., while still in the process of collecting basic objective facts and information. Case study in the preferred manner is a device for bringing assistance to the child as seen necessary.

The case study reports data and proposes tentative conclusions. It makes recommendations and records results. Consequently it draws from divergent sources its data and its observations. In its earlier days and particularly among teachers whose source of data was limited, the case study depended chiefly on interviews. This is not as true today. Current exponents of the case-study approach do not show so much dependence on this technique as formerly. This does not imply that personal contact with the child is not worthwhile. It is only to emphasize the idea that all evidence should be given consideration and that none should be depended upon exclusively.

The broad concept of child study as discussed should not be taken to preclude less comprehensive handling of a child's problem. Some problems require only short abbreviated observation and study. For example, a certain child may be having difficulty in reading. If the child is in the first or second grade, examination of the instructional program might point out that there is little relationship between the offering and the needs of the child. Attention should then be directed toward a change in program. If it is discovered that the child happens to have an organic reading difficulty, observation would point it out and steps could then be taken for its solution. The point to be made is that when solution of a problem has been accomplished, the case can be concluded temporarily without instituting a complex and elaborate study of the individual and his environment. It is essential, however, that when brief informal studies have been completed they should be recorded and made available for possible more comprehensive later study.

---

[1] A case may be considered complete only when the child is no longer available for study. Final statements and interpretations may then be made.

B. Some Problems of Child Study

1. *The Statistical Barrier*

Almost all well-known studies of children defend the idea that significance and scientific reputation depend upon the adaptability of data to statistical handling and interpretation. As a result of this viewpoint, interpretations abound with norm comparisons, standard deviations, correlations, significance of differences, and the like. Much is thereby learned about averages but little about growth as it takes place in a single child. Something of a revolt to this concept is indicated by increased interest in case study which has gone to the other extreme of considerable dependence on interpretation from subjective data.

The particular problem of the statistical hurdle has been of concern to investigators of children for a number of years. Gruelich analyzes the problem as follows:

Not the least obstacle in the furtherance of this study is the conceptual apparatus of analytical science which has for so long insisted that all scientific problems be stated in terms of the relation between two variables as revealed in the data obtained from a large number of subjects. The great prestige and fruitfulness of this tradition cannot long prevent the recognition that there are other important scientific problems the study of which in no way denies or rejects the analytic knowledge and methods of analytic science for this newer problem of organic growth and development, as seen in the life career of an individual organism moving through time, students of this problem are finding support in the studies of quantum physics, in the concept of relativity, the organic conception, and in the concept of "field", wherein individual structures and events are to be seen, not as isolated items in a casual sequence, but rather as components in an organized whole that cannot be dismembered or analyzed without jeopardizing that organic whole.

Gruelich not only protests the domination of the analytic tradition in research schemes clearly inappropriate for its utilization and thereby providing a block to the development of techniques that might be more applicable, but likewise sees in the devotion to it some reason for the dearth of conceptual frameworks of analysis. He says:

The conceptual framework for a study of organic growth and development is still to be created, since at present we have only a few tentative attemps at stating the problem and enunciating the theory of organic growth and development.................

It is significant that today, there is no adequate formulation of physiological development and maturation, largely because of the preoccupation with purely analytic questions and morphological changes.

2. *The Longitudinal Versus the Status Approach*

GENERAL ADVANTAGES OF LONGITUDINAL STUDY

Frank, perhaps better than most, has summed up the significance and general problem of longitudinal study. What he says is of tremendous importance since it finds so little application in the field:

Up until recently it has been assumed that one could study the growth of an organism or any of its constituent parts or functions by examining large groups of children of different age periods and aggregating the observations and measurements of this large array of subjects. Relatively smooth graphs have been constructed from such multiple collections of cross-sectional data and they have been regarded as offering an essentially valid delineation of the growth process..

In the intervening period various studies have shown that when, in place of these large statistical aggregates, attention is focused upon the growth sequence of single individual organisms over a period of years a somewhat altered picture emerges. Some established quantitative findings have begun to yield the modification and amendment, as shown especially in the Harvard Growth Study,[1] which showed not only how the longitudinal picture differed from the cross sectional, but also that chronological age categories produced large distortions and errors in the picture of growth and maturation.

Experimental methods are being developed to reveal the peculiar, idomatic growth and functioning of the individual and increasingly attention is being given to the pattern or configuration of responses given by individual subjects to standardized test procedures and experimental setups. Instead of statistically derived norms for a group, the individual's own growth curve may be used as a norm.

Macfarlane has done an equally fine job in analyzing the advantages of longitudinal study but in addition points out specific difficulties and problems in its usage.

We chose the longitudinal as opposed to the cross-sectional procedure, feeling that the former offered us possibilities for more valid comparisons between early and later environmental factors, behavior and personality characteristics. If offered us possibilities for measuring the persistency of patterns completely lacking or inadequately available to cross-section methods. Obviously much less has to be assumed in comparing two-year-old behavior with six-year-old behavior if we are dealing with the same children at each grade level. Obviously contemporaneous records are more accurate than retrospectively obtained histories. Yet one must be aware of certain basic difficulties in a longitudinal study which encompasses a growing psycho-biological organism in a shifting environmental setting.

First, there is a dilemma of choice between fixed and flexible procedures over a span of time. Certain procedures appropriate at one grade level become inadequate or inappropriate at a more mature level...
Moreover, one becomes aware during a cumulative study of important trends which were not systematically sampled by the initial plan or which represent developmental emergence. And one is faced with omitting new leads which appear fruitful, or with introducing procedures to tap such phenomena................................

Second, a frequent source of infertility in developmental studies is that a routine established may go on without evaluation or without check upon its productiveness. It is true of course that the pertinence of much data cannot be established until the presence or absence of relationship to later behavior is ascertained...................

Third, large environmental changes of the nature of shifts in cultural mores may be exerting unmeasured or unmeasurable influences—for example, propoganda on parental practice external to that of the study may have exerted considerable influence over a

[1] Original Harvard Growth Data now in the custody of the Child Development Laboratory, Michigan State College.

period of years—and the longer the longitudinal study the more change would be expected...

Fourth, in such an undertaking as this the very process of clinic contacts influences the group and to the extent that the study is successful it becomes an increasingly influenced group as the years go on.

Fifth, the shrinkage of sample, either through loss of rapport or moving from the community, over a long period could easily disturb cumulative records.

3. *Types of Longitudinal Study*

Dean C. V. Good's *Dictionary of Education* defines the longitudinal approach as "the continuous record of growth for one individual, as contrasted with cross-sectional views of growth". The most limiting aspect of the definition lies in its reference to the growth of one individual. If cumulative record taking rather than number of cases is the key to its meaning, then there are several different types of study approaches.[1]

The Continued-Measurement Series: Most of the well-known studies conducted by special agencies such as clinics at universities, Child Welfare stations, the Harvard Studies, the Antioch series, etc., are of this kind.

Studies under this classification are quite restricted to objective data—height, weight, grip, etc. Data may be directed toward a study of individual differences, the computation of averages at continuous age or maturity levels, or a combination of both. Particular studies under this classification are the following:

(a) HARVARD GROWTH STUDY[2]

In the present study the basis of classification is age at the close of the year of maximum growth in standing height. This method of grouping cases, unlike classification by menarcheal age, may be applied to both boys and girls. The present study, accordingly, is concerned with the growth patterns of the two sexes and of groups of cases with early or late growth spurts in standing height. The repeated physical measurements on 1553 cases collected by the Harvard Growth Study constitute the basic data.

(b) THE BRUSH FOUNDATION STUDY OF THE GROWTH AND DEVELOPMENT OF NORMAL CHILDREN[3]

This volume contains a summary and a careful statistical analysis of the anthropometric

---

[1] According to Stuart, Monog. of the Soc. for Res. in Child Development, Volume IV, Serial No. 20, No. 1, p. 2, the term longitudinal is used to denote continuing or repeated studies of the same children in contrast to cross-sectional studies of different groups of children at specified ages.

[2] Shuttleworth, Frank K., *The Physical and Mental Growth of Girls and Boys Age Six to Nineteen in Relation to Age at Maximum Growth,* Monog. of the Soc. for Res. in Child Dvelopment, Volume IV, Serial No. 22, No. 3, 1939.

[3] Simmons, Katherine, *The Brush Foundation Study of Child Growth and Development, II, Physical Growth and Development,* Mon. of the Soc. for Res. in Child Development, Vol. IX, Serial No. 37, No. 1, 1944.

Also see Ebert, Elizabeth, and Katherine Simmons, *The Brush Foundation Study of Child Growth and Development, I, Psychometric Tests,* Monog. of the Soc. for Res. in Child Development, Vol. VIII, Serial No. 35, No. 2, 1943.

data from the Brush Foundation study ... data are based on observations made on a rather homogeneous population of children over a period of years ... (p. xvii)

Regular Series children were examined at 3, 6, 9, and 12 months of age, then at every six months until and including the fifth birthday and thereafter at yearly intervals, at or near the birthday. By an examination is meant a visit by the child to the laboratory where he was measured anthropometrically, roentgenographed (6 areas, hand, foot, elbow, knee, hip, and shoulder), and examined psychometrically. At the same time a health history covering the examination interim was obtained.

The Regular Series does not then comprise one group of children examined from infancy through adolescence. It was preferred that children be enrolled at the age of 3 months and a larger number was enrolled at this age than at any other, but as stated above, some children were permitted to have their first examinations at any age up to 14 years and new enrollments were made throughout the program's duration. Altogether, 999 Regular Series children, 515 boys and 484 girls, were given 9,182 examinations, the number of examinations ranging from 2 to 17 per child, averaging 9 ... (p. 1).

... There is no single series of measurements from 3 months to 17 years; there are, however, cross-sectional data over this entire age range and there are discrete longitudinal series of adequate numbers overlapping segments of this age range. Obviously, the cross-sectional data are not truly cross-sectional since at every age except 3 months by far the greater proportion of the children measured were also among those measured at the next earlier age and the next later age. Nevertheless, the personnel of our cross-sectional age groups did change from age to age to the extent that at age 11 years there was no child measured who was measured at 3 months. It seems however that our sampling method kept our enrollment losses to a minimum of randomly selected individuals and that it ensured the comparability of children enrolled early and late in our program ....

Cumulative Multi-Observation Series: This category designates studies which use all kinds of data. Continued measurements tend to provide over-all direction but every opportunity is taken to supplement the objective continuum by using status measures, environmental evaluations, and the purely subjective appraisals.

In reality there are two branches of the main category. One is the case study and the other is the *program* approach. Illustrations of the case study are Jones, *Development in Adolescence,* and in many respects the material presented in this book as a study of Patricia. Both of these blend available estimates of the child into a picture of an emerging pattern of development.

The *program* approach might be found in a school system, research center, or child study clinic. *Program* does not commit itself to a specific limited type of operation but instead issues reports of various kinds of researches. Studies that might be so classified have been carried out at the following centers:

(a) INSTITUTE OF CHILD WELFARE, UNIVERSITY OF CALIFORNIA[1]

Methodological aspects of longitudinal study of personality development in a normal group of children. Essentially clinical in nature, this study purports to be different in

[1] Macfarlane, Jean W., *Studies in Child Guidance, I, Methodology of Data Collection and Organization.* Monog. of the Soc. for Research in Child Development, Vol. III, Serial No. 19, No. 6, 1938.

that it attempts cumulative observation of "contemporaneously developing adjustive patterns" in a normal sample rather than the unravelling of the antecedents of already developed maladjustment. The group studied, 252 children and their respective families, was selected from inhabitants of Berkeley, California.

Data collected covered the years from birth to age eight. With respect to each child, circumnatal data and systematic cumulative records of physical and mental development, regime and illness have been secured as well as records of personality development. Data on personality and behavior patterns were secured as seen through the eyes of parents, siblings, teachers, classmates, the child himself, and the clinic staff. Likewise, shifting, family and situational data have been cumulatively recorded.

(b) PSYCHOLOGICAL CLINIC AND THE DEPARTMENT OF CHILD HYGIENE, HARVARD UNIVERSITY[1]

A clinical and exploratory study of the growth of the "whole child", an investigation of numerous factors of different types, with special attention to how they become organized in the individual and to how this organization changes as the child grows. Subjects were forty-eight children between the ages of 5 and 14 years, 43 of them over a three year period. Physiological, intellectual, personality and environmental aspects furnished the areas of study. The main concern of the research was to study each of these variables in relation to the others.

In order to learn something of how the individual child changes in time our procedure was mainly to compare portraits—formulations of the whole—made at different times. Some such comparisons were made for the periods within the three-year study, e.g., a child as he was at the beginning of the study and that child as he was at the end of the study; other comparisons brought into account periods—as reconstructed from biography—before the study began, e.g., early childhood. In addition, single variables or groups of variables were sometimes abstracted and studied longitudinally in attempts to reveal the manner of their development. . . . .

In the present research we hace studied sequences by both longitudinal and cross-sectional methods. But our special concern has been with the more fundamental relations among intra-individual factors, so that we could see with some clarity what were the conditions under which age changes occurred.

(c) THE CENTER FOR RESEARCH IN CHILD HEALTH AND DEVELOPMENT, HARVARD UNIVERSITY[2]

The scope of the research activities at the Center is very broad and deals with the problems within or impinging upon many different disciplines. The project has become a coordinated research in the borderland fields of human biology and has as its central theme the more precise understanding of the phenomena of human development and their relation to problems of child health. Although there has been emphasis on problems of health and fitness, an attempt has been made to explore, in so far as possible, all

---

[1]Sanford, R. N., and Others, *Physique, Personality and Scholarship*. Monog. of the Soc. for Res. in Child Development, Volume VIII, Serial No. 34, No. 1, 1943.

[2]Stuart, H. C., and Staff, *The Center for Research in Child Growth and Development, School of Public Health, Harvard University, I, The Center, The Group Under Observation, Sources of Information, and Studies in Progress*. Mon. of the Soc. for Res. in Child Development, Volume IV, Serial No. 20, No. 1, 1939.

major aspects of development in the same children and all forces which may have a bearing upon the developmental progress of these children.

The principal research objectives of the center have been:

(1) to add to the available knowledge concerning the changes which occur in man during the period of growth; (2) to determine the differences in these changes in nature, extent, or time of occurrence, as manifest by different individuals; (3) to discover the relations which exist among these differences in themselves; and (4) to discover the relation between these differences and known experiences in the past lives of the individuals. The cross-sectional norms resulting from these studies are considered a by-product which should prove of interest and value. The objectives are being carried out by persons with very different training and by use of a great variety of procedures, but in all cases on the same children and in so far as possible at the same points in chronological age.

(d) THE BERKELEY GROWTH STUDY[1]

The Berkeley Growth Study is one of several long-term developmental investigations comprised in the research program of the California Institute of Child Welfare.

The problems investigated have dealt chiefly with mental, motor, and physical development, observed from birth and with the plan of continuing to maturity. The program of psychological study is essentially descriptive, involving (a) the assessment, seriation, of each individual's status in the group in a wide range of characteristics, (b) the study of trends and other age variations in status, and (c) the analysis of certain correlated factors. While interest has not been directed primarily toward personality nor toward attempts at the detailed intepretation of growth dynamics, considerable use has been made of qualitative observations and of material from interviews in addition to the more largely quantitative records. . . . .

Each child was brought to the Institute for a series of tests and observations at one-month intervals from birth to fifteen months, at three-month intervals from fifteen to thirty-six months, and at six-month intervals thereafter. Some additional visits have been made at irregular intervals for group observations or to collect material for special purposes. Below are listed the principal categories of data:

Mental Tests
Motor Abilities
Reflex Functions
Physiological Measurements
Anthropometric Measurements
X-Rays
Photographs
Pediatric Examinations
Emotional Reactions and Personality
Rating Scales
Projective Techniques
Home Interviews
Field Excursions

[1] Jones, H. E., and Nancy Bayley, "The Berkeley Growth Study". *Child Development*, 12, No. 2, June 1941, 167-173.

C. Principles Demonstrated in the Record of Patricia

The two previous sections have been presented with the purpose of sketching the full horizon of approaches to the study of children. They also serve to show that the total field of endeavor is much broader than the range of activities employed in arriving at an understanding of Patricia. It may be said, however, that many of the techniques described were utilized in this analysis. The main departure from the over-all ideal was the fact that the material presented on Patricia represented in fact a "post-mortem" analysis although the data utilized were collected as "live" observations. Thus judgments as to inadequacies in the environment or in the school program were entirely subjective, although reasonable, and not testable by the criterion of changed circumstances in its effect on the child.

One of the outstanding contributions may be found in the comparative maturity patterns shown in the preceding chapter, and the illustration of principles of growth and development which emerged throughout the entire study. The latter are summarized in the following sections.

Growth is Both Quantitative and Qualitative: Patricia well illustrated the point that growth is quantitative, that is, that the increments of growth increase with age. Physiological measures of height and weight became increasingly greater as she became older. Her mental age increased, her achievement scores, with a few marked regressions, showed higher grade levels as she progressed through school.

Illustration of a qualitative characteristic is more difficult. Quality usually refers to a position or relationship, i.e. one quality is better than another. The employment of the word here is one that designates *performance as more reliable at one time than another*. It is a word chosen to distinguish one test performance from another, during a plateau period, when there has been no quantitative increment. Patricia, for example, showed little or no increase in height and weight between 70 and 80 months. This was no accident! Her unfolding developmental design included a rounding-off period towards a definite maximum at this time. Although neither height nor weight showed increases, she was at 80 months a girl quite different from what she was at 70 months. There was undoubtedly a consolidation and integration of growth processes during this time which was necessary before she could travel quantitatively on a new growth cycle. Mental growth and academic growths showed the same characteristic. To the extent that any part of the cyclic manifestation can be characterized as a time for an inner organismic integration of forces, growth can be said to be qualitative.

Growth Is Continuous: This means something more than the mere fact that growth accompanies chronological age—the older the child the greater the magnitude. It also means something more than progress without a break. Basically it refers to two quite distinct characteristics.

The first of them is well illustrated by the data presented on Patricia. Continuous, in this sense, means that growth followed a definite pattern with very little deviation. The fact that all data were reducible to equations, with an average deviation of only 2.4 months from a perfectly smooth mathematical curve, may constitute documentation for this point. Regardless of what went on in her environment for seven years, regardless of the variation in teaching from grade to grade, regardless of the onset of adolescence, etc., she plodded along in a very definite and precise fashion.

The second point can not be illustrated with data at hand. This point employs the word "continuous" to indicate that where frustrating factors (illness for example) depress growth from its natural design, there is a return to it when the frustrating circumstances are removed. If Patricia had such experiences, losses and recoveries were made in between the testing periods and consequently were not detected.

Growth Is Individual: There is no possibility of illustrating the principle of individuality with the data of this study when proof of individuality requires comparison. Since only one case furnished the data, comparison is out of the question.

Nevertheless the equations computed on Patricia, and the comparative maturities portrayed in chapter eleven provide a picture of individuality which cannot be questioned. Starting points of the various growth processes, ages at which she arrived at her various maxima, and the specific rates of growth assigned her by the equations were definitely those of Patricia and of no one else. The technique by which these were derived had no dependence on comparative growths and consequently did nothing to distort the picture of individuality. If any other child possessed the same growth rhythms and relationships, this was entirely coincidental.

Growth Is Modifiable: Modification refers to deviations in the growth pattern. This means that there is a possibility of bringing about a shift in the growth pattern when environmental factors are changed. As noted previously the data showed no deprivation. Nor did the Journals indicate enrichment procedures. It was evident that nothing of this nature occurred in the school. The records, although casual, probably were sufficient to judge likewise that no such enrichment occurred in the home enrivonment.

The Cyclic Nature of Growth: The data on Patricia illustrate beautifully the cyclic nature of growth. In the case of height and weight, three cycles were demonstrated. Mental age presented two cycles, and the academic-learning curve likewise followed this pattern. Outstanding was, of course, the narrow age range between which all curves manifested the emergence of adolescence. Likewise significant was the relationship between the pre-adolescent upsweep in height and weight closely followed by the beginning of the pre-adolescent learning curve.

Growth and Learning Are Complementary: Certain implications may be drawn from the data regarding the relation of the physiological curves to the emerging learning curves. Teachers generally regard height growth as a physiological phenomenon and academic learning as the result of school activity alone. Actually in the data on Patricia we have an illustration of the idea that physiological growth and academic learning are parts of the same process. They maintain a relationship with each other throughout the entire time of the child's development. Witness the proximity of the cyclic breaks in both the physiological and the academic pre-adolescent and adolescent cycles!

The maturing individual grows and learns at the same time. For this reason it is at present absolutely impossible to measure accurately the effect of teaching with conventional tests. We have no way of separating the effect of teaching from the effect of maturation by the use of the common devices. Most teachers are unaware of this point of view. They commonly evaluate learning (or teaching) in terms of differences in test scores. What is being measured is not growth or learning, but both growth and learning currently inseparable from each other.

D. Evaluation and Summary

There are both weaknesses and strengths in the approach to an understanding of a child as presented in this book. Let us consider first its limitations.

1. *Limitations*

From the standpoint of the criteria developed in the two previous sections of this chapter, illustrated by the descriptions of outstanding child-study efforts, there are several limitations. These are:

(a) A 'post-mortem'—contains no record of improvement efforts and their effect;
(b) Study of the child contained no carry-over into the school program;
(c) Infrequency of testing periods;
(d) No clustering of observation and testing periods with reference to key maturity stages—hypotheses emerged but with no opportunity to test them.

(a) *No record of diagnostic and remedial efforts:* The story presented in this volume on Patricia represents exclusively a laboratory reconstruction of her emerging personality documented by longitudinal measurement and observations, plus a familiarity with this child through year-to-year contact with her. There was no attempt to relate emerging understanding of this child to instructional programming.

It is not too difficult to decide at what points the routine of data collection should be interrupted for preliminary analyses and prognoses. For the child who is obviously a problem, special attention should be given at any point in the growth sequence. For the "average" child who presents no special problem, tentative analyses may advantageously be provided at the end of the second, fourth, and sixth grades. Remedial treatment, better called an improvement program, could then be initiated at two-year intervals to be carried out along with the continued program of child study. The question of whether gains made, at the end of the two-year periods, could reliably point to treatment as the dominant factor in the situation is not so important as the question of whether the child finds himself in a continuously improved environment. Nevertheless, a comparison of progress made at different periods would give some clue as to the effect of a special factor.

The time sequences suggested are important. Near the end of the second grade the child should be well started on his pre-adolescent (childhood) maturity patterns. Data at this time would ascertain if this was so, and, if true, could be used to estimate anticipated projection up through the third and fourth grades.

Continued measurement would indicate the reliability of the estimate and would be used to plot growth through these two rich developmental years. Appraisal at the end of the fourth grade would provide estimates of the anticipated time of the approaching "levelling-off" period. End-of-the-year evaluation at the sixth-grade level would result in appraisal and correction of the earlier estimates, along with an accurate computation as to time and effect of the manifestation of adolescence on the various developmental patterns. A study as done on Patricia along with a record of bi-annual correction, appraisal and prediction would come close to representing an ideal situation.

(b) *No carry-over into the school program:* As stated above, there was no carry-over into the school program of the implications of the collected data. Since the school district was handicapped by limited funds, little of general enriching activities was provided for the children. Arts and crafts for a short period of time promised to develop but were over-shadowed by demands for housing and consequently shrivelled into a non-consequential offering.

A more striking neglect, or perhaps we should say an area of cooperation between data collection and instructional procedure more easily activated but ignored in this case, was school reports. Teachers continued to write the banal type of letter saying, e.g., that "Patricia should study harder", etc., in spite of evidence that she was growing normally and learning in accord with her evolving developmental design.

(c) *Infrequency of testing periods:* The data on Patricia fell too easily into definable growth designs. More testing periods would have been advantageous in determining whether this was a coincidence as the result of measurements which could be fitted nicely to a curve or whether the measurements obtained were reliable appraisals of true performance.

Earlier mental testing would have given full documentation as to the question whether mental age rightfully was a two-cycle growth affair, or whether it would have been demonstrated by three-cycle growth as was the case for both height and weight. This deficiency would suggest that in such a situation cooperation between home and school sufficient to bring pre-kindergarten children to the clinic for semi-annual measurement and observation would contribute greatly. The opportunity so offered would sharpen the preciseness of the maturity estimates and would enable investigators to predict within accurate limits the time at which academic achievement (reading, spelling, etc.) would become a natural part of the child's developmental design.

Likewise, more tests as soon as the child showed the first signs of adolescence would have resulted in predictive authenticity of the time of beginning of growth in this cycle.[1]

(d) *Lack of clustering of testings at significant maturity periods:* As indicated in the paragraph above, frequency of testing is essential near the beginning and the end points of cycles. The question of overlapping—the effect on the child of maturing in two cycles of development contemporaneously—and the way it affects different children is most significant with reference to emerging personality patterns. Obviously, increased frequency of objective measurement at this time must be accompanied by increased frequency of behavior ratings and personality measures. Only by such practices may the hypotheses suggested in the grade-six characterizations of Part One be adequately probed.

2. *Contributions of the Study*

There are three main contributions which this study brings to the literature. They provide:
 (a) an illustration of principles of growth and development as seen quantitatively;
 (b) several new hypotheses as to the effect of maturation itself on the behavior pattern of the child;
 (c) evidence of existence of a technique for a closer approach to revelation of growth inter-relationships.

(a) *Illustration of principle:* Research in child study whether it be a regular part of the school program or a laboratory experiment should be organized around principles and hypotheses as to how a child grows and develops. Many studies fail to be so oriented and consequently end up as pleasant but rather bland expositions.

The story of Patricia is quite the opposite. The exposition begins innocently enough without hypothetical or principle association. This was done in order to provide a simple picture of Patricia without arousing prejudice and without arousing a challenge before the main facts were established.

The concluding chapters, however, arrive at the point of maximum challenge. It is believed that data, although not novel as to type, have been presented in a fashion that is entirely new and thereby challenging to all who deal with hypotheses and principles of development. It is our belief that all serious presentations in the child-study field should rise to the height, at least, of challenging imagination and creative thinking as well as exposing important cause and effect relationships.

(b) *Several new hypotheses:* There are two main hypotheses brought out by this study. Discussion of the first is found in the section dealing with the sixth-grade

[1] As computed by the equations.

eleven-year-old child. The problem revolves around the question of the amount of maturity achieved in pre-adolescence at the time of the beginning point of the adolescent cycle. Related to this hypothesis and secondary to it, but part of the same problem, is the question of the effect on behavior when the adolescent cycle considerably overlaps the pre-adolescent cycle.

The second hypothesis may be found in Chapter XI. It was pointed out that at given ages there are definite ratios between maturities of physiological, mental, and academic growth. The question raised is that of the matter of universal relationships. In a previous study[1], it was discovered that three quite different children demonstrated similar developmental inter-relationships. For example, all three reached a 36.9±1.3 per cent of maximum mental growth before the academic curve began to manifest itself. Patricia, likewise, fell within a similar relationship between these two aspects of development. Other ratios showed greater discrepancy but within a reasonable range of the ratios found among the three other children.

(c) *Illustration of a new technique:* Although perhaps somewhat difficult to understand, the technique demonstrated in Chapter XI has the potentials for the kind of pin-pointing of relationships between various kinds of growths which is necessary for a complete understanding of child development.

Up to this time it has been possible only to say that "various kinds of growths are inter-related", or to say that "the child shows a natural evolving design." Courtis has provided a method by which "growth design" can be specifically defined. Without this aid none of the hypotheses mentioned would have emerged. It is also believed that only through the use of this technique can any orderly investigation of such ideas be probed.

Selected References

S.A. Courtis: "Maturation Units for the Measurement of Growth." *School and Society*, Vol. 30, 1929, pp. 683-90.

W.F. Dearborn and J.W.M. Rothney: *Predicting the Child's Development*, pp. 213-37. Sci-Art, Cambridge, Mass., 1941.

L.K. Frank: "Research in Child Psychology: History and Prospect." *Child Behavior and Development*, R.G. Barker, J.S. Kounin, H.F. Wright, eds., p. 10. McGraw-Hill, New York, 1943.

Arnold Gesell and Catherine S. Amatruda: *Developmental Diagnosis*, p. 349. Hoeber, New York, 1952.

W.W. Gruelich and Others: "A Handbook of Methods for the Study of Adolescent Children." *Monographs of the Society for Research in Child Development*, Vol. III, Serial No. 15, No. 2, p. xv. National Research Council, Washington, 1938.

[1] See C. V. Millard, *Child Growth and Development in the Elementary-School Years*, pp. 40-50. Heath, Boston, 1951.

Jean W. Macfarlane: "Studies in Child Guidance, 1. Methodology of Data Collection and Organization." *Monographs of the Society for Research in Child Development,* Vol. III, Serial No. 19, No. 6, pp. 7-8. National Research Council, Washington, 1938.

C.V. Millard: *Child Growth and Development in the Elementary-School Years,* pp. 30-54. Heath, Boston, 1951.

T.J. Nally and A.R. DeLong: "An Appraisal of a Method of Predicting Growth." Child Development Laboratory, Series II, No. 1. Michigan State College, East Lansing, 1953.

Daniel A. Prescott and Others: *Helping Teachers Understand Children.* American Council on Education, Washington, 1945.

Appendix

EXCERPTS FROM THE JOURNALS

FIRST-GRADE OBSERVATIONS

General Attitude: Patricia's attitude to those around her seems to be one of indifference. Her attitude toward her work however is one of earnestness. She sticks with it until she has completed it, looking up only a few times. She is attentive to her teacher. When she is talking Patricia sits quietly and listens.

Physical Health: Patricia seems to be very healthy. She has had measles and chicken pox. She doesn't seem at all run down and has a very healthy look about her. She is about the right height and weight for her age and she has a lot of pep.

Work Habits: Patricia works by herself and does all her work promptly. She has the hardest time with her reading, and yet she likes that better than any other subject. Her attention span is fairly long. When she becomes tired or distracted she gazes around for a while before going back to work. She is very neat about taking care of her materials and equipment. She hands all her work in on time and it seems well done.

Social Status: Patricia is definitely not friendly with the other children, that is, she doesn't giggle with them or act silly. Nor does she look as though she wanted to. She frowns a great deal and appears rather disgusted with them at times. She is not disliked and they do not pay much attention to her. I think, perhaps, the fact that she is Syrian makes her this way. She is probably close to her family and feels no need for outside friends. She is by no means snobbish, but more or less indifferent.

SECOND-GRADE OBSERVATIONS

1. *Fall-Quarter Observation*

Report Card: The following letter was sent to Patricia's parents in November of this year.

Dear Parents: I wish to report at this time that Patricia is doing very well in her classes. However, I would like to see Patricia work a little harder on reading.

Patricia works and plays well with the other children.

Sincerely yours,
Miss——

(No answer from parents)

Handwriting Lesson: This lesson consisted of using the grade spelling list to make sentences. Patricia had to do hers over. According to her teacher when youngsters begin to think of themselves as older than the rest they write smaller than they should at this age. Patricia did just that with her first paper. Also, she made several mistakes with her sentences.

General Work Attitude: Patricia was definitely not interested in her seat work. Late in the afternoon her group was called to the front of the room to read and Pat was unprepared.

Patricia pays more attention to the rest of the room than she does to her own work. She is not too interested and frequently wastes the whole afternoon. On another day she paid but little attention to the lesson in the Weekly Reader and ate candy when the teacher was not looking. She seems to "flutter" when walking or moving about.

Clothes: Patricia has been wearing the same dress every Thursday, every week. Today however she had a new coat. It seems that she belongs to the "Brownies." She often wears the uniform. From seeing Patricia every week I imagine that she doesn't have many clothes. Those she has are always messy and inclined to be soiled. Her hair looks as though it had never seen a comb.

Playground: On the playground she is active—running and jumping. She is ignored to a certain extent but she tries to be one of the group. Strangers (observers) do not confuse her particularly. In fact she likes any attention she gets.

General Summary: Patricia is a good child but is not industrious. From all appearances she hasn't much of a home environment. Her teacher has little time and too many pupils. Pat appears to have little desire to learn.

2. *Spring-Quarter Observation*

General Observation: Pat seemed to be doing her work but spent a great deal of time gazing around and getting up and sharpening her pencil. During the reading class she was attentive.

Playground: While playing outside Pat didn't try to mix with the group. One of the other girls gave Pat a shove and she hit back. Once I tried talking to Pat but she refused to speak and ran away.

Seat Work: Pat spent all of her time today just gazing around. First she would chew on her pencil and then look around at the other children. When working on the sentences assigned she would really be engrossed but this lasted only several seconds.

Pat took the opportunity to go up to Miss——to tell her that several of the children were creating a disturbance in the back of the room.

Reading Group: In her reading class Pat follows the book very faithfully while other children are reading. She is anxious to read orally but none of the group will choose her until all others are chosen.

When she finally gets the opportunity she displays a very pleasing voice, reads well, but does not seem to comprehend what she is reading. She appears to be nervous when reading aloud and shows this by bending stiffly at the waist.

Personal Interview: Today I went with Pat to a vacant room to discuss what she liked, disliked, and to attempt to draw Pat out.

At first she was nervous, moving her hands continuously and sitting on the edge of the chair. Later however on the playground she became relaxed and friendly to the point of slapping me on the arm and saying, "Hi, kid."

When asked about school Pat said that she liked reading best of all but doesn't like seat work that she has to do. She said she would rather sit and look around. It is a very rare thing for Pat to finish her seat work.

Extra class activities don't interest Pat at all. A great many of the girls in her grade belong to the Brownies. Pat went to a few meetings and then decided that it was all "baby stuff". I believe the real reason for her quitting is that she couldn't make friends with the girls.

Pat said that on school nights she is allowed to stay up until 10:30. Summers are usually spent in just playing around the house. One week each summer the family goes to a cottage. According to Pat this makes all happy except her mother who says that the rented cottages are dirty.

I asked Pat if she liked school. She said, "Yes, I guess so!" I asked her if she would keep going to school if she didn't have to. Again the answer was "Yes." When asked why, she said that she should learn as much as she could.

In spite of her inability to make many friends, Pat seems to be a happy child. It would seem that her peer situation will improve with some help. Her family with its foreign culture will probably hinder somewhat Pat's social development. This can be overcome by Pat herself if she has a strong desire to do so.

THIRD-GRADE OBSERVATIONS

Spring-Quarter Observation

Report Card: The following letter was sent to Pat's parents on November 1.

Dear Parents: Patricia has shown good improvement in following school regulations such as going home promptly after dismissal. She also is taking care of herself in the room much better than she did at first.

She has been tardy once and absent one-half day.

She is doing very good work in 3rd-grade subjects. Her reading is good except she repeats herself. If she can stop repeating herself, she will read more smoothly. Her arithmetic work is very good. She works fast and is quite accurate. Her writing work is good, but she should write larger. In spelling, her final scores are a little less than her trial scores. She should study more to correct this. She expresses herself quite well in art.

Sincerely,
Miss——

(No reply—just the father's signature)

A second report was sent to the home on January 17.

Dear Parents: Patricia's attendance record for the half year shows one tardiness report and seven and one-half days absence.

She is doing average work in arithmetic. If she would be a little more confident of her ability to work problems, she would get better scores.

In reading, her work is satisfactory. She could improve by reading more and by being careful to understand when she is doing exercises. She is doing good work in *My Weekly Reader*.

Her written work in language has been quite good. In writing she needs to be neater about her work.

Her spelling work is above average. On review tests she has had a little over half of the words right. To improve she can study harder.

Her interest in social studies is good.

I am sorry Patricia was unable to finish her Christmas art work. She wasted time when she was in school when she might have accomplished more.

Patricia is a good girl in school. If she would take better care of her own property and hustle a little more there would be no complaints.

Sincerely,
Miss——

Reply from parents:

Could Patricia please bring her school books home so that she can study at home? Thank you.

Mrs.——

A third report was issued April 4:

Dear Parents: Patricia did her best work in spelling. Her work in reading, health, arithmetic, and language is satisfactory. Her work in art was not so good, mostly because she did not do neat work in following directions.

She was tardy eleven times in eight weeks.

Patricia has been helpful in the room. She has made good gains in her work and behavior.

Sincerely,
Miss——

(No reply from parents)

First impression: My first impression of Patty was that she was a very quiet and shy little girl. In class, today, she didn't enter into the discussion at all but when the work books were passed out she settled right down and went to work right away. Only a few times did she look up from her work. Even during the confusion when the work books were passed out and everyone was talking, Patricia sat very quietly in her seat.

During recess we went out on the playground but Patty didn't seem too eager to participate in any of the games that were being played. I tried talking to her but she was quite unresponsive. She would answer my questions but would not volunteer any comment.

In the classroom, after returning from recess, she appeared to be a very conscientious little worker.

General Behavior in Room: Patty was wandering around quite a bit today. However, once settled down, she seems to work, is quiet and a good listener. Very seldom though does she participate in class discussion. I believe her teacher is partially to blame. She scarcely ever calls on her and Patty never volunteers. Therefore she does not appear to be very interested. Today Patty had a pencil which had a multiplication scale on it. She was completely fascinated by this little gadget.

Peer Status: Patty has a little chum in the room who helps her with her reading workbook. According to the second-grade observer Pat had very few friends. She seems now to have acquired more. She is very friendly with almost everyone. She has probably acquired more self-confidence during the past year. In fact she acts very much like a typical third-grader going through the giggle-stage.

Another Interview: Pat was acting very silly again today. While I was talking to her she giggled most of the time. She said that reading is her favorite subject but that she also likes spelling. She likes art even though she does not do too well in it. Patty was very proud of the fact that she had had a hand in the painting of Tar-Baby, a mural on the "Song of the South." She saw the movie and said that she liked it very much. In fact, she confesses to liking all movies.

In reference to vacation plans she didn't know what she was going to do except "play and have a good time."

Self-Consciousness: Today the third grade was practicing a play for their parents.

Patty was in several group songs. I noticed that she acted very self-consciously. She displayed several kinds of mannerisms—folding and wringing her hands, playing with her hair, etc. In two of the songs the children had to clap their hands to the music and I especially noted that Patty has an exceptionally good sense of rhythm. She never missed a beat.

Apathy: Also, today, and as I recall other days, I noticed that Patty acts as though she were in desperate need of rest. She wanders around at times with an indifferent attitude toward everything.

General Summary: Patricia is an average third-grade student but because of her Syrian parentage seems to have acquired an ethnic-minority inferiority complex. I believe that she has felt a separation from her classmates because of this.

If a stranger came into the classroom he would not pick Patty out as being particularly different from the rest. She is at most times a very timid, quiet and unpretentious-looking child possessing the same likes and dislikes as any other eight-year-old. She is somewhat over-weight for her age but this does not entirely distract from her cuteness—and she is cute. She has deep, beautiful, large brown eyes, long dark hair, and a rather dark, soft, smooth skin.

At first, this spring, on the playground, Patty did not participate too eagerly in games with other children. As the semester progressed she seemed to gain considerable status. I believe that her classmates are beginning to accept her more and more.

She still does not freely participate in class discussions. I did not hear her say one word in all of the afternoon sessions I observed. The teacher is partially responsible as she seems to favor a selected few and overlooks the others. Therefore a child like Patty receives very little encouragement and motivation.

In subject-matter learnings, Patty is average. Although she is best in spelling, reading is her favorite subject. She does well in writing when she takes her time but usually she is careless in the formation of letters. She is interested in social studies but is not exceptional in her work. This holds true also for art. Pat might do better if she were given more freedom to create what she feels. From my observations it would seem that the children are given very few creative activities. Everything was handled in a stereotyped fashion.

From talking to Patty I learned that she had two sisters, one in the sixth and one in the eighth grade.

FOURTH-GRADE OBSERVATIONS

Spring-Quarter Observation

General Observation: Patricia appeared neatly dressed in a cotton frock, clean, and not cheap. She had on red sandals, anklets, and her hair was combed in bangs with the rest long and curled. She did not readily make conversation with me but did answer any questions directly asked of her. She appeared somewhat nervous and shy and wiggled her hands and feet as we talked. She is a big heavy girl with pretty hands and beautiful brown eyes.

Habits of Work: In an art class the children were working on cutting out paper flowers. They were cutting out patterns and pasting them together. Patricia worked very slowly and without much interest. Her flowers were very small and not neatly done. I approached her and asked, "How are the flowers coming?" She shrugged her shoulders and said, "No good, I threw them away!" As the period ended Pat was still fussing around with her material. She was the last one to get her desk cleaned up.

She apparently didn't care if she finished her work or not and seemed relieved when her teacher asked her to stop and put away her things.

Her flowers being so small may reveal some personality trait—shyness and a sense of insecurity.

Small Satisfactions: In the course of the afternoon when the children were informally doing seat-work, Pat got out of her seat and walked up to the teacher's desk. She whispered into her ear and the teacher cut a piece of string and put it on her (the teacher's) finger. The teacher explained to me later that this was to remind her to bring some things for the Chinese exhibit which she had forgotten.

Patricia didn't appear shy in this little act. She was greatly pleased by the attention given her and returned to her seat with an air of great satisfaction.

Self-Conscious Again: During the period when the children were having some grapefruit juice Miss—— asked us to help. I paid no more attention to Patricia than to the others but did ask her how she liked it. She said, "O.K. but it is awful sour."

She appears very ill at ease as we try to get acquainted. She seems to be wishing, "Oh if it were only time to go home." She seems to be inside a shell and resents any attempt to bring her out of it.

Indifference to School Work: Pat seems quite indifferent to the teacher's story hour. All other children seemed quite interested as a story was read to them. Patricia, however, was bent over her desk with her notebook working very studiously at something. Occasionally she would look at the clock. She would thumb through the papers, stop and write a little, and then continue looking through the note book.

Aggressiveness Displayed: While I was waiting for the bus I saw Patricia come across the street. She rushed up to the intersection guarded by a Safety Patrol boy. She grabbed his stick and flag, and after a fight for it began to poke him with it. He could not readily retrieve it. Finally he did manage to get it back. Patricia at this point ran across the street, against the light, and kept running. It would seem that Patricia will not only fight when necessary but will frequently pick a fight.

After class today I talked with Miss——. She said that Patricia does not like to be called Pat or Patty. She said that she had talked to Patricia about Syrian foods and asked her to bring some recipes. Patricia did not seem interested and tended to shy away from the idea. Miss――says that Patricia is very hard to know and that it is very difficult to get a rise of enthusiasm from her.

Reaction to Attention: Today is Patricia's birthday. When we came into the room we immediately noticed a comic mouse on the blackboard holding a big card which said, "Happy Birthday, Patricia." Patricia however appeared to show little enthusiasm. While the children were playing Patricia sat back and didn't participate very actively. She would wait until several others had volunteered and then she also would volunteer.

When the children decided to play "automobiles," Patricia seemed to pep up and act more interested. She very eagerly wanted her team to run around the rows of desks.

When the children got into the music period and began to sing songs Patricia stood in the back row and tried to be inconspicuous. When the teacher asked for songs they wanted to sing, she showed signs of wanting to suggest one. Instead of volunteering directly, Patricia whispered her suggestion to the girl next to her. Finally the girl made her suggestion and Patricia was greatly pleased.

I feel that Patricia would like to take a greater part in group activity but is too shy. When her opportunity was past she would make a suggestion. When this was ignored she gave the appearance of boredness or indifference. When the children were singing Patricia didn't seem to know the words and just mumbled them. This might explain her desire to be inconspicuous.

Today being Patricia's birthday, several of the observers brought her a little book. Just before school was dismissed, we gave the present to her. Of course all of the class wanted to see what it was. The children crowded around her but Patricia didn't want to open the package. With urging from Miss――the book was opened. The class liked the book and Patricia said, "Oh, thank you!"

Patricia was pleased with the gift. She was quite hurt when a boy pulled on the ribbon and broke it. I believe she wanted to show her family the gift as it was originally given to her. She put the book in the package, carefully replacing the ribbon. She actually showed some emotion for a change. Usually nothing bothers her.

Further Pressures: One day Patricia was appointed among a group of others to pour out the grape juice for the children. This was being done during recess when the other children were out of doors. Patricia was quite messy in performing this task, pouring carelessly and occasionally spilling some. I happened to be in the room with the children. I asked Pat, "Do you help your mother at home?" Patricia said, "Yes." I then asked her if she liked to do this and she replied, "Oh, it's all right, I guess."

When the class returned Miss――asked several children to pass the juice out. When they had almost finished, they discovered that they didn't have enough. Some of the glasses were larger than others and the girls had poured more in these than in the smaller glasses. Patricia realized she had made a mistake. She apologized with an "Oh, I'm sorry, we had some left and filled them up full."

Patricia had tried hard to do what was right. She was proud to have done what she thought was proper but upon discovering her mistake she felt genuine disappointment.

Growing Aggressiveness: During the art class Patricia was cutting out a felt doll for a pincushion. She needed to borrow scissors. As she walked to the back of the room she roughly poked another girl. She seems to be acquiring a growing roughness in manner.

From an Interview: Pat told us that her mother only went to school through the second grade. At home Syrian is spoken for the greater part by parents. Pat can understand it but can't speak it.

Pat says that she intends to finish high school and that her father is saving money to send the girls to college. She thinks that she would like to be a teacher. When asked what she would like most, she decided that she would like a swimming pool in the back yard and would like to take a trip to Syria to see what it is like.

Her favorite actress is Yvonne De Carlo. She has no favorite actor. She likes Walt Disney movies and on the radio likes Baby Snooks and the Juke Box Review which is an afternoon program featuring the latest hit tunes.

Miss——is her favorite teacher since her beginning in school. Her best friends are her cousins. Sometimes when they visit her they laugh and talk in bed. She likes pets, especially dogs which she will take in preference to cats. Softball is rated very high and she likes to play any position. She has little interest in reading for she could not think of a book she had read aside from the one we had given her.

After school Pat goes to the store which was mentioned previously. The family eats dinner there. Punishment is given her in the way of curtailment of privileges. She receives no regular allowance but can have money as she needs it.

Pat was quite elated with the interest which we had shown in her. When we got back to the room a very interesting demonstration of foreign clothes was being presented. Pat paid little attention but dug through her belongings to find some samples of work for our journals. The interview which we had had was really the first occasion on which Pat had talked to us freely without continual prodding.

Miscellaneous Incidents: The minute we walked into the room Pat came up to me and asked to see the pictures I had taken of her the preceding week. After she looked at them she said she wished she had a picture of all of us. This seemed to me to indicate how much progress we had made in getting acquainted with Pat. She is a most friendly child once she gets to know a person.

When Virginia, the little girl in front of Pat, could not find her place in the spelling lesson, Pat got up and helped her locate it. Such rare occasions as this one seem to bring out another side in Pat's character.

FIFTH-GRADE OBSERVATIONS

Spring-Quarter Observation

First Glance: Pat has on jeans which did not seem to be worn by other girls. At no time during this first hour did Pat talk to her seat partner or to any of the children sitting in her vicinity.

Social-Science Class: Miss——was leading a discussion on Michigan when we came in. The topic dealt mainly with the Upper Peninsula, Mackinac Island, and the Straits. Most of the children entered freely into the discussion. Miss——told the children about a trip she had recently taken to the Island, along with some of its history.

Pat listened quite attentively to the discussion but she had no comments to make. Miss——asked the class a question about Michigan. Pat volunteered but did not seem to answer the question. She, apparently, merely wanted attention and recognition—perhaps from us. She kept looking back at us during the discussion. As the discussion proceeded she became less and less attentive.

Further Attention-Getting: In the spelling class which followed, Pat volunteered to pronounce the first word on the list and to put it into a sentence. She pronounced the word correctly but did not seem to find an appropriate sentence. She was attentive throughout the lesson and listened carefully to the sentences proposed by other children.

During recess period two of us had the opportunity to say "Hello" to Pat. Although she did not seem too involved in the play of the children she was very friendly with us.

General Interaction With Group: During the music class Pat sang along with the rest of the children but she didn't show much pep or enthusiasm. When the children requested some two-part songs certain girls in the grade got up to lead the others. Pat was not one of those selected.

On the playground, however, Pat showed more aggressiveness. She ran down to the swings, pushed the other girls in a friendly fashion, and proceeded to be very talkative. She was reluctant to come in, waiting until all others were entering before she left the swings.

During the period following Miss——read stories which had been written by various children. Most of the group enjoyed the stories, laughing a great deal. Pat listened attentively but was not amused. It later turned out that Pat had not yet finished her story. She promised Miss——that she would get it in tomorrow.

General Disinterest in School: When we came to visit the second time the children were working on geography. Pat was following the discussion rather carefully although she had nothing to say. She sat with her elbows on the desk casually watching. One of the boys was asked to read and Pat listened. As the discussion resumed Pat alternated between chewing on her fingers and sprawling in her seat.

Friendly and Mischievous: At the end of the social-studies period the children got up from their seats to put their books on the shelf. On the way back to her seat Pat picked up a leaf that had fallen from one of the plants on the window sill. She took it to her seat and showed it to the child next to her. After visiting a moment with him she placed it on the neck of the boy in front of her. He turned around and they laughed and talked together.

A Conversation With Pat. On our second observation as before we went out on the playground. Instead of playing with her group Pat was watching the sixth-grade girls play soft-ball. Another observer and I walked up to Pat and started to talk to her.

"Aren't you playing?" we asked. "No, I am just watching, this is the sixth grade playing."

"Don't the girls in your room play ball?"

"No", answered Pat. "They don't like sports."

"Do you?"

"Yes, I like all sports. Out at our store there is a vacant lot. We play ball there every night."

We inquired, "Why don't you get the girls in your room to play ball with you?"

Pat said, "I am going to bring it up at the next meeting when we talk about our trip to Canada, Detroit, and Greenfield Village."

"When are you going on your trip?"

"May 22," responded Pat very promptly.

We asked, "How are you going?"

Pat was very proud of her answer. "We're going to the depot and then take the streamliner to Detroit. Then we're going to take a bus to Canada."

We wondered about this and asked Pat, "How did you earn the money?"

Pat was well informed about this. She immediately answered, "Oh, we all put in, we've got $105.88."

"Is Miss——going?"
"Yes, and some of the mothers and Mr——."

Following this interview on the playground the children all came back to the room. Pat seemed restless and couldn't get organized for the class that followed. She went up to Miss——. Since we were sitting nearby we were able to hear the following conversation.

Pat, "May I go out and get a drink?"
Miss——, "Didn't you have one when the rest of the children did?"
"Yes, but it's so hot and I'm so warm."
Miss—— was quite unmoved. She answered, "If I let you go out then all the children would want to go out too."
Pat was persistent, "Just one, please?"
Miss——, "No!"

Pat went back to her desk and took out her Weekly Reader. During this discussion the other children were busy getting their readers out and didn't pay much attention.

The blunt "No" Pat received to her plea for a drink didn't seem to hurt her feelings at all. She accepted it and was not resentful.

Sociability Improving: An interesting incident occurred one night after school as the children were leaving. This incident seems to indicate a growing friendliness on the part of Pat toward other children, friendliness toward us, and further, it illustrates the natural reaction of children which would not be seen in the formal school class. The story follows:

Pat went to Miss—— and asked if she could stay after school and look at the "map." Miss—— said yes and then two other girls decided to stay with Pat.

The three girls each took a stick and began playing with them. I watched for a while and was puzzled. The girls still weren't looking at a map. So I went up to Pat (she was balancing the yard stick on her hand) and asked her,

"What map are you going to look at?"
She said, "Oh this one!", and unrolled one that was a map of the world.
"What are you looking for?" I asked.
"Oh, anything. We just point to places and name them."
With that she pointed to Syria and said, "This is where my mother and dad used to live. They lived in a small town there but I can't pronounce it."
"Can you try?" I asked.
"Not very well," Pat answered. "My mother told me one night but I still can't say it."

At this point one of the other girls pointed to Hamburg and pronounced it. They all laughed and said "Hamburg" again as if it were an extremely funny name for a place. When I left they were still having a good time with the map.

Need for Attention: The following incident, during our third day of observation (third week), deals with a typical afternoon and Pat's reaction to it.

The class was reading the "Golden Touch." First one child and then another was called on to read. During this time Pat was writing something. She was not paying any attention to the story at all. She seemed to be copying from one paper to another. I was quite surprised at Pat's behavior at this time. She is frequently restless but usually pays fairly good attention. Finally Pat raised her desk top, put away the book she was copying from, returned the pencil to Nancy's desk from which she had apparently borrowed it and took out her reading book. She found the story and gave it her attention.

Pat finally was called upon to read. When she was not sure of a word she would try to pronounce it and then look at Miss———to make sure that she was correct. She read very well and I was pleased to see that Pat tried to pronounce words before asking for help.

After she finished reading and answered a couple of questions she started to lose interest. Pat looked at the clock and around the room at the other children. Putting her head on her arms she deliberately ignored the continuing reading. Feeling a little guilty perhaps with her head still on her arms she kept the place but every now and then looked at the clock.

As the story period ended it was time for recess. Pat brought two pieces of paper to me as she was leaving the room. They were samples of her handwriting. This is what Pat had been working on when we first came into the room. It seems that Pat is greatly pleased when she can attract an interest toward herself. Apparently neither children in the room nor the teacher give her quite enough.

This point seems to be substantiated by her interest in and attention for me. As we were going back into the room after recess we had quite a conversation. I had heard Pat mention that she had a birthday recently so I asked her, "When was your birthday?"

She said, "Yesterday."

"How old were you?"

"Eleven", she answered.

"Did you have a birthday party?"

"Yes, but just a little one."

"Did your friends from school come?"

"No, just my cousins and a couple of girl friends."

At this, Pat grinned and said, "Oh, yes, I got three dollars and a soft-ball glove from dad and blue jeans and a plaid shirt from my mother."

During this discussion Pat kept one eye on the ball game. She would interrupt to yell, "Run, run", or "Throw it", "Hurry." She certainly is very interested in soft-ball and baseball.

When we walked back into the room I said, "Do you think Miss———would mind if I got a drink?"

"No, she doesn't care."

Getting inside the building we found a long line of children at the fountain. Pat went close to the front of the line and said, "Cuts!" The children let her in line and she beckoned for me to follow.

As we assembled in the room the children were all looking at the baby white rats which had been born a few days previous. I said,

"I think these babies are funny looking. Do you like them?"

"No, not until they get some fur on them," Pat answered.

Incidents of Disinterest in School: This particular day was very warm and the whole classroom atmosphere was relaxed and without much motivation although Miss——— was trying to interest the children in some informal activities. Making scatter-prints and oral reading took up most of the time before recess.

The oral-reading class was being conducted by one of the children. She called on the children in turn. Pat alternated between attention and complete withdrawal. At one point she went over to Miss———to watch her help some other children. On returning to her seat she was called upon to read but could not do so since she did not have her place. Someone else was then given her turn.

Increased Peer Status: Pat's general reactions seem to indicate increased peer status and group acceptance. The following incidents seem to lead to this conclusion.

Coming in from recess with the children I stopped to observe the silhouettes of some of the children which had been made in the art class and pasted on the board. As I was observing these Pat entered the room. When she saw me she came right over to where I was standing. I told her I thought I had found her silhouette and pointed it out to her. She said, "Yes," that was it. She commented however that it didn't look like her. As we were talking, some other children came over and joined in the discussion as to the resemblance of the silhouette to Pat. Most of the group were interested and it seemed to me by their interest that the children showed that they liked and respected Pat.

As the children were settling down Pat followed me to the back of the room where I was sitting. She seemed to want to talk so I asked her if she had any hobbies.

"Yes, I used to collect bottle caps but now Nancy and I have an ear-ring collection."

"How many ear-rings do you have?"

"Oh," answered Pat, "we just started a couple weeks ago. We only collect one of a pair, not both."

The class was assembled and our conversation was interrupted. Opening the period Miss———asked the children if they would like to sing some songs. The children agreed and several girls raised their hands to volunteer as leaders. Pat and two other girls were chosen. They went to the front of the room and faced the group. They led songs of their own suggestion and some suggested by the group. Pat really wanted to lead the singing but did so with little enthusiasm and considerable self-consciousness. There was no question however of her acceptability to the group.

Home Responsibilities: As I left the building and was waiting for our bus I had another opportunity to visit with Pat.

I asked Pat if she worked at her dad's store very much.

"Yes," she said, "I go there every night after school."

"What do you do there?" I asked.

"Oh, I burn the paper and bring in the buns. Then my sisters and I play in the gas station. My oldest sister drives the car up and my other sister looks at the oil and I fill it with gas."

I was surprised. "Can you really work the gas pump?"

"Oh, yes!"

Boy Friends: Just at this point in the conversation two boys rode past us on their bikes. They both called, "Hi, Pat!" Since I did not know the boys I asked who they were. Pat said that they were boys that often came to the store. This led to a discussion of Pat's boy friends. After some coaxing she let Nancy tell us that it was Roy. Then Pat herself told us that he was cute.

This incident pleased Pat. She liked the attention she received and was proud to acknowledge that she had a boy friend.

Apathy and Self-Consciousness: On our next visit we entered the room during the reading of a mystery story by Miss———. Most of the children were very engrossed, often uttering, "Ohs" and "Ahs". Pat was listening but without the enthusiasm of the others. During the latter part of the reading Pat turned completely away from the front and faced the back of the room where I was sitting.

Although Pat is very friendly with us, she didn't respond with any enthusiasm when I led some singing. Sometimes Pat sung and sometimes she didn't. Most of the children went through the motions I suggested but Pat didn't.

Sometimes Pat gives me the impression that she feels silly making these motions. Perhaps she is self-conscious because she is now so over-weight. Even so she is a very pretty child. When she responded at all to the songs she had very good rhythm. Although they are chubby Pat has very graceful hands and uses them considerably in her conversation.

Action Her Delight: On our next visit a game was played which really interested Pat. The game was called "Initial Tag". A boy would write a girl's initial on the board. The girl chosen must rush to the board, erase the initials and catch the boy before he got to his seat. Pat was chosen by Carl. Before she erased her initials she said, "Now where do I sit?" All the children laughed as did Pat. Although the children thought Pat was being funny she was really figuring out in advance the strategy she was to use. After she had her turn she began to be the life of the party. She would pretend to put a "hex" on the runners, or she would stand up and say, "And there they go around the bend"—simulating the Spike Jones recording. Pat really enjoyed herself and the other children really enjoyed her humor.

Improved Friendships: On the next observation the highlight was the planning going on in regard to the Detroit trip to be taken by the children.

Miss——asked the children to pick five that they would like to ride with them in their parent's car. Nancy, the first child making a selection, chose Pat to go with her. Pat was pleased and looked over at me and smiled. I was glad to see Pat chosen but felt sorry for the girls that were not selected until the very last. Of course, the selection here was based on friendships with the children whose parents were providing transportation and not necessarily on peer status in the total group. It would seem, however, that Pat's status has greatly improved during this year.

Teacher Reports: The following report was sent to her parents in November:

Dear Parents: I am happy to say that Patricia has done good work this past period.

She reads well and spells well too. She always tries to do her best and hands in her work well done.

Patricia has a most refreshing sense of humor. She is well liked by the group and is helpful and kind in the room.

Sincerely,
Miss——

From parents: I'm glad Patricia is doing well and hope she will keep it up.

A February report also carried a letter to the parents from Patricia:

Dear Parents: I'm doing good in arithmetic, spelling, and other studies too. Our student teacher is teaching us about weather and it is very interesting. I try very hard to do my work. I'm a very good citizen except for talking.

Pat

Dear Parents: Patricia is a very good citizen except for talking and visiting. She does nice work in all her subjects and I am quite pleased with her.

Sincerely,
Miss——

SIXTH-GRADE OBSERVATIONS

Spring-Quarter Observation

Reactions During First Observation: On my first visit to Pat's room the children were discussing courtesy and good behavior. The children took turns calling on each other to give examples of behavior. How to act during conversations on the telephone seemed to be the theme of the discussion. Pat was called on by one of the boys. She gave an example and answered several questions asked by the teacher.

Following this period the children took out their music books. Pat quickly offered hers to me with a "Please take my book." I thanked her and she returned to her seat. The teacher asked for suggestions on what song to sing. Pat immediately volunteered.

"Pat, will you start the song?"

Pat replied, "I don't know how to."

During the session that followed Pat pulled at her mouth, scratched her head several times and constantly shifted her position in her seat. She yawned occasionally. She was not singing and at intervals merely formed the words with her mouth.

Continued Disinterest in Music: Pat again showed a lack of enthusiasm toward music on my second observation.

While the other children were suggesting songs and singing them, Pat looked at the book but only now and then sang a few words. She kept time to the music by drumming her fingers on the desk top. Miss——walked up and down the aisles. Pat glanced from the book to her teacher. Occasionally Miss——stopped and put the syllables on the blackboard. Pat followed the syllables but hesitated to say them until after the first sounds were made by the rest of the children. Pat put her head down and supported it on her hands. She pulled at her mouth in this position. As Miss——played a difficult passage on the piano, Pat moved her fingers across the desk as if she, also, were playing the piano.

For one of the songs it was suggested that some of the boys should sing it. They went to the piano and Miss——drilled some of them on a tenor part. Pat laughed at them, then looked around, rubbed her eyes and yawned. A girl two rows over signalled a silent message to Pat. She sat up, looked at her book and started to sing again.

Two boys sang, "It Looks So Good in the Window". The rest of the room joined in on the chorus but Pat only sang a few words. When the group laughed about something, Pat was apparently thinking about something else.

A Typical Afternoon With Pat: After the music period it was time for history. The children took out their books and Miss——immediately started asking questions about trade routes during the feudal period. Miss——asked Pat where they were located.

Pat, "Most of them were by the sea coast."

Miss——, "Good, Pat, that's another one."

Later when the class was discussing monasteries, Miss——asked,

"What is a monastery?"

Pat, "They were where the monks lived."

Miss——,"What are monks?"

Pat, "I don't know."

Pat sat down seemingly embarrassed by not knowing the answer. The children were then assigned to read silently the next few pages. Pat read in earnest. I noticed that she formed some words with her lips as she read. Miss——called on her again and Pat was able to give the answer almost verbatim as it was in the book. Pat smiled as Miss——— praised her and then looked at me and smiled.

The children then went out for recess where they immediately started playing "dodge-ball." Pat participated enthusiastically, running and laughing with the others. On the way back to the room Pat walked beside me. I asked her if she liked playing games, and she said yes with a great deal of enthusiasm. She said that she especially loved soft-ball and baseball.

Her Teacher's Impression: After class I had an opportunity to visit with Miss———. She said that Pat is pretty well adjusted. She also commented on her personality. She said Pat was well liked and was considered somewhat of a clown with her spontaneous sense of humor. Miss———stated that her health was good and that she was a fairly good student.

To me, Pat does not seem interested in school except when she is reciting and then only because of the opportunity that it gives for gaining approval.

Repetition of Previous Reactions: Today was somewhat different in that Pat played more or less of a starring role. The reason? It was her birthday. On entering I immediately noticed that she was sitting at the side of the room opposite to her former seat. It appears that in this room it is more or less standard practice to change seats every month or so.

Miss———had written on the board, "Today is Pat———'s (Peaches) Birthday. Happy Birthday, Pat!" Miss———asked Pat to select the first song. Pat suggested that the children sing, "Zippy, No Biddiby, Bobbiby Bo." One of the children corrected her pronunciation of the song-title and she laughed saying, "That's right!"

As the children looked for further songs to sing, Pat found one and made some comment to the girl next to her. She then raised her hand and said, "Miss———, my father said that they used to march to this song." Miss———answered that she thought it would be a good song to march to.

When Pat withdrew from the center of attention she returned to her old pattern of slight boredom punctuated only by attention-getting gestures with a new birthday handkerchief. She sang a little but from a position in which she supported her head with her hand. In this hand she held the new handkerchief and occasionally waved it in the air in time with the rhythm of the music. Occasionally she would look at her new blouse and flick her fingers at a thread or bit of dust. She yawned several times in succession covering her mouth with the hand holding the handkerchief.

At another point, when Miss———was at the piano in the back of the room accompanying the singing, Pat turned in the opposite direction. She scratched her head, folded her arms, yawned and disarranged her hair. She became awake however with the next song. It required motions. Pat smiled and made definite sweeps and sharp movements with her arms. She even swayed with her body.

Following this period the children studied poetry. Miss———read and re-read a poem to the group. She then asked them to say aloud the last word in each line. Apparently she was trying to impress them with the rhyming element in poetry. Pat's performance wasn't exactly enthusiastic. She was slow in most cases, repeating the word only after she had received a cue from the others speaking slightly ahead of her. To a few of them she responded rapidly.

Miss———then decided to have the children write out the poem. She passed out paper to all the children. She wrote a portion on the board and asked the children to copy it as neatly as they could. In carrying out this assignment Pat rested her arm and hand on the desk and copied slowly.

The Observer's Reaction to Pat: I was quite interested in Pat's new birthday presents. She seemed very happy with them and took advantage of every opportunity to show them off.

Pat seems to have lows and highs of animation. Her weight is excessive for her height and age. I believe that her size more than anything else makes her self-conscious, restless and tired. This would seem to explain her yawning, resting her head, sitting side-wise in the seat, etc.

When Pat is the center of attention with the whole class, she seems alert and interested. When the group is working individually or working together on passive or sedentary activities, however, she shows little interest.

After school Miss——gave me Pat's report cards to look over. They indicated that she was well liked, enthusiastic, enjoying a variety of situations, and contributing to the group. She is regarded as an above-average student. She is strong in arithmetic and spelling. She could volunteer more in reading, social studies, and English. The reports indicate that Miss——is fond of Pat and her "sunny disposition." All of her reports were complimentary and indicated faith in Pat's abilities and potentialities. Some of these reports were answered by her mother. She said that she was glad to hear that Pat was doing so well and added that she would be glad to help Pat at home in any way she could.

A Busy Afternoon: On this particular day Pat seemed to show more interest, cooperation, participation, and proper role playing than in any previous day. The following series of events seemed outstanding. These show some apathy but in the main they indicate enthusiasm, interest, and good sociability.

As I came into the room Pat was working at the desk, her head and shoulders down, and her book on the upper right-hand corner of the desk. Pat took out a piece of paper and went to work quickly on her handwriting. When she had finished, before the other children, she picked up the work-book and held it above her. She looked at it closely, tapping her pen. Pat put down the book and looked for something in her desk. She moved her books, lifted several loose papers but did not find what she wanted.

The children were now through with their handwriting and Miss——asked them to take out the song books. Pat was indifferent at first. She looked around, pulled at her hair and sang a little. She pepped up when Miss——asked me to lead some songs. I taught the children the song, "I Went to the Animal Fair." Pat laughed along with the other children at the words and the different parts, and sang most of the time. Miss—— then asked for further suggestions. Pat requested, "Take Me Out to the Ball Game" and sang all the way through.

The children then took up their spelling. Miss——said that they might play "Hangman's Noose" with their spelling words. Pat contributed several times and kept her hand up in the air almost continuously, anxiously signalling her desire to be called on. She finally was chosen to lead the team. She jumped up and hurried to the board. She chose the word "mixed" to spell out. As she called on each pupil for a letter she jumped from side to side, and waved her finger in an exaggerated fashion at the children. She quickly wrote down the letters as they were given and then turned around and called on another pupil. Time was running out and both sides were fairly even. Pat was again chosen as leader. She moved rapidly with an excited manner. Children were yelling their answers and cheering from all sides. The other side won and Pat graciously accepted the defeat.

When the children went out for recess, playing various small group games, Pat joined the "keep-away" group. She entered into the game and eagerly snatched the ball. She threw it high and far. Becoming warm she stopped to wipe her face with her hand and to catch her breath. I asked her if she was tired, "Gee, am I!" she answered.

It seems to me that I have noticed a difference in Pat's reactions. She seems to be very nervous yet she speaks and acts with assurance. She seems to be gesturing more and using her whole body in expression.

Pat's energy seems to come in great spurts. In any physical activities she plays hard and moves quickly but almost immediately her energies are spent. She breathes heavily and perspires freely.

A Routine Afternoon: Miss——was telling a story when we came in. Pat was listening to the story with her head resting on her arm. Then she stretched out and laid her head on the back of her seat. Miss——asked a question concerning the story. Pat jerked around in her seat. A few seconds of attentiveness on her part followed. Then she laid her head back again and gave herself up to her daydreaming.

Miss——asked the children to take out their pencils and penmanship books. Pat complied and went to work quickly. Her head and shoulders were bent low over her work. She continued until her lesson was completed and then put her materials away. She gazed around the room and then began to bite her fingernails.

The other children finished and the teacher organized a discussion around the theme of the visit to the College Museum.

On answering the question as to what they saw, Pat replied, "They had some reptiles down there. A whole bunch of snakes and things."

Miss——asked, "Tell about the moulds."

Pat then described the moulds for making snake models. She repeated words several times and constantly gestured with her hands. Her fingers were spread apart and she waved them or shaped something with them. She also moved from foot to foot and occasionally twisted her body.

Following this lesson I was asked to teach the game, "Who Is Knocking At My Door". Pat enjoyed this, laughed heartily and clowned for the children when she had her chance.

At the end of the day when the children were dismissed Pat went out arm-in-arm with her girl friends. She seems to be a very affectionate child. Miss——speaks of this in contrast to her earlier behavior. Pat seems to have important social abilities. She can absorb and profit from criticism. Her fun, sense of humor, game interests, plus her sincerity are definite social assets which she can use in making friends.

If she could lose more of her self-consciousness and develop a group spirit to a larger degree, I feel that she would gain a great deal more poise and social stability. A direct attack on the problem might be made through encouragement to lose weight. This is a sore subject with her. She is very conscious of her size. Perhaps working on a clothes consciousness that would minimize her size would be helpful.

Pat's mother is very stocky so it is likely that heredity plus the starchy dishes prepared for the family are natural causes for Pat's weight. The children had a health discussion recently. As a consequence Pat decided to go on a diet. She told Miss——that she had already lost four pounds.

Index

Academic: picture, 113; STANFORD scores, 95; status, 15, 27, 38, 50, 62, 73
Achievement tests, 181
Adjustment profile, 145
AMATRUDA, C. S., 154, 196
AMES, L. B., 16, 29, 39, 52, 63
Arithmetic: achievement, 101; curve, 102
AVERILL, L. A., 154
BAILEY, E. W., 39, 52
BALDWIN, B. T., 93
BARKER, R. G., 29
BAUER, W. W., 16, 29, 40, 52, 63, 74
BAYLEY, N., 93, 190
BEAUCHAMP, M., 115
Behavior: and goal, 151; and personality, 151
BENEDICT, R., 154
BIBER, B., 29
BISHOP, E. L., 39, 52
BLACK, I. S., 29
BLAIR, A. W., 63, 74, 154
BLATZ, W. E., 65, 74
BLOS, P., 154
BONNEY, M. E., 29, 52
BOTT, H. M., 65, 74
BRECKENRIDGE, M. E., 79, 93
Brush Foundation study, 187
BURROWS, A. T., 39, 52, 74
BURTON, W. H., 63, 74, 154
California study, 186, 188, 190
Case study, 183
Character and ideals, 120

Check lists, 180
Child study: approaches, 178; journals, 183; problems, 185; purpose, 177; statistics, 185
CONRAD, H. S., 74
Constants, 165, 167
COURTIS, S. A., 93, 115, 165, 175, 178, 196
Creative ability (dramatics), 33
Cultural effects, 20, 65
CUNNINGHAM, R., 39, 52, 63
Cycle: early childhood, 164; growth, 192; implications, 151; overlapping, 66; PATRICIA, 166, 168
DEARBORN, W. F., 93, 175, 196
DELONG, A. R., 176, 197
Development, per-cents of, 171
Discipline: teacher domination, 7, 39; teacher-pupil relations, 140
EBERT, E., 187
Emotional behavior: characteristics, 126; effect of maturation, 12, 128, 152; reactions, 12, 25, 35, 48, 59, 70; theories, 124
ENGLISH, H. B., 52
Ethical-moral: behavior, 15, 29, 34, 39, 52, 62, 73; character and ideals, 120, 151-2; property respect, 22-3
Faculty (Ohio State University), 16, 29, 39, 52, 63, 74
FINLEY, M., 66, 74
FLORY, C. D., 94
FORREST, I., 16, 29
FRANK, L. K., 143, 185, 196
FREEMAN, F. N., 94
GESELL, A., 16, 29, 40, 52, 63, 94, 154, 175, 196

GOOD, C. V., 187
GOSLIN, W. E., 115
Grouping, value of, 142
Growth: age curve, 175; age equivalents, 161; analysis, 160, 162, 163; patterns, 19, 20, 31, 151; principles, 91, 191, 195; relations, 170; studies, 187-90
GRUELICH, W. A., 143, 185, 196
Harvard studies, 186, 187, 189, 190
HUGGETT, A. J., 115

ILG, F. L., 16, 29, 40, 52, 63, 175
Individuality, concept of, 139, 192
Intelligence: breadth, 88; quotient, 89; relation to achievement, 90; tests, 181
Interrelations, 165, 170, 171
Isochron, 165

JENKINS, G. G., 16, 29, 40, 52, 63, 74
JONES, H. E., 65, 74, 190
Journal records, 183

Language achievement, 111
LATON, A. D., 39, 52
LEARNED, J., 16, 29, 39, 52, 63
Learning: climate, 9; relation to growth, 9, 44, 93, 162, 192; types and kinds, 33, 44
LERNER, E., 143
Literature achievement, 111
Longitudinal study: approach, 178, 185; arithmetic, 104; personal-social, 135; types, 187
LOWREY, G. H., 16, 40, 52, 63, 74

MACFARLANE, J. W., 143, 186, 188, 197
Maturation: curve, 173; meaning, 67-8
Maxima, 169
MEEK, L. H., 144
Mental age: curve, 88, 90; development, 33
Mental development: functioning, 86; general characteristics, 84
Mental hygiene: adjustment profile, 145; behavior mechanisms, 147
METRAUX, R., 16, 29, 39, 52, 63
MILLARD, C. V., 94, 115, 144, 154, 176, 196, 197
Moral-ethical, *vide*: Ethical-moral
Motor development: aspects, 83; basic skills, 84; measurements, 182; needs, 9; performance, 11, 24, 34, 48, 59, 70; principles, 84
MURPHY, L. B., 29, 74, 143

NALLY, T. J., 176, 197

OLSON, W. C., 160, 176
OLSON technique, 160, 178
Organismic: age, 160; developmental curve, 176
Parent-teacher relations, 11
Peer-group relations, 43
Personal-social: development, 13, 26, 36, 50, 61, 71; general factors, 136, 137; needs, 7-8, 13-4, 43, 56; structure, 131
Personality: and behavior, 151; conditioning factors, 136, 137; definition, 117; direction of, 8; development pattern, 21-2, 151
Physical development: comparative growth, 79; factors influencing, 83; general energy, 83; height and weight, 81-2
Physiological measurements, 182
PIAGET, J., 65, 74
Play interests, 14, 27, 38, 50, 61, 73
PRESCOTT, D. A., 63, 74, 183, 197
Principles of growth: continuity, 91, 191; demonstration of, 191, 195

Rating scales, 180
Reading: achievement, 96; curve, 97; stages, 98
Recreation, *vide*: Play interests
REDL, F., 65, 74, 154
REYNOLDS, E. L., 40, 52, 63, 74
ROTHNEY, J. W. M., 93, 175, 196

SANFORD, R. N., 144, 189
SCHACTER, H., 16, 29, 40, 52, 63, 74
SCHOEN, G., 40, 52, 63, 74
School: effect on development, 137; function, 10, 20; limitations, 138, 140
Science achievement, 109
Sex: differences, 47, 58, 69; interests, 31-2, 46, 56; knowledge, 37, 46-7
SHUTTLEWORTH, F. K., 94, 187
SIMMONS, K., 81, 94, 187
Social development, 131; *vide* also: Personal-social
Social-studies curve, 110
Sociometric: rating, 134, 180; status, 133
Spelling: achievement, 105; curve, 107
Starting points, 168
Statistical barriers, 185
STECKER, L. I., 93
STENDLER, C. B., 16
STRANG, R., 16, 40, 74
STUART, H. C., 187, 189

TABA, H., 154
Teacher: parent relations, 11; pupil relations, 21; role played, 140
THOMPSON, G. C., 154
THOMPSON, H., 94
THORPE, L. P., 154
TRAGER, H. G., 154
TRYON, C. M., 144

VAUGHN, W. F., 154
VINCENT, E. L., 79, 93
WALKER, R. N., 16, 29, 39, 52, 63
WATSON, E. H., 16, 40, 52, 63, 74
WOODCOCK, L. P., 29
WRIGHT, H. F., 29
YARROW, M. R., 154
ZACHARY, C. B., 65, 74